D1034543

THE ECUMENICAL VANGUARD

The Ecumenical Vanguard

The History of the Una Sancta Movement

BY

LEONARD J. SWIDLER

Foreword

BY

HANS KÜNG

DUQUESNE UNIVERSITY PRESS, PITTSBURGH, PA.

Editions E. Nauwelaerts, Louvain

Other Fine Duquesne Books

Leonard J. Swidler, editor
SCRIPTURE AND ECUMENISM
$4.95 cloth

Albert Dondeyne
FAITH AND THE WORLD
$5.00 cloth

Peter Schoonenberg, S.J.
GOD'S WORLD IN THE MAKING
$3.95 cloth

William H. van de Pol
ANGLICANISM IN ECUMENICAL PERSPECTIVE
$4.75 cloth

In Preparation

CHURCH-STATE RELATIONS IN ECUMENICAL PERSPECTIVE
Elwyn A. Smith, editor

BULTMAN-BARTH AND CATHOLIC THEOLOGY
Heinrich Fries

Library of Congress Catalog Card Number 66-15156

Printed in the United States of America

Acknowledgments

I wish to express my thanks to all those who helped make the production of this book possible. Some few, however, should be thanked by name. It was the *Deutsche Akademische Austausch Dienst* of the Western German Federal Republic that made the research possible by generously giving me two grants—in 1957 and 1958. Professor Heinrich Fries of the University of Munich initiated me into the whole study and guided me much of the way. Professor Hans Küng of the University of Tübingen reviewed the first part of the book and offered valuable criticism, and later generously consented to writing a foreword. Professor George Mosse of the University of Wisconsin read an earlier version of the entire manuscript and contributed many constructive criticisms. To all these I wish to express my deep appreciation.

Often authors have been helped in their scholarly efforts by their wives; none could have been assisted more capably and selflessly than I was by my wife Arlene.

Duquesne University LEONARD SWIDLER

TABLE OF CONTENTS

Foreword

How did it come about so suddenly, this amazing shift of the Catholic Church to a more open, more understanding, more ecumenical attitude? The question is asked often today, both within and without the Catholic Church. One refers to John XXIII, and rightly so, for he, a man of charism in the office of Peter, provided the decisive spark. But the spark would not have ignited, nor would this far-shining fire of the Church, gripped anew by the Holy Spirit despite all its frailties, have kindled, were it not that already for decades the material had been piled up by many known and unknown men in the Church, so that the spark could take fire.

These forerunners of renewal suffered greatly. It would be wrong to forget this today. They suffered under the imperfection, the weakness, the darkness and unholiness of the holy Church of God which they loved. They suffered under the erroneous developments and erroneous attitudes which had crept into liturgy and pastoral work, into preaching and teaching, into discipline and piety, into the relationship to other Christians and to the world. But these solitary forerunners did not give up! Within the Church they were often suspected by fellow Christians and by some Church leaders, hindered in their work, disavowed, accused of heresy, persecuted. They were considered dangerous, extremist, radical, even revolutionary. But they did not give up. They went farther, as far as they were permitted and sometimes beyond—in persevering patience but at the same time in fearless courage. Often they stood in the foremost line of fire without any human protection with only the gospel of Jesus behind them. Only decades later was their work affirmed and acknowledged by Church authorities; some of them were rehabilitated only by the Second Vatican Council. Do not we of the younger generation, for whom all is easier and who may stand on their shoulders, have every reason to bow in gratitude and respect before the Christian contribution of these lonely heroes of the battle for the renewal of the Church and the reconciliation of Christians—a battle which often seemed hopeless?

History alone can teach us how modest and unpretentious was the beginning, how slow and laborious the progress: in the ecumenical movement, in liturgical reform, in biblical renewal, in the lay movement, in Reformation research, and in ecumenical theology. Anyone knowing this history will see the Church of the present in a different perspective. Some things he will judge more skeptically, some more positively. He will observe that the truth does not always lie with the majority, that often it is only a few who proclaim the future, and that some outsiders are not outsiders but the daring small vanguard of a sometimes rather sluggish and in any case slow main force which follows. He will perceive that some goals set decades ago are still far from being accomplished. And he will above all gain the courage and hope, even though alone and unappreciated, to go ahead unwearied, despite all the so often well-intentioned and yet so unilluminated opposition, on the way which, if he will fulfill the task laid upon him, he must go.

In the ecclesiastical and ecumenical break-through of our century the land of the Reformation has a special significance. Dr. Leonard Swidler, professor at Duquesne University in Pittsburgh, is admirably prepared through his theological studies in Germany to conduct the American reader through the history of the ecumenical renewal in the German-speaking areas. As editor of the *Journal of Ecumenical Studies,* the first inter-confessional magazine in the United States, he stands in close contact with the present intellectual currents in ecumenism. In a German form, the first part of this book was accepted by the Catholic theological faculty of the University of Tübingen as a thesis for the Licentiate in Theology. With much labor and great professional knowledge the author has thoroughly acquainted himself with the complicated problematic, so that he is able to draw a detailed and plastic picture of the various movements of Church renewal in Germany which have become meaningful for the entire Church in these years.

I wish Dr. Swidler's book a sensitive audience who, out of the Church's past, will build in the present strength, courage and hope for the future.

Hans Küng

Tübingen, September 9, 1964

Introduction

THROUGH the Second Vatican Council the Roman Catholic Church has suddenly been catapulted into prominence in the movement toward Christian unity. While it is true that Pope John and Vatican II have occasioned a "great leap" forward in this and many other areas, it would not have been even remotely possible had there not been a long and arduous preparation in at least one significant section of the Roman Catholic Church. If the promotion in Vatican II of Catholic involvement in ecumenism had depended, for example, on the American or English Catholic Church, it never would have materialized.

But the preparation was accomplished—in the country which also, ironically, was the source of one of the major divisions in the Christian Church: Germany. Germany has long been the locus of intellectual, cultural and other kinds of fermentation in the world—for evil as well as good. This one was good. The name given to this fermentation in Germany toward Christian unity is the Una Sancta Movement. It is to be distinguished from the ecumenical movement, which has broader historical roots but which did not, until Vatican II, substantively include Roman Catholics. The Catholic-Protestant dialogue was of the essence of the Una Sancta movement, which became vanguard of Roman Catholic involvement in ecumenism.

The term "Una Sancta," (coming from the Nicine Creed, "Credo . . . unam sanctam . . . ecclesiam,") was used by a number of people interested in reunification work, particularly in the decades following the first World War. But the term "Una Sancta Movement" seems to have crystallized only as a result of the work done by Father Max Metzger and to have gained general currency only after he founded his Una Sancta Brotherhood in 1938.

It was in Europe, after the devastation of World War I, that the several forces arose which greatly changed the religious situation and prepared the conditions necessary for the growth of the Una Sancta Movement. These forces behind the Una Sancta Movement appear to fall into six major categories. In the past forty years, first of all, a very important element of Protestant theology has turned away from the liberalistic point of view to reemphasize the position of Scripture. The "Church" has grown in importance in Protestant theology, and the desire for reunion of the Church of Christ has been visibly exhibited in the extraordinary growth of the ecumenical movement. The Protestant Church has experienced a "Luther-renaissance" and in re-finding Luther has moved closer to the Catholic Church, while Catholics, in a searching reappraisal of Luther and the Reformation, have attained a much more sympathetic view of Protestantism. The liturgical movement within both Churches has brought them into a very intimate contact with each other, each benefiting from what have long been considered by many to be exclusive traits of the other. The Catholic Church has experienced a biblical renaissance which is attempting to place the Scriptures more readily in the hands of the layman. Again, the rise of the lay apostolate in the Catholic Church stresses the importance of the layman in the Church, thereby bringing the Catholic Church closer to the Protestant position. Added to these forces was that of the Nazi persecution, which drove the two Churches together in the face of a common enemy, and the displacement of the peoples after the war, which has led to unprecedented personal contact between Catholics and Protestants.

A number of pioneering attempts were made during the 1920's and 1930's to build bridges between the Protestant and Catholic Churches in Germany. Some of them grew directly out of the various background causes of the Una Sancta movement, such as the *Hochkirchlich-ökumenisches Bund* which was both liturgical and ecumenical in inspiration and worked with both Catholics and Protestants for a while.

By the middle 1930's some Protestant-Catholic groups were being formed as a result of the cumulative force of the liturgical, biblical and other movements. The growth of these groups was accelerated by the Nazi persecution.

Just before the outbreak of World War II, Catholic-Protestant study groups of laymen and clergy began to mushroom throughout Germany. These were given a loose organization and further stimulation by the Catholic priest, Max Metzger, who founded the Una Sancta Brotherhood in 1938. After the war the Una Sancta cricles spread and grew so greatly that they were referred to as part of a popular movement. But this initial post-war period was followed by a period of uncertainty and suspicion, when several decrees from Rome greatly restricted the Movement's activities. For a while it looked as if the Una Sancta Movement would disappear, but it recovered in the middle 1950's and has grown stronger than ever before.

Chapter One

The Change in Protestant Theology

SINCE the First World War there has arisen in Protestant theology a school which approaches the Catholic theological position to such an extent that many Catholic and Protestant theologians now find it possible to hold intelligent theological discussions with one another. This trend, called "dialectical theology," has been led by Karl Barth and is still considered one of the strongest influences on contemporary Protestant theology.[1] Of course there were, during the same period, other less important and less dramatic tendencies in Protestant theology (such as the emphasis on "the Holy" by Rudolf Otto and Karl Heim's "positive theology"), but these trends had no real influence on forming the historical conditions necessary for the Una Sancta Movement.

EARLY PERIODS OF PROTESTANT THEOLOGY

Historically, the first period of Protestant theology was the time of the confessional writings, when the distinguishing doctrines of the different confessions were crystallized and set down in writing either by the reformers themselves or their immediate followers. For Lutheranism the period lasted until 1588, when the Concordance Formula was established. In Reformed Protestantism it lasted somewhat longer, until the Synod of Dordrecht in 1619. Protestantism then entered the era of "orthodoxy," when the dogmas were clothed in philosophical, often Aristotelian, formulas, and rigid submission to the "correct" interpretation and wording was demanded. This unbending dogmatism reached its zenith in

[1]Anders Nygren, "Das Gespräch der Theologie," *Dokumente,* XIII (1957), 188.

the seventeenth century, and by its stringency called forth two strong countermovements, Pietism and the theology of the *Aufklärung*. Both of these countermovements, and particularly the latter, were of course parts of a much larger intellectual movement.

Pietism, springing up in the latter part of the seventeenth and the first half of the eighteenth century, placed great emphasis on finding personal sanctity by living Christianity in daily life, while quickly passing over doctrinal matters as not decisively important. From this stream of Christianity there have come many champions for peace and unity among the Christian Churches, starting with its great eighteenth century leader, Graf Zinzendorf. But because it stressed the personal and practical, Pietism had little effect on the development of dogma.

This was not the case with the theology of the *Aufklärung*, which was important in the latter half of the eighteenth century and the first half of the nineteenth. Where orthodoxy had given man's reason room to explain the meaning of divine revelation and to protect it from the attacks of nonbelievers, the *Aufklärung* theology attempted to subject the truth of revelation to critical judgments and empirical methods of research. Reason, and not the authoritative Church or the confessional writing, became the standard against which doctrines were measured.

The application of critical reason and critical historical method to the Bible was led by J. S. Semler (1725-91), "the father of German rationalism," whose popularity lasted until 1779, when he attacked the views of Reimarus and Bahrdt, who carried rationalistic biblical criticism further than he thought justified. Reimarus (1694-1768) took a purely deistic position, denying the necessity or possibility of revelation. Bahrdt (1741-92), following Reimarus' lead in biblical criticism, eventually set up a natural religion "moral system" to replace supernatural Christianity. He stated, "I looked upon Moses and Jesus, Confucius, Socinius, Luther, and myself as the instruments of Providence through which he is working for the welfare of men."[2]

The most radical and rationalistic elements of the *Aufklärung* theology were continued in the work of Philippe Henke (1752-1809), Heinrich Paulus (1761-1851) and, even later, in the work of David Strauss (1808-74), who interpreted the biblical life of Jesus as a myth made up more or less consciously by the followers of Jesus. The divinity of Christ and propitiary power of his crucifixion were denied. The importance of the doctrine of original sin was greatly lessened or disappeared altogether as the other side of the balance, the importance of man and his reason, surged upwards. The deemphasis of sin naturally eliminated the necessity for Luther's prime doctrine of justification by faith alone, as there was nothing from which man needed to be redeemed except possibly his own ignorance and subservience to authority, and this reason could do. While the old Protestantism focused on the visible Church as the community of believers, the *Aufklärung* theology declared the autonomy of the individual. Luther and Calvin were seen as champions of the freedom of the individual from the Church, and this principle of freedom was then used to free the individual from Luther and Calvin themselves. All of these positions in Protestant theology were met by strong counter-movements, however, and after World War I there was a return to the earlier stress on the Bible as the Word of God, on Luther, and on the supernatural, and a corresponding deemphasis suspicion of the self-sufficient reason of man.

Not that the *Aufklärung* theology had held the field of dogmatics uncontested after the beginning of the nineteenth century. As a general intellectual and cultural movement the *Aufklärung*, with its stress on the abstract and rational, provoked the rise of its antithesis, romanticism, with its

---

[2]Andrew L. Drummond, *German Protestantism Since Luther* (London, 1951), 85.

emphasis on the feelings and emotions of man, so also the rationalistic theology was met by the theology of Friedrich Schleiermacher as he worked to free Protestant theology from the abstraction and naturalism of rationalistic theology and yet avoid what he considered the sterile dogmatism of Protestant orthodoxy. Like the Pietists, Schleiermacher made the personal experience of faith the *sine qua non* of true religion. He accepted Kant's denial of the ability of the pure reason really to know any thing of a metaphysical nature or anything about God, or even the fact of His existence, but at the same time rejected his moralism under the direction of the practical reason. Schleiermacher thus made religion not a thing of knowing or of doing but, under the influence of romanticism, a thing of feeling. "Piety is neither a knowing nor a doing, but rather a definiteness of feeling or immediate awareness of self."[3]

For Schleiermacher, feeling as the center of religion meant that when man becomes conscious of his own being and the universe about him, he becomes aware of, he feels, his and its utter dependence on something "other," something nonfinite and therefore infinite. This infinite "other" on whom man feels absolutely dependent is called God. Thus the religious man grasps and holds on to God by personal intuition and feeling not, as the rationalists held, by intellectual knowledge. "If man is not one with the Eternal in the unity of intuition and feeling which is immediate, he remains, in the unity of consciousness which is derived, forever apart."[4] What then are dogmas and what is the purpose of the theologian? Dogmas are nothing but the expression and description of the communal feelings resulting from a people's experience of the infinite, of God. The work of the theo-

[3]"Die Frömmigkeit ist weder ein Wissen noch ein Tun, sondern eine Bestimmetheit des Gefühls oder des unmittelbaren Selbstbewusstseins." Friedrich Schleiermacher, *Der christliche Glaube,* quoted in Konrad Algermissen, *Konfessionskunde* (Paderborn, 1957), 668.

[4]Friedrich Schleiermacher, *On Religion* (New York, 1958), 40.

logian is not to investigate the truth or falsity of these expressions, for neither can be proved, but rather to study their origin in the history of the Church. It is this emphasis on the subjective and historical, and his distrust of the speculative powers of man that made Schleiermacher the father of "liberal theology."

In nineteenth century Protestant theology there were two main currents. The first was liberal theology, which flowed out of Schleiermacher's subjectivism, rationalism, liberalism and the development of the critical historical methods of the time. The second was the "awakening theology" (*Erweckungstheologie*), which sprang from Pietism and the confessional theology which stressed the Bible as interpreted by the confessional writings. In addition a *Vermittlungstheologie* attempted to combine the advantages of both movements by maintaining a belief in the Bible and at the same time giving free rein to scientific research and thought. However, it was the first, liberal theology, that became dominant by the end of the century.

Liberal theology in the latter part of the nineteenth century and the first part of the twentieth century was influenced by Kant and Schleiermacher particularly through the theology of Albrecht Ritschl (d. 1889) and the religious-historical school. Ritschl saw in the truths of Christianity not objective religious facts but, in the final analysis, only phenomena of the subjective consciousness. This subjective and historical approach was carried even farther by his student Ernst Troeltsch (d. 1923) and by Adolph Harnach (d. 1930). Harnack looked upon Christian dogma as a product of the Greek spirit built upon the foundation of the gospel, as a falling away from pristine Christianity.[5] Troeltsch, with his religious-historical and religious-philosophical method, denied any absolute character to Christianity. Christian dog-

[5]Cf. Rudolf Bultmann, "Introduction," in Adolf Harnack, *What is Christianity* (New York, 1957), ix-xviii.

ma could make no unqualified claim to truth but had to be tested and interpreted by religious psychology and Troeltsch's own philosophy of history.[6]

In thus applying modern historical and philosophical thought and methods to religion, Ritschl and his followers drew censure as well as applause.[7] But by the turn of the century and up to the first World War, liberal theology was dominant in the Protestant world, or at least appeared to be engaged in a final heavy battle aganist rapidly disappearing opponents.

Dialectical Theology

Then came World War I and all civilization seemed to be bankrupt. Progress, the nineteenth century's god, now appeared a phantasy and both reason and liberalism were discredited. This same reaction showed up strongly in Protestant theology, where Troeltsch, Harnack and likeminded liberal theologians found themselves violently attack by the new "dialectical" theology under the leadership of Karl Barth. Barth's *Commentary on the Epistle to the Romans* was the first effective salvo in this attack, and he and similar thinkers like Emil Brunner and Eduard Thurneyson wore, at least for a time, the mantles of prophets. They announced that the old ways of theology lead to death; that theology must seek a new way of life, and give its allegiance once again to

---

[6]Cf. Friedrich von Hügel, "Introduction," in Ernst Troeltsch, *Christian Thought* (New York, 1957), 13-32.

[7]The Reformed theologian Adolf Zahn referred to their work as a "rational scepticism and a Pelagian moralism which to no avail is poorly camouflaged with the Reformation truths, with the threadbare mantle of Lutheranism; the most brilliant sign of the exhaustion and impoverishment of Protestantism is that by the end of the century it could discover nothing newer than that which the lowly people always had known: 'Act justly and fear no man.'" Adolf Zahn, *Abriss einer Geschichte der evangelischen Kirche auf dem europäischen Festlande im 19. Jahrhundert* (Leipzig, 1893), 64-65.

the one true God, the God of revelation, and traffic no longer with false gods of this world.

Thus Barth's *Commentary on the Epistle to the Romans* "fell like a bomb on the playground of the theologians."[8] Liberal theology had attempted to accommodate itself to the thought and world view of modern man with his new discoveries of science, psychology, philosophy and historical criticism. Christian theology was to be the crowning of the spiritual evolution of man, the highest development of the *naturally* religious man; theology was the apex placed on and based on the pyramid of all man's achievements. But Barth declared that if theology lived by a worldly, merely natural civilization, it would also die by it—and in the eyes of many modern Europeans, civilization was certainly in its death throes.

Barth maintained that theology needed to speak not the language of the history of religions or psychology, but rather the language of revelation, of the Bible. Here too was its proper subject matter: the revealed acts of God, not the philosophy of religion and the historical evolution of man's spirit. There was a need for a new dogmatics which would be exclusively a theology of the Word of God in its content, method and vocabulary. For when man attempts to synthesize revelation with "reason," theology suffers both from malformation—casting revelation in a particular intellectual form—and from constant change, since man's knowledge is always being remolded to new shapes or even cast aside completely.

Barth himself led the way by attempting to reshape his thought along biblical lines. However, his first attempt at writing a prologue to a new dogmatics (*Die Lehre vom Worte Gottes, Prolegomena zur christlichen Dogmatik,* 1927) was so sharply attacked for basing its theology on a new

---

[8]Karl Adam, "Die Theologie der Krisis," *Hochland,* XXIII (1925/26), 271.

anthropology—exactly what he was trying to avoid—that Barth dropped the project and started anew in 1932 with his *Church Dogmatics,* the first book of a series not yet finished. In 1939 he said, ". . . in these years I have had to rid myself of the last remnants of a philosophical (in America one says 'humanistic' or 'naturalistic') foundation and exposition of Christian doctrine."[9]

In calling theology back to the Bible and insisting on its own norms and ends, Barth was emphasizing God as transcendent, as "completely other." The proper study of theology is not the inner self, nor is it the development of the forms of expression of the inner selves of a group or groups of people, as it was to the historical school following Schleiermacher. Rather, it is God Himself, as He is revealed in Christ.

> In the meantime we have lost sight of the Almighty God before whom we are as nothing, who is praised in the truly religious language of the Psalms. Here is the note which is unmistakable in all the great religions; it is what gives force to the Institutes of Calvin, however much we may dislike some of his doctrines, and it has been restored in the teaching of Karl Barth. . . . He is convinced that this tradition makes far too little of the transcendence of God, that it is not sufficiently theocentric. . . .[10]

Along with his return to the Bible and a transcendent God who has manifested Himself in Jesus Christ, Barth and others returned to the reformers. At the beginning of this century a renewed interest, particularly in Luther, had arisen in an attempt to use modern historical methods to recreate the image and message of the reformer in their original forms; this "Luther renaissance" has continued to grow even to the present. Partly as an effect of this general growing concern

---

[9]Karl Barth, "How My Mind Has Changed in This Decade," *Christian Century,* LVI (1939), 1132.

[10]Martin C. D'Arcy, "The Groups and the Spirit of Worship," in *Oxford and the Groups* (Oxford, 1934), 183-185.

with the reformers, dialectical theology, and Barth in particular, tried to reach back beyond the "New Protestantism" of the eighteenth and nineteenth centuries, beyond the period of rigid orthodoxy to the spirit and often letter of Luther and, for Barth as a Reformed Protestant, also Calvin. However, the theology of Barth was arrived at not only through a radical return to the sources, to Calvin and Luther straight through all the "developments," misrepresentations and watered down versions of New Protestantism, "but more essentially still through a cleansing and radicalization of these sources themselves. . . . Barth avoids a certain 'orthodoxy' just as decisively as he does 'Liberalism.' "[11]

Lastly, Barth asserted that theology is the teaching *by the Church* of the revelation of Jesus Christ as found in the Scriptures. It is the purpose and duty of the Church to transmit the "Word" of God to men. "Theology follows the word of the Church"[12] Barth took special pains to point out that his protest against the Catholic Church's concept was not at all like the objection of the modern "educated" man who rejected the very idea of authority. "Protestantism protests not against, but for the Church. . . . Protestant Church not only means not less, but more, not only not weaker, but stronger, than the Catholic Church—it means precisely *Church*."[13] Such positive emphasis on the Church had been quite alien to liberal theology, which rather stressed the individual, who should be made as free from all limitations as possible: "We want for ourselves still more freedom, still more individuality still more expression and teaching."[14]

---

[11]Hans Urs von Balthasar, *Karl Barth. Darstellung und Deutung seiner Theologie* (Cologne, 1951), 32. Cf. also J. McConnachie, "Reformation Issues Today," in F. W. Camfield, *Reformation Old and New* (London, 1947), 106.

[12]Quoted in Nygren, "Das Gespräch," 187-188. Cf. the last chapter of Heinrich Fries, *Kirche als Ereignis* (Dusseldorf, 1958).

[13]Quoted in von Balthasar, *Karl Barth,* 41.

[14]Adolf Harnack, *Wesen des Christentums* (Leipzig, 1901), 112.

NEW RELATION TO CATHOLICISM

It is just these essential characteristics of the dialectical, especially Barthian, theology that have gradually created a new relationship to the Catholic Church. The whole psychological and historical approach so typical of the liberal theology had found a very determined opponent in the Catholic Church. But Barth had this in common with the Catholic Church: he too was an opponent of the liberal theology. He went so far as to say:

> If today I became convinced that the interpretation of the Reformation developed in the direction of Schleiermacher-Ritschl-Troeltsch . . . were correct, that Luther and Calvin in their efforts had really meant things *so,* I would indeed not become a Catholic tomorrow, but at the same time I probably would have to take leave of the would-be Evangelical Church. Faced with the *choice* between the two evils, I would in fact rather become a Catholic.[15]

Likewise, the turning back to Luther by Protestant theology has *ipso facto* brought it much closer to the Catholic Church than it was under the aegis of liberal theology. Luther himself was much nearer to Catholicism in his notions of the Church, the Bible and dogma. A reemphasis on his advocacy of a liturgy similar to the Catholic Mass and such things as private confession and morning and evening prayers has led many Protestants into teaching and doing things often thought to be exclusively Catholic. Karl Adam even felt that a "*rapprochement* between Catholicism and Protestantism will only be possible *if it takes Luther as its starting point.*"[16]

With this shift of theology away from psychological, historical and philosophical approaches to a biblical theology and a greater cooperation between exegesis and systematic theology, Protestantism has again perforce drawn closer to Catholicism. The Scriptures are one essential constituent of

---

[15]Karl Barth, *Die Theologie und die Kirche* (Munich, 1938), 339.

[16]Karl Adam, *One and Holy* (New York, 1951), 68.

faith that both confessions have in common—even though they may be differently interpreted. The unifying force of the Bible, moreover, has been strengthened by the growing interest of the Catholic Church in spreading the use and understanding of the Bible more and more widely, as is shown by the Bible movement. Bishop Besson has said, "Through the Gospel our fathers were divided. Through the Gospel we must find each other again."[17]

From this intensive biblical study has arisen a greater concentration of Protestant theology on the "Church." This is particularly true of the dialetcical theology which sees "the Church as the unique bearer in history of God's purpose and grace,"[18] and "not merely another social institution since it is also the Body of Christ in history."[19] In addition German Protestant concern about the Church was greatly intensified by the development of the ecumenical movement and the collapse of the monarchy in the first World War (the Protestant Churches had been very closely connected with the individual princely states) and the *Kirchenkampf* during the Nazi time. As a result "today Protestantism works with a concept of Church which is continually coming ever closer to that of Catholicism."[20] The Catholic Church had been

[17]Marius Besson, *Nach vierhundert Jahren* (Lucerne, 1934), 1.

[18]Langdon B. Gelkey, "Neo-Orthodoxy," in *A Handbook of Christian Theology* (New York, 1958), 257.

[19]*Ibid.*, 259. "The recovery and elaboration of the doctrine of the nature of the Church is one of the chief aspects of Protestant theology in this century. It was preceded by a long period of unrestrained individualism, which regarded the Church as being extraneous to the Christian faith and a strictly human, mundane organization. For this important change there are at least three reasons: the wide consensus of biblical scholars that the Church belongs to the saving works of Jesus Christ; the struggles of Christians during the two world wars and under tyrannical persecution and their need to distinguish the Church from the rest of mankind; the encounters of the divided denominations in mission fields and in the ecumenical movement." J. Robert Nelson, "Church," in *A Handbook of Christian Theology,* 53.

[20]Konrad Algermissen, *Konfessionskunde* (Paderborn, 1950), 858.

accused of being a "juridical Church," it being assumed that the Church of Christ should be something other. But the Lutheran Church in the twentieth century, because of the collapse after the first World War and the *Kirchenkampf*, has also found itself in the position of having to emphasize the juridical aspect of the Church, along with renewing the stress of the Church's teaching office.

A whole new emphasis on the position of dogma and tradition has flowed from the new concept of Church. In Protestant theology since the Enlightenment, dogma had a primarily historical significance. Not only the formulations but also the essence of church doctrines were thought to be conditioned by the circumstances under which they arose. Although the pejorative connotation of dogma—which reached a high point with Adolph Harnack who said, "The history of dogma is the dissolution of dogma"[21]—has by no means completely disappeared, Protestants especially Lutherans, are again emphasizing the importance of being precise in the meaning of doctrine and firm in its adherence. "Advocates of a 'dogma-free Christianity' can no longer be considered by us as representative of the Evangelical Church."[22]

Another old quarrel, the problem of Scripture and tradition, has grown milder. Protestant theologians no longer rigidly insist on the "Scriptures alone" principle in opposition to the Roman Catholic formula, "Scripture and tradition." They ackowledge that the New Testament itself arose out of an oral tradition, and that it was this oral tradition that brought about the formation of the canon of the New Testament. The oral tradition preceded the written. And with a new sense of their own past, Protestants have become aware that through the past four hundred years there has grown up a

---

[21]Quoted in Jaroslav Pelikan, "Dogma," in *A Handbook of Christian Theology*, 81.

[22]Thomas Sartory, "Besteht Hoffnung auf Ueberwindung der Glaubensspaltung?" *Oekumenische Rundschau* VII (1958), 72-73.

vital Protestant tradition.[23] All this brings the Protestant Church much closer to the Catholic position, that the source of the Christian faith is found in both Scripture and tradition. On the Catholic side there recently has been much research and thought given to this problem, particularly in the extended discussions at two sessions of Vatican Council II. Many theologians have insisted that the teaching of Trent was that the whole content of faith is found in *both* Scripture and tradition rather than partly in one and partly in the other, and that until Trent there was no sharp distinction between the two. Thus, a growing Catholic opinion now holds that "Scripture" means the Bible as read by the Church, and hence includes "tradition." This position is, of course, more acceptable to Protestants.[24]

Even the externals, the form and manner, of much of the new Protestant theology is strikingly like traditional Catholic theology. Barth's monumental *Church Dogmatics,* for example, is very much like the great medieval *Summae.* Barth has not restricted himself to the Bible, Reformation and post-Reformation writers, but has drawn from the scholastics and Fathers, so much so that his co-theologians quickly accused him of rationalism and philosophism, and of giving up the reformed fiducial faith and falling back into the middle ages. A Catholic finds that the theology of Barth's dogmatics has a breadth in subject matter and history that is as extensive as his own.[25] In Barth's own words:

> We must direct our attention to a Thomas and Bonaventure, and also an Anselm and even further back to an Augustine, just as keenly to the much attacked characteristics of the then

[23]"Ueberlieferung," *Christliche Religion,* ed. by Oskar Simmel and Rudolf Stählin (Frankfurt, 1957), 315.

[24]Cf. Josef Geiselmann, "Das Misverständnis über das Verhältnis von Schrift und Tradition und seine Ueberwindung in der katholischen Theologie," *Una Sancta,* XI (1956), 131-150; and George Tavard, *Holy Writ or Holy Church,* (New York, 1959).

[25]Von Balthasar, *Karl Barth,* 32.

> still not "reformed" [*verbesserten*] Church. We must concern ourselves with the recognized teaching of a Church which is also ours, at least in so far as it had not then avoided reform. They have the right to be heard by us along with the Reformers. And it would have gone better with Evangelical dogmatics if they had been listened to more instead of acting as if the Reformation in its well known tumultuousness were the beginning of all wisdom.[26]

Barth has ofen spoken out clearly against the divisions within Christianity. For him a plurality of Churches cannot be justified. It must be "carried about as one carries one's own and another's sins. . . . It should be seen as guilt."[27] One must work for the unity of the Church of Christ at the express command of Jesus. And there can be no escape into the subterfuge that the unity of the Church is meant to be found only in the invisible Church, as if the multiplicity of the Churches were a necessary characteristic of the visible, empirical Church in contrast to the invisible, ideal, essential Church. "There is no flight from the visible to the invisible Church."[28]

Like the Catholic Church, Barth believes that unity between the Churches can come about only on a theological basis, not on a practical-social basis. As a consequence, he was distrustful of the union at the time of Friedrich Wilhelm III in the nineteenth century, when a fusing of the Lutheran and Reformed Churches in Prussian lands was forced politically. Barth was also skeptical of the early efforts of the ecumenical movement, at least until the founding of the World Council of Churches at Amsterdam in 1948.

Despite his early reluctance to involve himself with the ecumenical movement, Barth had already in the 1920's entered into an earnest theological discussion with the Catholic

---

26Karl Barth, *Die kirchliche Dogmatik* (Munich, 1932), 375-376.
27Karl Barth, *Die Kirche und die Kirchen* (Munich, 1935), 9-10.
28*Ibid.*, 9.

Church, delivering a lecture, for example, on the "Concept of Church" before the *Hochschulgruppe* of the Catholic *Zentrum* party in 1927 at Münster.[29] Elsewhere he stated that it must in principle be possible "to come to an understanding" even with a Catholic theologian, for the Christian gospel will in the last analysis also stand behind the post-Tridentine Roman Church. "There remains enough of the Catholic in us Protestants that we are forced to assume that the goals and hopes of the Reformation also cannot be completely dead on the other side."[30]

Among the Catholic theologians who have entered into public, non-polemical exchange with Karl Barth in periodicals and books is Hans Küng, who has compared in great detail the doctrine of justification as explained by the Council of Trent with Barth's teaching on the matter.[31] The startling conclusion is that they are identical: In a letter to Küng, which was printed along with his analysis, Barth says: "If that which you unfold in your second half as the teaching of the Roman Catholic Church really is her teaching, then I must certainly grant that my doctrine of justification agrees with hers."[32] He then asks that similar attempts at mutual understanding be made in other areas of theology.

This does not mean, of course, that Barth has only praise for the Catholic Church, that he has no criticism to direct at it. At times his criticism becomes strong, even bitter, as at the Amsterdam ecumenical conference, where he took note of the Catholic Church's absence: "We are not disappointed that no cardinal delegated by the Vatican is here to sit

---

[29]Von Balthasar, *Karl Barth,* 18.

[30]Karl Barth, *Das Wort Gottes und die Theologie* (Munich, 1924), 103.

[31]Hans Küng, *Rechtfertigung. Die Lehre Karl Barths und eine katholische Besinnung* (Einsiedeln, 1957).

[32]Karl Barth, "Geleitbrief von Karl Barth," *Una Sancta,* XII (1957), 122.

at our head table. And I suggest that no useless tears be shed over Rome's absence among us, as some have attempted to make an appearance of doing."[33] But these criticisms are more than balanced by exchanges like the one with Küng.

Since the sixteenth century there has been little opportunity for a non-polemical discussion between the Catholic and Protestant Churches. Certainly there was no such chance in the first fury of the battle, nor in the period of strict "orthodoxy" that followed it. The conditions were not improved by the theologies of the *Aufklärung,* of Schleiermacher, or of the liberal school. However, with the break toward dialectical theory at the time of World War I, the theological situation has become more favorable for a fruitful and more irenic exchange. The turning away from the rationalistic, psychological and historical approach in theology to a bible-centered approach, stressing a common possession of both confessions; the return to Luther, who was vastly closer to Catholicism than was the New Protestantism; and the renewed stress on the importance of the Church, the cornerstone of Catholic doctrine, have helped set the stage on the theological level for an Una Sancta Movement.

---

[33]Quoted in Heinrich Hermelink, *Die katholische Kirche unter den Pius-päpsten des 20. Jahrhunderts* (Zurich, 1949), 140.

Chapter Two

Catholic Reformation Scholarship

Polemical Period

Since the time of Johannes Cochlaeus in the sixteenth century, Catholic Reformation scholarship has not been disposed to look upon the Reformation in a very favorable light. Johannes Cochlaeus (1479-1552), one of the bitterest and, in the long run, most influential opponents of Luther's acts and writings. His *Commentaria de Actis et Scriptis Martini Lutheri Saxonis* came out in 1549, three years after Luther's death. Cochlaeus did not go about his difficult work with the coolness and detachment of a non-partisan historian, nor did he think it a fault not to do so. He felt his readers should not only be informed about Lutheranism, but also made fully aware that Luther had devastated the Church and brought unutterable misery to his German homeland. Every deprecation, slander and evil legend was snatched up by the author. He asserted, for example, that Luther entered into the indulgence battle against Tetzel because, as an Augustinian, he was jealous of the lucrative indulgence trade enjoyed by Tetzel and the Dominicans. Another story had it that Luther, already as a fifteen year old lad, was indulging in immoral relations with his benefactress, Frau Cotta zu Eisenach; that he lived a riotous student life in Erfurt; and that during his first period in the cloister, Luther lived in concubinage with three nuns, from which experience he contracted venereal disease. Some of the stories about Luther, because they are handed on in all seriousness, take on an air of humor. For example, when Luther wanted to emphasize a statement he might say, "I am not drunk now—I know what I am saying," which was immediately taken by his calumniators as an admission that he often *was* drunk and did not know what he was saying.[1] Only the completely baseless legend of Luther's suicide, which Paul Majunke revived as late as 1890, is missing in Cochlaeus. Any really first-hand reports coming from Protestants, especially Luther's close companions Melanchthon and Mathesius, are conspicuously absent, since they would be favorably to Luther.

The practice of seeing Luther as all evil and the Catholic Church as all good continued through the centuries. The nineteenth century historian, Johannes Janssen, for example, maintained that the Church had already begun a brilliant and profound reform in the fifteenth century, and that this reform was suddenly disturbed in a most unwarranted manner by Luther's revolution.[2] But the high point in controversial literature was reached in the writings of Heinrich Denifle and Hartmann Grisar shortly after the turn of the century. The Dominican Denifle attempted to perform a "moral and scholarly execution" of Luther as a fallen-away monk with unbridled lust and a theological ignoramus. Luther was an evil man, and the Reformation fundamentally sprang from immorality. Denifle wrote "Luther, there is nothing godly in you!"[3] Luther was

> an ordinary, or if you will, an extraordinary destroyer, a revolutionary, who went through his age like a demon, ruthlessly trampling to earth what had been reverenced a thousand years before him. He was a seducer who carried away hundreds of thousands with him in his fateful errors, a false prophet who in his contradiction-burdened teaching as in his sin-laden life manifested the exact opposite of what one should expect and

---

[1]Sebastian Merkle, "Gutes an Luther und Uebles an seinen Tadlern," in Alfred von Martin, *Luther in ökumenischer Sicht* (Stuttgart, 1929), 17.

[2]Johannes Janssen, *Geschichte des deutschen Volkes* (8 vols., Freiburg, 1890).

[3]Quoted in Johannes Hessen, *Luther in katholischer Sicht* (Bonn, 1949), 11.

> demand from one sent from God. He was a liar and deceiver who, through the very overthrowing of all moral limitations under the banner of Christian freedom, attracted to himself so many deluded souls.[4]

The violence of this attack on Luther came about as a reaction to the Luther-cult which, growing out of the then rising Luther renaissance, did not hesitate to speak of a "*sanctus et divinus Lutherus*"; Denifle wanted to attack this cult and destroy it once and for all.

For the Jesuit Hartmann Grisar,[5] Luther was not so much a morally evil man as a mentally sick man. We should turn not our hate but our pity toward Luther the psychopath, who was subject to illusory visits by the devil and terrible fits of depression. It is granted by Protestants that Grisar went about his work with a great deal of scholarly zeal and that his work "contains a powerful denial of the old Catholic Luther-fables and calumniations as well as the deep-rooted view, most lately upheld by Denifle, according to which Luther was driven down the path of the Reformer by lust of the flesh."[6] However, this improvement over Denifle was hardly satisfying to Protestants. Grisar's polished style merely poured salt in the wound, and his apparent objectivity convinced no one. Without a doubt all the terrible words of Luther, full of hate, anger, "*Wildheit und Rohheit*" are actually found in Luther's writings. But the complaint was raised that this was far from all that was in Luther's writings. This was only a one-sided picture, and therefore a distortion, though one with a certain refinement. In the end, "Grisar, just as Denifle, wishes to annihilate Luther."[7]

---

[4]Heinrich Denifle, *Luther in rationalistischer und christlicher Beleuchtung* (Mainz, 1904), 33.

[5]Hartman Grisar, *Luther* (3 vols., Freiburg, 1911-12).

[6]Friedrich Heiler, "Martin Luthers Leben und sein Werk," in von Martin, *Luther*, 259.

[7]*Ibid.*

Grisar and Denifle, of course were supported in their attitudes by the highest church authorities. Pope Leo XIII in the encyclical *Militantis ecclesiae,* written for the *Canisius-jubilaeum* August 1, 1897, described the Reformation as the "*rebellio lutherana,*" which brought about the ultimate ruin of morals. St. Pius X in his encyclical on St. Charles Borromaeo, *Editae saepe,* May 26, 1910, said:

> There arose haughty and rebellious men, 'enemies of the cross of Christ . . . men with worldly . . . minds whose god is the belly.' They strove not for the betterment of morals but rather for the denial of the foundations of faith. They cast everything into confusion and cleared for themselves and others a broad path of undisciplined wilfullness, or sought, indeed openly at the bidding of the most depraved princes and peoples and under the disapproval of the ecclesiastical authority and leadership, forcibly to obliterate the Church's teaching, constitution and discipline.[8]

SHIFT FROM POLEMICAL APPROACH

This polemical approach to Luther and the Reformation, particularly by Denifle, soon found critics among German Catholics. Already in 1906, historian Hermann Mauert accused Denifle of wanting not to find the truth but only to win his argument. "With Denifle one finds onself all too often listening to the prosecution of the state attorney who wants to subject the accused to an unconditional condemnation, and one misses the just, all-around careful weighing, objective probing of the non-partisan judge, and in this case of the calm, collected historian."[9] In 1929 Sebastian Merkle said that to contend that such a completely base Luther was able to cause such a deep-going and long-lasting split in Christendom is "to stand all philosophy of history on its head

---

[8]Quoted in Walther von Loewenich, *Der moderne katholizismus* (Witten, 1956), 314.

[9]Hermann Mauert, *P. Heinrich Denifle O.P.* (Freiburg, 1906), 35.

and to view the entire history of humanity through the eyes of a worm."[10] And by 1931 Hubert Jedin stated that no Catholic church historian in Germany any longer shared Denifle's view of Luther's moral personality.[11]

A change occurred in Catholic Luther scholarship with the appearance of an article in the *Hochland* in 1917 entitled "Martin Luther's Religious Psyche as the Root of a New Philosophical World View."[12] Like Grisar, the author, Franz Xaver Kiefl, formerly a theology professor at Würzburg and the Dean of the cathedral of Regensburg, treated the psyche of Luther. However, as the title indicates, he treated it not as the object of depth psychology, but rather as a religious soul. He maintained that Luther's starting point and his main interest were religious. It was from Luther's religious psyche, as the "most profound and vital source," that "as out of a seed everything later grew."[13] The trend toward a more favorable interpretation of Luther continued to grow gradually in the next years.[14]

---

[10]Merkle, "Gutes an Luther," 17.

[11]Quoted in Ernst Wolf, *Neue Wege katholischer Reformationsgeschichtsschreibung* (Essen, 1940), 1.

[12]Franz Xaver Kiefl. "Martin Luthers religiösepsyche als Wurzel eines neuen philosophischen Weltbildes," *Hochland,* XV (1917/18), 7-28.

[13]*Ibid.,* 7.

[14]In 1929 Alfred von Martin, then Lutheran, said that any interconfessional agreement on the religious significance of Luther still lay in the distant future, but that there were hopeful signs of at least the beginnings of a *rapprochement* over Luther. Johannes Albani, a Catholic convert, declared "that a decontamination of the inter-confessional atmosphere . . . can be hoped for only if and when the person and works of Luther are given their just due." Max Pribilla, S.J., wrote in 1929 that the sixteenth century Reformation never would have taken place if the church and her representatives had been living up to their mission. "Protestants and Catholics—both bear the guilt for the present circumstances and neither has the right to raise himself above the other." The professor of Catholic theology Paul Simon expressed the same idea: "the split would never come if at the time of the Reformation the burning questions had been handled as religious questions from religious men." Von Martin, *Luther,* 2-3.

The editing of *Luther in ökumenischer Sicht* in 1929 by Alfred von Martin was among other things an extraordinary attempt to foster among Catholics a new attitude toward Luther and the Reformation. The book originally was to be a supplement to the fourth volume of the periodical *Una Sancta,* edited by von Martin with both Protestants and Catholic contributors, but because of difficulties with Rome it did not appear as a part of the *Una Sancta.* Von Martin said, "What is presented here is *no longer* an 'Una Sancta' periodical. It forgoes for the time the attempt to find a united objective ground on which the Christians of the separated confessions can meet each other."[15] Rather, the book is a series of individual essays by both Catholics and Protestants which can claim only the individual conviction and responsibility of the several authors. Nevertheless, von Martin maintained that there was a certain perceptible unity within the volume and that the book would serve as a step toward reconciliation.

In one of the essays within the volume, Sebastian Merkle attempted to redress what he considered wrongs done to Luther and the Reformation. He pointed out that while Luther and many of his biographers exaggerated both the seriousness and the extent of the bad conditions in the Church —or Janssen would not have been able to bring up so much oppposing documentation—it was at the same time true that there were a great many abuses rampant—or Luther would not have found such an enthusiastic following among strongly religious circles. "He would have to appear much more as the greatest wonder-worker of history, if he had brought about the mass defection from a flourishing Church, a Church

---

[15]Von Martin, *Luther,* 3.
[16]Merkle, "Gutes an Luther," 11.

at the zenith of fulfilling its task."[16] He quoted with approval the statement St. Clemens Maria Hofbauer made in 1816:

> Since I have been a papal delegate in Poland I have become certain that the defection from the Church has come about because the Germans had and still have a need to be pious. The Reformation was not spread and held by heretics and philosophers, but by men who were really searching for a religion for the heart.[17]

In the same collection of essays Johannes Albani asked the question, "Did Luther break with the Church? Did the Church break with him?" His answer was Luther broke not with the Church but with the priesthood, and then only after the priesthood had first broken with him. Although Luther made the mistake of thinking the hierarchy was dispensable, he was correct in recognizing that too little attention was given the individual soul.[18] In another essay in the same col-
die Kirche mit ihm?" in von Martin, *Luther*, 72.
lection, Albani outlined five types of subjectivism: scholastic, springing from Occam; rationalistic, coming from Zwingli; mystic, from Meister Eckhart; enthusiastic (*schwärmgeistige*), led by Thomas Münzer; and humanistic. Luther's subjectivism was none of these, for revelation stood before him with "incorruptible objectivity."[19]

A third Catholic theologian, Anton Fischer, wrote what was probably the most positive estimate of Luther of the time. Fischer presented a side of Luther seldom seen by Catholics. He called Luther a "great Christian man of prayer,"[20] and maintained that it was through Luther as a man of prayer

---

[17]Friedrich Perthe, *Leben von Clemens Theodor Perthes II* (Hamburg, 1851), 160.

[18]Johannes Albani, "Hat Luther mit der Kirche gebrochen? Brach

[19]Johannes Albani, "Luthers Subjektivismus," in von Martin, *Luther*, 80-88.

[20]Anton Fischer, "Was der betende Luther der ganzen Christenheit zu sagen hat," in von Martin, *Luther*, 188.

that an understanding of his great religious genius was to be found. Although Luther as a fighter belonged only to a part of Christianity, as a man of prayer he belonged to all, and he had something to say to all Christian groups. "Though a Church be ever so rich in truly great Christian men of prayer, it should not pass by without noticing this great man of prayer, his priceless statements on prayer and his incisive instructions on how to pray."[21] Even Catholics must admit that there are few masters of prayer like Luther, with his "quickening freshness, genuine popular appeal and biblical vitality."[22]

"The *fighting* Luther *wounds*—even today after four hundred years," Fischer writes. "The *praying* Luther heals: The *fighting* Luther *divides;* the *praying* Luther *unites* Luther the *fighter* belongs to the *past*; Luther the *man of prayer*—may his mission begin in the present."[23]

In 1929, the same year he edited *Luther in ökumenischer Sicht,* von Martin joined with another Protestant, Friedrich Heiler, in calling for a Roman Catholic historian who would write a Luther biography "which presents to us the real, whole Luther, the Luther who destroys and renews, who has brought misery and blessing."[24] Ten years later their wish was to a very large extent fulfilled in the work of the Catholic church historian, Father Josef Lortz. Lortz, born in Luxemburg in 1887, became deeply involved in Reformation history when in 1917 he was made the scientific secretary for the "Corpus Catholicorum" at the University of Bonn. The "Corpus Catholicorum" is an organization whose aim is to publish significant documents of Catholic tradition. It did much to lay a scholarly foundation for later works, not least for the work of Lortz himself.

[21]*Ibid.,* 187-188.
[22]*Ibid.,* 191.
[23]*Ibid.,* 194.
[24]Heiler, "Luthers Leben," 260. Cf. von Martin, *Luther,* 8.

LORTZ'S EPOCH-MAKING WORK

Josef Lortz published his epoch-making work, *Die Reformation in Deutschland,* in 1939 and 1940. The trend in Catholic Reformation and Luther scholarship, which had gradually departed from the Denifle and Grisar-like approach, took, with the appearance of Lortz's work, the most decidedly irenic direction it has had in its entire history. Just how very different this new direction was and what a stir it caused—and still causes—can be appreciated to some extent from the comments of the editors of the Protestant journal *Zeit im Querschnitt* in 1941, a year after the second volume was published. They wrote that *Die Reformation in Deutschland* had excited both Catholic and Protestant minds intensely as was indicated by the very numerous stands, pro and con, taken toward the work, and this not just in professional magazines, nor just in Germany.[25]

In the foreword Lortz indicated that he took for his guiding aims the overcoming of the much too prevalent "counter-Reformation" attitude toward his subject matter, the maintaining of an openness and sensitivity for the religious goals of the Reformation and, in conjunction with this, a substantial, though not polemical, criticism of the weaknesses of the Reformation. Critics pointed out that though these aims were not particularly new, the manner with which Lortz carried them out was new indeed, and that on every page it was evident that "here history has become the object of Christian meditation and examination of conscience."[26] They noted that it was not just the divisive and differentiating that was brought into focus, but also the shared and unifying. The result was a work "characterized by a rigid scientific objectivity born

[25]Herman Wendorf, "Luther, Erasmus und Karl V.—so oder so?" *Zeit im Querschnitt,* XLI (1941), 280.

[26]Georg Smolka, "Die Reformation in Deutschland," *Die Schildgenossen,* XIX (1940), 165.

out of a deep religious sense of responsibility, and it is exactly this combining of these two elements which can become effective religiously if it be accepted in the same spirit."[27]

Two aspects of Lortz's book have drawn the main attention: his description of the late-medieval conditions leading to the Reformation, and his description and estimation of Luther. One Protestant writer described it thus: "Any Evangelical Christian who reads Lortz's *Reformation in Deutschland* carefully will be pleased by Lortz's willingness both to acknowledge the sins and failings of the Catholic Church and because of his readiness to give the aims of Luther their just due . . ."[28]

Lortz drew a picture of a late medieval Christendom filled with strong forces tending toward the break-up of its unity. Medieval Europe was long in need of a reform. The prestige and power of the papacy were shattered with the "Babylonian captivity," the long schism that followed it, and the conciliar movement that grew out of the situation. All of Bohemia was a heretical land. But even more destructive than these were the intellectual and spiritual forces that had been eating at the very foundation of medieval civilization, theology.

Lortz laid the degeneration of the medieval theology at the feet of William of Occam, or more exactly, Occamism. This Occamism taught the doctrine not of a paternal God, but rather of an arbitrary one, a God who on no "objective basis" orders one soul to hell and another to heaven, a God who by mere accident calls one thing good and another evil,

---

[27]*Ibid.* This sympathetic interpretation of the Reformation and Luther, however, should not be taken as an indication of a weaker Catholicism on Lortz's part, as one Protestant writer hastened to add. ". . . On the contrary, his vital Catholicity expresses itself on every page of his book; indeed it appears that it was out of this Catholicity that he drew the power for an unencumbered vision and judgment." Wendorf, "Luther, Erasmus," 280.

[28]Richard Haug, "Das Objektive. Zum Gespräch mit der katholischen Kirche," *Für Arbeit und Besinnung,* I (1947), 220.

commands and praises something today and forbids and condemns the same thing tomorrow. This same Occamism placed an extraordinarily heavy emphasis on the part man played in the process of salvation, leaving a smaller role to be played by grace. (It is easy to see how Luther later reacted against this doctrine by moving to his position of "*sola gratia.*") Occamism also split nature and supernature apart almost to the point of erecting a double standard of truth. Revelation could declare something true in theology, at the same time that reason declared it false or impossible in philosophy, by reason. This led to Luther's fight against philosophy and reason.[29]

Lortz also discussed another intellectual movement undermining the Church's strength in the pre-Reformation period, that of Humanism, which made man rather than God the center of attention. Humanism was by nature subjective and anthropocentric. In Lortz's words, "It is premeated to its foundation with an outspoken spiritual, moral and–if the expression is permissible–religious secularization."[30] Often and especially in the cases of the Erfurt Humanists and Erasmus, it took the form of an undervaluing of dogma and of dogmatics; but it was the lack of definiteness in theology, the relativeness of Erasmus and those influenced by him, that was one of the "most important pre-conditions of an ecclesiastical revolution. It is one of the keys that explain to a large extent the riddle of the terrible defection."[31] It is the finding of the root of the Reformation here rather than in the evil of Luther that particularly distinguishes Lortz from his polemical Catholic predecessors.

Lortz showed how these and other disintegrating forces had their effect even in the highest places of Christendom:

---

[29]Josef Lortz, *Die Reformation in Deutschland* (2 vols., Freiburg, 1949), I, 172 ff.
[30]Josef Lortz, *Wie kam es zur Reformation?* (Einsiedeln, 1950), 52.
[31]Lortz, *Die Reformation,* I, 137.

the pope, his curia and the hierarchy. The abuses of the renaissance papacy were well known, reaching their zenith, or nadir, in the last three reigns before the breaking of the storm, those of Alexander VI, Julius II and Leo X. The first, of course, was known for his scandals concerning sex, the second for his warring intrigues, and the third for his all-consuming concern for humanism. As was then said: "First Venus reigned, then Mars, and now Pallas Athene."[32] It was the last, Leo X, who had to meet the first religious challenge of Luther, and it was he who chose as a motto, "Let us enjoy the papacy since God has granted it to us."[33] From this Renaissance papacy there flowed the Roman "super-curialism," with its arbitrary multiplication of clerical privileges, its actions approaching simony, its wealth spent in a luxurious life. Just as the curia was ruled by the desire for money, the members of the hierarchy also engaged too often in a hunt for as many lucrative benefices as possible, leaving the care of souls connected with the benefices in the hands of a poorly paid substitute, a "hireling."

Lortz maintained that this was not a one-sided picture he had outlined. He offered as one proof of this the statement that Pope Adrian VI, the last Germanic and non-Italian pope, made through his delegate Chierigati at the Reichstag in Nuremburg in 1522/23. "We know well that for many years there have come forth also from this Holy See itself many despicable things: abuses of spiritual things, transgressions of commandments. Indeed, in everything there has been a turn for the worse. Therefore it is not surprising that the illness has transplanted itself from the head to the members, from the popes to the hierarchy."[34] Lortz granted that there were bright spots as well as shadows, that on all levels one

[32]*Ibid.*, I, 80.
[33]Lortz, *Wie kam es?* 65.
[34]*Ibid.*, 67.

could find "a correct Church life." But if mediocre correctness was the best one could find, if "exemplary heroic life of faith was almost everywhere lacking," then the religious situation was indeed bad.[35]

Lortz drew this startling conclusion: "A 'Reformation' had become historically necessary."[36] It was hardly possible for the Church to avoid an uprising; the split was already latent. Lortz went further and laid part of the blame for the evil of the Reformation on Catholics. ". . . The Reformation is a Catholic affair in the sense of a partly Catholic causation, and thus a partly Catholic guilt."[37]

The central point of Lortz's Reformation history is the figure of Martin Luther. Some 300 of the first volume's 437 pages are concerned mainly with him. Lortz, following in the twentieth-century Caholic tradition, studied the soul of Luther, but with a much different perspective. Luther was no longer the ignorant and lustful monk or pitiable psychopath, but a sea of inexhaustible power, a genius, an "*Urkraft.*" Above all, Luther was a fundamentally religious man, a "*homo religiosus,*" a man who stood alone with his conscience before God. In referring to the years of deep depression in Luther's life, 1527-37, called a period of spiritual illness by the Danish psychiatrist Paul Reiter, Lortz refused to extend the diagnosis of "spiritually ill" to Luther's entire life. One could fill a thick volume with examples of Luther's idiosyncracies but, if correct proportion is to be kept, then ten more volumes would have to be added to bear witness to the intellectual, spiritual and religious sanity of Luther.[38]

---

[35]*Ibid.*, 70. Cf. also Lortz, *Die Reformation*, II, 82 ff.
[36]*Ibid.*, 79. Cf. also Lortz, *Die Reformation*, II, 37.
[37]*Ibid.*, Cf. also Lortz, *Die Reformation*, II, 37.
[38]Josef Lortz, *Die Reformation als religiöses Anliegen heute* (Trier, 1948), 112-116.

According to Lortz, Luther was a "cascading fullness." He had within himself a great power of prayer. In fact, he was a master of prayer, which he centered and fed on the Scriptures and particularly on the Lord's Prayer. His power of speech and pen was often that of a genius, a vulcanic genius. It is not just his translation of the Bible that gives testimony of this power with words; many of his books, sermons and verses do likewise.

On the other hand, Lortz saw Luther's main fault as subjectivism, though not an "autonomous arbitrariness" as the eighteenth and even more the nineteenth and twentieth centuries understood the term, for tradition was still very strong in Luther. He fought, for example, the attempts of the Enthusiasts and Zwingli to empty the Divine Service of the sacred. His attachment to the "Word" was so strong that one can speak of an objective subjectivism, or even of a subjective objectivism. Nevertheless, at root it was the subjective element that ruled Luther. For him there was no living teaching office of the Church, but only the individual conscience standing before the word of the Bible. "Luther's objectivism is a self-deception. . . ,"[39] because his principle of explaining the Scriptures according to one's own conscience was fundamentally a revolutionary elimination of the objective teaching office, without which every attempt at being objective really becomes subjective.

Despite this accusation of radical subjectivism Lortz has made a revolutionary approach to Luther, acknowledging his greatness, depth and fundamentally religious character. "They are poor students of history who believe that a superficial spirit without religious depth would have sufficed to deliver the terrific blow which ripped open the Church. That would

---

[39]Lortz, *Die Reformation,* I, 402.

be a severe accusation against the holy Church were it possible."[40]

The reception of Lortz's work in Catholic circles was for the most part favorable, though often tempered with criticisms of one or several aspects of his work.[41] Lortz called attention to some of these reviews himself when, in the preface to the third edition of *Die Reformation in Deutschland,* he listed a goodly number of favorable reviews, including foreign and even Roman periodicals. Many of these contained constructive criticisms which Lortz attempted to utilize in this edition. Even the sharpest critics of Lortz's work almost always began with strong praise of his book.[42]

Protestants received Lortz's two volumes with approval that approached jubilation. Readers on almost any intellectual level were bound to come across references to it. There was, of course, occasional adverse criticism, some quite brief and some quite detailed; but even more than the Catholics, the Protestant writers maintained a lauda-

---

[40]*Ibid.,* I, 192.

[41]Paul Simon, for example, pointed out that Lortz's often severe condemnations of Luther's opponents and the ecclesiastical conditions of the time should lead to an elimination of mistrust between Catholics and Protestants. See Paul Simon, "Die Reformation in Deutchland," *Hochland,* XXXVII (1941), 440-442. Joseph Schmidlin wrote: "The work of Lortz has characteristics . . . which make it an undertaking worthy of the closest study." Joseph Schmidlin, "Zur Reformationsgeschichte von Josef Lortz," *Schönere Zukunft,* XV (1940), 343. As far as building a bridge of understanding, reconciliation or at least of fruitful religious discussion between the confessions is concerned, Adolf Schremmer maintained that Lortz had done everything humanly possible. See the review by Adolf Schlemmer in *Klerusblatt Organ des Klerusverbandes der Diozösanvereine in Bayern u.d. Pfalz* (Munich), January 1, 1941. Bishop Buchberger of Regensburg espoused the same idea when discussing the Una Sancta Movement and the causes contributing to its phenomenal growth. See Michael Buchberger, *Aufbruch zur Einheit und Einigkeit im Glauben* (Freiburg, 1948), 19.

[42]Such as Joseph Schmidlin or Johannes Hessen.

tory tone throughout their discussion of *Die Reformation in Deutschland*.[43]

In writing his two-volume work, Lortz hoped that his efforts would result in more than mere description and interpretation of a past period for its own sake. He wanted to prepare a common ground on which the two confessions could meet in ecumenical discussions, to break a path toward the *Una Sancta*. In the conclusion he restated this. "If something of the deepest aims of this book lies beyond its scholarly task, or better is only accomplished through it, it is this, that it might participate in the discussion between the confessions, and might give this discussion new possibilities."[44]

LORTZ'S CONTRIBUTION TO THE UNA SANCTA

Lortz's interest in the Reformation went beyond writing and publication on the specifically academic level. Already

---

[43]Georg Smolka viewed this objective, scholarly presentation of the Reformation as something long overdue from the Catholic side. He expressed the wish that this work of Lortz would become effective "in the sense of the overcoming of the division of faith, of the completion of the true reform through the unity of the Church, without which the genuine aims of the Reformation remained and must remain piecemeal work." (Smolka, "Die Reformation," 170.) Georg Merz noted that there were no cheap confessional polemics to be found in this work. (Georg Merz, "Realität der Kirche oder singuläres Geschichtsphänomen?" *Bethel,* XXXII (1940), 124.) Otto Urbach saw in Lortz's book justification of great hope. (Otto Urbach, "Ist der Gegensatz von Katholizismus und Protestantismus unüberbrückbar?" *Theologie und Glaube,* XXXIII (1941), 15.) Herman Wendorf, in an exchange with Lortz, paid him a great tribute: "It is astounding how far Lortz's ability to enter the feelings of others extends, without stepping outside the framework of a strong Catholicism." (Wendorf, "Luther, Erasmus," 282.) As late as 1956, Walther von Loewenich congratulated Lortz for having the courage to write this book, for it was not at all certain that such a work would receive the imprimatur. He also praised the responsible ecclesiastical authorities "that they did not allow themselves to be frightened away from it in narrow anxiety." (Von Loewenich, *Moderne Katholizismus,* 340.

[44]Quoted in Buchberger, *Aufbruch zur Einheit,* 19.

since the 1920's he had been giving lectures throughout Germany on the Reformation, attempting to eliminate the inter-confessional polemics so prevalent in this field. One Protestant, in relating how Lortz spoke all over Germany at Una Sancta meetings in the late 1930's, referred to Lortz as "the wandering preacher of the Una Sancta."[45]

Following his writing and lecturing in the interest of the Una Sancta Movement, Professor Lortz, with the urging of Father Max Metzger, published at the beginning of the war a small booklet of forty-eight theses. The theses contained certain main points based on an historical analysis of the Reformation and its consequences, whose discussion would be especially important and fruitful in an ecumenical sense. Typical of the theses might be the third and the last. "A particular guilt weighs on Catholics in that especially in the beginning of the Reformation the real religious aim of the Evangelicals were not taken seriously enough.."[46] "Those returning home lose nothing, but rather are enriched; they in turn enrich those to whom they return, namely 'in all that of positive value which they have embraced and cherished with particular love.'"[47] Later on in the war, when the Nazis no longer allowed the theses to be printed because of the alleged paper shortage, they were copied and spread by many individual typists and by hectograph.

A second publication flowing directly from Lortz's lecturing came out in 1948: *Die Reformation als religiöses Anliegen Heute, Vier Vorträge im Dienst der Una Sancta* (*The Reformation: A Problem for Today*, Westminster, Md.: Newman, 1964). This is a group of four lectures on the sources of the Reformation in relationship to Catholicism today.

---

[45]Heinrich Hermelink, *Katholizismus und Protestantismus* (Stuttgart, 1949), 27.
[46]Josef Lortz, *Die Reformation, Thesen als Handreichung bei ökumenischen Gesprächen* (Meitingen, n.d.), 2.
[47]*Ibid.*, 30.

Later, Lortz continued his support of the Una Sancta Movement by publishing in 1950 the fruit of further lectures as *Wie Kam es zur Reformation* (*How the Reformation Came*, New York: Herder and Herder, 1964), in which the basic facts and conclusions found in the first part of his earlier larger work are reiterated.

In 1949 Lortz's reputation was so great that the leader of the Una Sancta Movement, Matthias Laros, addressed to the government a request which he considered absolutely necessary "for the unity of the confessions and internal peace among Germans." He urged the establishment of a "Reformation History Institute" at one of the universities for the consideration of scholarly questions concerning unity in a comprehensive and objective manner. And Father Lortz, according to Laros, was the one man from either side of the confessional line best suited to direct such an institute. "Lortz must be freed for this great task. This is certainly the desire of all those who have any insight, of those who are intimately concerned with the intellectual-religious unity of our people."[48]

In the following year, 1950, Lortz was appointed director, along with Professor Fritz Kern, of the *Institut für europäische Geschichte* at Mainz University. Lortz is in charge of the department of Religious History of Western Civilization, which is doing research and publishing on the immediate and remote pre-conditions of the Reformation, the complex of the Reformation itself with particular attention to Luther, and the development of the Reformation up to the present.[49]

---

[48]Matthias Laros, "Was ist zu tun?" *Begegnung*, IV (1949), 123.

[49]Erwin Iserloh and Peter Manns, eds., *Festgabe Joseph Lortz* (Baden-Baden, 1957), xix.

HERTE, HESSEN AND OTHERS

Only a few years after the appearance of Lortz's major work, the Catholic church historian Adolph Herte published his study on the influence of the polemic writing of Cochloeus, *Das katholische Lutherbild von Cochlaeus bis zur Gegenwart.* The important thing about Cochlaeus was not that he wrote such a tendentious work on Luther, for there were many written on both sides, but that this amazing collection of stories "exerted an influence which is without parallel. . . . Like a comet it drew almost the entire Luther-literature after it in a gigantic tail, and it determined in the final analysis the features and form of this literature."[50] Just how widespread and long-lasting the influence of Cochlaeus on the Catholic view of Luther has been can be appreciated only after reading through Herte's three volumes. Herte gathered an enormous amount of material of all sorts: Luther-monographs, polemic and popular writings and essays, and "heretic stories." He listed his material through the centuries with what has been called "staggering monotony,"[51] and showed the very frequent ultimate connection with Cochlaeus.

Of course among Catholics interested in bettering relations between the confessions the book was well received. But at least one, the Jesuit Max Pribilla, was somewhat cynical. He felt that Herte expected that the Protestants would balance the picture by also confessing their faults, and Pribilla doubted that they would.[52] On the Protestant side, von Loewenich admired Herte's "ruthless openness in the face of

---

[50]Von Loewenich, *Moderne Katholizismus,* 329.
[51]*Ibid.*
[52]Quoted in Max Pribilla, "Um das katholische Lutherbild," *Stimmen der Zeit* CXL (1947), 469.

his own tradition."[53] "His plea to the Protestants to do the same on their side is thereby justified and well founded."[54]

Continuing in the same non-polemic vein is the work of Johannes P. Hessen, a booklet much smaller than the comprehensive works of Lortz and Herte. In it Hessen insists that if "catholic" means universal, all-embracing, Catholics must "express a full 'Yes' to the real values which are in Luther's personality . . ."[55] He follows Lortz in maintaining that a Reformation was needed and echoed the position of Friedrich Heiler, that a "reformation of the Reformation" was needed because the matter had gone to extremes. For Hessen, Luther as the center and the principle of Protestantism must be the main concern in all ecumenical efforts. Luther is "the way to Una Sancta."[56]

However, Hessen directly opposed Lortz's position that Luther was radically a subjectivist. "Nothing stands so in contradiction to the innermost spiritual structure of the reformer as modern subjectivism, which makes the human

---

[53]Von Loewenich, *Moderne Katholizismus,* 330. Herte's work found a widely favorable reception among Protestant theologians and historians. Speaking of Herte's 1935 publication, the Protestant Otto Urbach wrote: "Herte's pioneering work is from beginning to end based on the sources, in the formal sense a gigantic project of German scholarly diligence." (Urbach, "Ist der Gegensatz," 64.) He very emphatically recommended the book to his readers, "for it is one of the keenest and most tightly reasoned works which serve to tear down the dividing walls between the confessions." (p. 64) A very favorable ten-page review of Herte's three volume work was written by the distinguished Evangelical Reformation expert Karl Meissinger in 1944. He referred to the book as a "pioneering experience" and declared that partly because of it "the atmosphere of the Reformation research has changed." See the review by Karl A. Meissinger, in *Theologie und Seelsorge,* XXXI (1944), 53. Hermelink, the Protestant church historian, also acknowledged the service done toward better interconfessional relations by Herte. See Hermelink, *Katholizisimus und Protestantismus,* 17.

[54]Von Loewenich, *Moderne Katholizismus,* 330.

[55]Hessen, *Luther,* 7.

[56]*Ibid.,* 66.

subject the measure of all things."[57] Rather he explains the Reformation and the key role Luther's personality played in it as a manifestation of the systaltic action of history. During the middle ages there was an expanding tendency toward a greater and greater synthesis. With Luther and the Reformation the historical pendulum swung in the other direction, toward concentration on principles. Hessen's booklet had a particularly warm reception in Protestant circles. Friedrich Heiler said of it that it "must fill every Protestant with bright joy and convince him that, with such broad and free Catholic spirits, an understanding over Luther and the central demands of the Reformation is not difficult to attain."[58]

Thus in a little more than a generation, the attitude of leading Catholic historians toward Luther and the Reformation has changed from the criticism and polemic of Denifle and Grisar to the objectivism of Lortz, Herte, and Hessen. And this list includes only the more outstanding scholars who have written on Luther and the Reformation specifically. In addition to a growing amount of monographic material, there are other Catholic historians, writing in kindred fields, who have also contributed to this pattern: Walter Zeeden with his two volume work on Luther in the eyes of Lutherans[59] and Hubert Jedin who recently brought out the
des deutschen Luthertums (2 vols., Freiburg, 1950-52).
second volume of his monumental history of the Council of Trent.[60] These men, though they are rarely ever mentioned in Una Sancta literature because they usually do not deal with controversial points such as Luther or the causes of

[57]*Ibid.*, 24.
[58]Review by Friedrich Heiler, in *Oekumenische Einheit*, I (1948), 140.
[59]Ernst W. Zeeden, *Martin Luther und die Reformation im Urteil*
[60]Hubert Jedin, *Geschichte des Konzils von Trient* (2 vols., Freiburg, 1951-57).

the Reformation, have also employed an objective and irenic manner of writing. This change has had a large effect on the inter-confessional situation by giving Catholics and Protestants more common ground on which to meet and by eliminating some points of emotional friction which had made a conversation between the Churches psychologically impossible in the past.

Chapter Three

The Ecumenical Movement

THE "ecumenical movement" is a term used to designate the recent striving of many Christian Churches toward some kind of union. Since the very beginning of Christianity, however, there has been a constant movement to maintain unity. The first really major split in the Christian Church, one which has lasted to the present day, was the fission between the Eastern Churches and the Roman Church, which became definitive in 1054. Since the eleventh century many attempts to heal the division have been made, with relatively meager results. The second Council of Lyons in 1274 and the Council of Florence in 1438 met with some temporary success, but their influence did not last. Then another surge of centrifugal energy arose in the sixteenth century, the force of which is by no means abated. In the United States alone, score upon score of Protestant Churches and sects have split off from the older Christian Churches.

Various efforts were made in the centuries following the Reformation to reestablish unity. One of the more interesting of these was that made by Leibniz and Bossuet in the latter part of the seventeenth century. However, these attempts at reunification, for instance those between Rome and the Eastern Churches in the middle ages, were essentially bound to political motives and conditions and, like all political agreements, unstable. Or less often they were the work of more or less influential individuals. The strivings to reinstate the *Una Sancta Ecclesia* take on organizational form only in the twentieth century.

NINETEENTH CENTURY BACKGROUND

The ecumenical movement, which burst upon the twentieth century scene with unprecedented force, has as one of its main sources the evangelical awakening among the Protestant Churches during the latter half of the eighteenth and early part of the nineteenth centuries. This awakening took on different forms in different countries. In Germany it sprang out of the Pietist movement of the eighteenth century; in England Methodism was the great force; while in America there had been great awakenings in the eighteenth and nineteenth centuries as a response to the needs of the Church on the frontier. The fact that this awakening knew no national boundaries that it brought with it an almost unparalleled missionary activity tended gradually to strengthen the centripetal forces of Christianity. "Missions and ecumenism are inseparable. Revival, missions, Christian unity, is an inevitable series."[1]

During the second quarter of the nineteenth century, this desire for unity among Protestants expressed itself more and more strongly through articles, books, and discussions, and in 1846 it finally culminated in the formation of the Evangelical Alliance.[2] During discussions leading to the formation of this organization two main alternatives were considered: Should there be some sort of union or at least federation of the Churches themselves, or should the union be merely of individuals from the various Churches? The decision was made in favor of the latter idea, and in August of 1846, eight hundred prominent Christians of fifty-two different Churches from both the New and Old World met in London, an extraordinary event for those days.

This Evangelical Alliance produced some significant results. The week beginning with the first Sunday of the year was set aside each year for prayer for unity by the Churches. The merely psychological effect of this for promoting a consciousness of unity among Christians was considerable.

---

[1]Ruth Rouse, "Voluntary Movements and the Changing Ecumenical Climate," in Ruth Rouse, ed., *A History of the Ecumenical Movement* (London, 1954), 310.

[2]Cf. J. P. Michael, *Christen suchen eine Kirche* (Freiburg, 1958), 21.

The world-wide conferences, such as those of London (1851) and New York (1873), increased the awareness of oneness of Christians on an international scale. The Alliance sponsored journals in different countries, which helped dispel mutual ignorance and its consequent prejudice among Christians. Nevertheless, the Alliance had some outstanding weaknesses, since the relations of the Churches as such with one another were ignored. There was a definite shying away from any discussion of plans for reunion, and at the same time the membership requirements as far as doctrinal belief were concerned were extremely rigid. (This last contributed greatly to the disappearance of the American branch in the 1890's.) Despite these weaknesses and a lack of central leadership and organization, the Evangelical Alliance paved the way for those ecumenical organizations of the twentieth century which were, to a greater or lesser extent, to overcome these same weaknesses.

About the same time, two other organizations which were destined to have an extraordinary effect on the ecumenical movement of the present century were founded. The YMCA and YWCA were founded in England in 1844 and 1854, and quickly spread to America and from there to the rest of the world. Although neither group was directly concerned with ecumenical problems, their international perspective and interest in the development of Christian student groups made them, along with the Student Christian Movement, the breeding grounds of four-fifths of the leaders of the future ecumenical conferences leading to the founding of the World Council of Churches in 1948.

Christian Unity and Rome

The second quarter of the nineteenth century also witnessed a series of ecumenical efforts directed toward the Church of Rome. Although these Rome-oriented efforts did not directly affect the formation of the great Protestant ecumenical organizations of the twentieth century, they are a part of the growing search for Christian unity of the time and have helped to pave the way for the later Una Sancta Movement by bringing Catholics and Protestants together for theological discussion. It was in Britain that these ecumenical efforts began.

In the 1830's there arose within the Church of England the Oxford Movement which, in emphasizing the importance of patristic theology and the need for a liturgical revival, insisted on the continuity between the Church of England and the medieval and patristic Church. It developed a theology of the unity of Christendom, which was therefore non-Protestant in its orientation. This "branch-theory" viewed the Church as an image of the Trinity, having its unity personalized in the Roman, Orthodox and Anglican branches, for only these Churches had apostolic succession. After the difficulties the Oxford Movement encountered with Newman's conversion to Roman Catholicism in 1845, it sought the solution of the problem of collective *rapprochement* in corporate reunion. This had been Newman's ideal even before his conversion, and also that of Pusey.[3]

In 1857 the Association for the Promotion of the Unity of Christendom (APUC) was founded by an Anglican, Frederick Lee, and two Catholics, A. W. Pugin and Ambrose de Lisle, as a league of prayer for the corporate reunion of the Anglican, Orthodox and Roman Churches. Lee was also the editor of a periodical, *The Union,* which agitated for the aims of the Association although there was no official connection. The Association had the sympathy of Cardinal Wiseman, Archbishop of Westminster, until his death in 1865, but it was opposed vigorously by Father Henry Manning who, as an avid ultramontane, had considerable influence in Rome. It was through *The Union,* which somewhat rashly published letters of priests who were not on the best terms with their

[3]Georges Tavard, *Petite Histoire du mouvement oecuménique* (Paris, 1960), 37-42.

bishops, that the Association was condemned by Rome. The letter of the Holy Office, *Ad omnes episcopos Angliae,* in 1864 forbade Catholic membership in the Association.

Lee later founded a semi-secret organization, the Order of Corporate Union, through which Anglican clergymen were to receive orders through an Orthodox or even Catholic bishop. The Order however soon proved abortive.

The first generation of the Oxford Movement was bitterly disappointed by the condemnation of the APCU, and even more so by the definition of papal infallibility in 1870. But a second generation followed, among which was Charles Lindley Wood, later Lord Halifax(1839-1934), who was haunted by the idea of union with Rome. In 1890 Lord Halifax met the French priest Fernand Portal who also was deeply interested in the problem of Anglo-Roman unity. Their first action was the publication of a series of articles in which Father Portal concluded that Anglican orders were not valid. These articles drew the attention of a number of Catholic intellectuals, particularly two celebrated church historians, Louis Duchesne and Auguste Boudinhon, and also Pietro Gasparri, later Vatican secretary of state during the pontificates of Benedict XV and Pius XI. In the meanwhile Lord Halifax and Father Portal contacted a number of Angelican clergymen and bishops with mixed success.

By 1895 the discussion of the validity of Anglican orders as a basis of a possible reunion of Canterbury and Rome had come to the attention of Pope Leo XIII, who accorded Halifax and Portal two audiences in the early part of that year. Halifax was extremely optimistic. He wrote, "It was impossible for the pope to have been more amiable and encouraging."[4] In April of the same year Leo XIII published an apostolic letter, *Ad Anglos,* which was conciliatory in tone and encouraged the patient study of the possibility of unity.

---

[4]Andre D. Toledano, *L'Anglicanisme* (Paris, 1957), 86.

The Anglican Archbishop of York declared that "reunion is in the air," and in December, 1895, Father Portal founded the periodical *Revue Anglo-romaine*. However, many English Catholic clerics and certain circles at the Vatican did not favor a corporate reunion which, they believed, would not command the adherance of the Anglicans in general. Also evident here is the feeling of the followers of Cardinal Manning, who had said, "Rather than being a rampart against irreligion the Church of England must be recognized as the mother of all intellectual and spiritual aberrations which today cover the face of England."[5]

The whole discussion rose to a climax when Leo XIII appointed a commission to study anew the validity of Anglican orders. The commission was divided in its conclusions, with men like Msgr. Gasparri and Father Duchesne giving a judgment in favor of the validity of Anglican orders. On September 13, 1896, the Pope issued the bull *Apostolicae curae* which declared the Anglican orders invalid. The Anglo-Roman discussions were then dropped for a quarter of a century until the Malines conversations were initiated.

The Malines conversations were a series of five discussions between Catholic and Anglican theologians from 1921 to 1926 at Malines, Belgium. They were carried on by a very small select group of six to ten outstanding scholars. On the Anglican side there was Lord Halifax; Walter Frere, bishop of Truro; Armitage Robinson, dean of Wells; and later Charles Gore, retired bishop of Oxford; and Beresford Kidd, a well-known historian. The Catholics were Cardinal Mercier, famous as a neo-Thomist philosopher and theologian; his Vicar General and later successor, Msgr. Van Roey; Father Portal; and later Pierre Batiffol, the celebrated church historian; and Canon Hippolyte Hemmer, a specialist on the Church Fathers.

The initiative came from the Anglicans, as a result of the statement of the Lambeth Conference of the Anglican bishops

[5]Tavard, *Petite histoire*, 57.

in 1920. At this conference the Anglican bishops were not dealing with the Anglo-Roman question at all, but were attempting to prepare the way for a reunion between Anglicans, Presbyterians and Congregationalists. To this end the bishops declared themselves and their priests prepared to undergo whatever regulation in connection with the Presbyterian and Congregational ministry necessary. Lord Halifax then concluded that in principle, it would also be possible for the Anglican bishops and priests to submit to a Roman reordination as a prerequisite to reunion with Rome. This meant that the Roman rejection of the validity of Anglican orders placed no insuperable block in the way of reunion. Consequently Lord Halifax set himself in contact with Cardinal Mercier, who offered to serve as host to Anglican-Catholic theological discussions.

The conversations were not an attempt to negotiate a reunion between England and Rome; the participants were not plenipotentiaries, but simply theologians expressing their own opinions. What transpired, however, was known to the leaders on both sides, and was of the greatest interest to them. The Archbishop of Canterbury himself, Randall Davidson, prepared some contributions to the discussions. From the popes, first Benedict XV and then Pius XI, there was blessing and encouragement. Cardinal Pietro Gasparri, then secretary of state at the Vatican, wrote to Cardinal Mercier, "The Holy Father authorizes your Eminence to say to the Anglicans that the Holy Father approves and encourages your conversations and prays to the good Lord with all his heart to bless them."[6] The immediate aim of the conversations was to clear the atmosphere by eliminating the misconceptions and prejudices of both sides; "the union itself will be a work of grace at an hour which divine Providence will deign to chose."[7]

[6]Jacques de Bivort de La Saudée, *Anglicans et catholiques* (Paris, 1948), 66-67.
[7]*Ibid.*, 50.

Unfortunately for all involved, Cardinal Mercier died in January, 1926, and in June of the same year Abbé Portal also died. With the two Catholic leaders gone only one final summarizing conference was held in October, 1926. The one result of the conversations was to prove that a dialogue between Catholic and non-Catholic Christians was possible even at a very high level. But while some Anglicans were thus involved in ecumenical exchanges with Rome, others had turned to Protestant groups to work for unity among the non-Catholic Christian Churches.

THE ECUMENICAL WATERSHED

In the latter part of the nineteenth century students began to play a significant part in Protestant missionary affairs. The Christian student movements forward in the 1880's and 1890's were evangelistic and missionary in aim. By 1945, 20,500 students from so-called Christian lands had gone into foreign countries to do missionary work. These young people soon began to take the divisions in Christianity seriously and were led very quickly to ecumenical projects. By 1895 many of the groups had gathered together in the World Student Christian Federation. The interest of the Student Christian Movment in things ecumenical proved a tremendous boon to the ecumenical movement. The Student Christian Movement, and more particularly its international conference, served as laboratories for ecumenical experiments which the Churches themselves would never have dared to venture. The experience gained and the personal contacts made served greatly in preparing the way for what has been called "the ecumenical watershed," the World Missionary Conference in Edinburgh in 1910.[8]

As those societies founded during the awakening to spread the gospel expanded, they tended more and more toward

[8]Ruth Rouse, *World's Student Christian Federation* (London, 1948), Chapters 8, 16.

cooperation, often through the holding of conferences. These reached a high point in the Edinburgh Conference of 1910. "Edinburgh 1910 summed up and focused much of the previous century's movement for uniting Christians in giving the gospel to the world."[9] It was not merely delegates from missionary societies, for there had been such delegates appointed to conferences in 1888 and 1900. But the previous conferences had been largely to educate, inform and impress the general public; the more thousands that came the better. Edinburgh, on the other hand, was to be a consultative body with a view to further cooperation. With this aim in mind the planners of the Conference tried to make the membership of the Conference as official and broad as possible. The result of this planning was a gathering that included more nations, races, and shades of belief than any previous Conference. It was mostly this breadth that made Edinburgh the beginning of a new ecumenical era, and it was "largely because of the influences which issued from Edinburgh 1910" that the "ecumenical movement became widely inclusive."[10]

The direct or indirect influence of Edinburgh on the founding of one of the first two world-wide ecumenical organizations, the World Conference on Faith and Order, also made that Conference important in ecumenical history. As a delegate to Edinburgh, Bishop Charles H. Brent felt there was a need to discuss the questions of faith and ecclesiastical order deliberately excluded from the Edinburgh Conference. Speaking from the floor of that Conference, he declared his intention to found an organization for that purpose.[11]

---

[9]Kenneth Scott Latourette, "Ecumenical Bearings of the Missionary Movement and the International Missionary Council," in Rouse, *A History*, 355.

[10]*Ibid.*, 357.

[11]*Ibid.*

FAITH AND ORDER

In the fall following the Edinburgh Conference, Bishop Brent, a Missionary Episcopal Bishop in the Philippines, addressed a mass meeting of the Protestant Episcopal Church of the United States, telling the members about the Edinburgh Conference and urging them to take the lead in founding a Conference on Faith and Order. As a consequence a committee was very shortly appointed, and work was energetically begun. The response was extraordinarily favorable throughout the United States and other parts of the world. Even the response of the Vatican was very sympathetic, though indefinite. However, the plans, which were rapidly approaching fruition, were almost completely disrupted by the outbreak of the first World War.[12] Immediately after the War, in the spring of 1919, a deputation from the American Episcopal Church Commisison left on a European trip in an attempt to contact the leaders of the Orthodox Churches and the Roman Catholic Church. Though they had success with the smaller Orthodox Churches, they met with disappointment in their contacts with the Russian Orthodox Church and with Rome. Nevertheless, efforts continued. A planning meeting representing some seventy Churches and forty nations was held at Geneva in 1920. Here a continuation committee was appointed to take over the responsibility for leadership from the Protestant Episopal Church of the United States, thereby giving the whole movement a more international and inter-Church basis. The continuation committee met again in 1925 and set the date for the first World Conference on Faith and Order.[13]

On August 3, 1927, 385 men and 9 women from 108 different Protestant and Orthodox Churches met in Lausanne,

---

[12]H. Sasse, *Die Weltkonferenz für Glaube und Kirchenverfassung* (Berlin, 1929), 5.

[13]Tissington Tatlow, "The World Conference on Faith and Order," in Rouse, *A History,* 407-419.

Switzerland. It is notable that the majority were not just interested private individuals or representatives of societies, but were officially appointed representatives of their Churches. After several weeks' work the Conference was able to agree unanimously on reports concerning six of the seven subjects on the agenda: the call to unity, the Church's message to the world—the Gospel—,the nature of the Church, the Church's common confession of faith, the Church's ministry, and the sacraments. The report on the seventh subject, the unity of christendom and the place of the different Churches in it, met with difficulty and was in the end referred to the continuation committee for further consideration. The list of subjects discussed shows the central concern of the Conference for the idea of the Church. This concept has continued to grow in importance in the ecumenical movement, as it has in modern Catholic thought.

Before the end of the Conference, a continuation committee of ninety-two men and three women was appointed with Bishop Brent as chairman. This committee, like the previous continuation committee, played an important part in advancing the work of the Faith and Order movement.

But already in 1929 it was felt that much of the same ground was being covered by both the Faith and Order movement and the Life and Work movement. That same year a small committee was appointed by Faith and Order to confer with a similar committee from Life and Work concerning their mutual relationships. From this first small cooperation grew the final fusion, which took place at the foundation of the World Council of Churches at Amsterdam in 1948.

The second World Conference on Faith and Order met in Edinburgh on August 3, 1937. It was attended by 344 delegates and 84 alternates from 123 Churches.[14] The absence of one group of delegates was very sharply noticed: passports

[14]Cf. Leonard Hodgson, ed., *das Glaubensgespräch der Kirchen* (Zurich, 1940), 380 ff.

had been refused members of the German Evangelical Church by the Nazi Government. Nevertheless, the Edinburgh Conference was a definite advance over the one held ten years previously at Lausanne. This improvement was due mainly to two things. Ninety-five persons at Edinburgh had also been at Lausanne; hence further exchanges of ideas and insights could be built on old friendships. And there was a vastly greater amount of theological preparation for the Edinburgh Conference than for the Lausanne Conference.

When the reports were finally drafted—the concept of the Church again figured very prominently in the discussions—they were all accepted unanimously by the Conference. Only one ran into some difficulties, the proposal for the formation of a World Council of Churches, which had been formulated by a joint committee from Life and Work and Faith and Order. In the end, however, this too was accepted unanimously.

LIFE AND WORK

The genesis of the second large ecumenical organization of this century, the movement for Life and Work, was intimately bound up with World War I and the World Alliance of Churches for Promoting International Friendship. At the very beginning of the war, the founding congress of an international Protestant peace league took place at Constance, Germany. War between Germany and Russia began August 1, 1914. The congress met August 2, and ended, perforce, August 3, the day Germany declared war on France. Although poorer circumstances in which to begin a peace league could hardly be conceived, the World Alliance was founded nevertheless. In 1915 the name of the World Alliance was changed to The World Alliance for Promoting International Friendship Through the Churches.[15]

[15]Nils Karlstroem, "Movements for international Friendship and Life and Work," in *A History*, 514, 517.

About the same time, May, 1914, Nathan Soederblom, a prime mover of the later Life and Work movement, was elected Archbishop of Uppsala, Sweden. Working through his own Church and the World Alliance, Archbishop Soederblom expended a great deal of energy in an attempt to bring about peace. As one writer later remarked, "From this time on, Nathan Soederblom gradually became a personal symbol of what was to be undertaken."[16]

The idea of calling an international Christian conference even while the war was still going on arose from many sides, and several attempts were made to make the conference an actuality. A date was set a third and final time, September 8, 1918, but once again the conference had to be postponed. Ultimately, the only result of these efforts was a telegram sent on September 8 by the Scandinavian leaders to their colleagues in different countries, "Our prayers are holding an ecumenical conference."[17]

The first world Christian conference actually to take place was that of the international committee of the World Alliance, held at Oud Wassnaar, Netherlands, on September 30, 1919. It was here that Archbishop Soederblom outlined his now ripened plans for the Ecumenical Council of the Church.[18] He maintained that a common organ of expression was necessary for the Churches, and that its formation could not wait until they had achieved unity on matters of faith and order. This had been demonstrated by the helplessness of the Churches during the crisis of the war. "We cannot afford to remain separated and in a state of unnecessary impotence caused by our separation, up to the time when we shall be truly united in faith and Church organization."[19] This Ecu-

[16]Charles S. McFarland, *Steps toward the World Council* (New York, 1948), 42.

[17]Karlstroem, "Movements for international Friendship," 421-430.

[18]Cf. Nils Karlstroem, "Ein oekumenischer Kirchenrat," *Oekumenische Einheit*, III (1953), 93-102.

[19]Nathan Soederblom, *Christian Fellowship, or the United Life and Work of Christendom* (New York, 1923), 1.

menical Council would not encroach on the independence of the Churches and would deal, not with matters of faith and order, but with social and international problems. As the planning committee of Life and Work expressed it in 1922, "Doctrine divides, but service unites."[20]

In August of 1920, ninety delegates from fifteen countries met in Geneva (the same month and location as that of the founding meeting of Faith and Order) to call into existence the Universal Christian Conference on Life and Work. A committee of arrangements was formed and it was this body which later set the time and place for the first world conference: 1925, in Stockholm.

The Stockholm conference "more than any other great Christian conference was the child of one heart and one brain; [for] in a most unusual way Nathan Soederblom, Archbishop of Uppsala, *was* Stockholm."[21] On August 19, over 600 delegates from 37 coutries gathered in the cathedral at Stockholm for the opening services. Afterwards they were received in the Royal Palace by the King and Queen of Sweden. For the first time, the delegates had assembled not merely as interested individuals but, in almost every case, as official representatives of the Churches.

The continuation committee which grew out of the Stockholm meeting helped direct the energy of the movement in many different projects, some of which did not find their fulfillment until later, in the World Council of Churches. The continuation committee also made a start in such new undertakings as inter-denominational inter-Church aid, an ecumenical training institute, the introduction of an ecumenical approach in the study of Church history and in theological education generally, and even the writing of an ecumenical history of the Christian Church.

---

[20]Karlstroem, "Movements for international Friendship," 540.
[21]*Ibid.*, 545.

It also took care of the planning and preparation for the second World Conference of Life and Work, which took place July 12 to 26, 1937, in Oxford, just a few weeks before the Faith and Order Conference at Edinburgh. The 425 regular members at the Conference from 120 Churches had come from over 40 countries. As at Edinburgh, a great absence was felt–besides that of the Roman Catholic Church–for the German Churches were barred from participation by the Nazis. In fact, Pastor Niemöller and others were already in prison.[22]

From the very beginning the Life and Work movement emphasized the practical application of Christianity to the social and international situations through the Churches' cooperation with one another. But theological aspects were never neglected completely. With the passage of time, the Life and Work movement found itself increasingly involved with problems of faith and church order as prerequisites to its more specifically social problems. This tendency became more and more marked, until the fusion of the Life and Work movement with the Faith and Order movement into a World Council of Churches became an obvious necessity.

WORLD COUNCIL OF CHURCHES

To quote the General Secretary of the World Council of Churches, Willem Adolf Visser 't Hooft, "The story of the origins of the World Council of Churches reminds one of the development of a theme in a symphony. At first one or two instruments introduce the new melody and one expects that the other instruments will take it up. But no, the theme disappears in the mass of sound. Here and there it tries to disengage itself, but its time is not yet. Suddenly it comes out clearly and dominates all other sounds."[23]

---

[22]Cf. W. Menn, *Oekumenischer Katechismus. Eine kurze Unterweisung über Werden und Wesen der Oekumene* (Stuttgart, 1950), 14.

[23]Willem Adolf Visser 't Hooft, "The Genesis of the World Council of Churches," in Rouse, *A History,* 697.

Immediately after World War I, several individuals raised their voices in favor of some sort of League of Churches corresponding to the League of Nations.[24] However, the tendency already noted to keep the two great ecumenical bodies separate under the slogan "Doctrine divides but service unites" remained strong until the great Conferences in 1925 and 1927. The idea of a World Council of Churches gained some momentum in Stockholm in 1925. For example, Dr. G. K. A. Bell spoke of the formation of an "international Christian Council as desirable but not yet feasible."[25] At Lausanne in 1927, Archbishop Soederblom came out in favor of forming such a Council out of existing organizations, but his position was severely criticized.[26] Nevertheless, support for a World Council continued to grow throughout the early 1930's, until Dr. Bell, bishop of Chichester, asked a large number of Church leaders on behalf of Life and Work whether or not the next world conferences of both Life and Work and Faith and Order should take place in the same place and at almost the same time. The answers were overwhelmingly in the affirmative.

The movement toward unification gathered momentum in the summer of 1936 when Dr. J. H. Oldham, feeling that the 1937 world conferences would be an opportunity which might never be repeated, submitted a memorandum to the committee meetings of both Life and Work and Faith and Order. He suggests that a joint committee be appointed to draft a report on the formation of a World Council of Churches, to be discussed by the two world conferences in 1937. The committee was appointed, met and concluded that the time had arrived to form a World Council of Churches as a perm-

---

[24]Cf. Hamilcar S. Alivisatos, "Report of Preliminary Meeting," *Internationale Kirchliche Zeitschrift,* XX (1921), 93 ff.

[25]G.K.A. Bell, ed., *The Stockholm Conference 1925* (Oxford, 1926), 682.

[26]H. N. Bate, ed., *Faith and Order. Proceedings of the World Conference, Lausanne, August 3-21, 1927* (London, 1928), 397 ff.

anent organ of the Churches. The Council was to be "a body representative of the Churches and caring for the interests of Life and Work and Faith and Order respectively."[27] This report was then submitted to both the Edinburgh and Oxford Conferences and, after some opposition and vigorous debate, was twice accepted *nemine contradicente.*

A committee of fourteen members was appointed by the Edinburgh and Oxford conferences to put the accepted plan into effect. It met in May of the following year and set up a provisional structure destined to last for ten years. Several plans for early meetings, including one for a General Assembly to be held in 1941, were completely disrupted by the war. The administrative committee of Life and Work transferred its responsibilities to the provisional committee, but the Faith and Order continuation committee continued to function separately.

The provisional committee made its headquarters in Geneva and, throughout the war and its immediate aftermath became increasingly more involved in relief work. Once the war came to an end, however, no time was lost in trying to reestablish the contacts broken by the war and in laying the foundation for the first General Assembley of the World Council of Churches. At first there was considerable anxiety over whether or not the problem of war guilt would have the same disruptive influence that it did after World War I. These fears were allayed, however, when in October, 1945, a World Council delegation met with the new Council of the Evangelical Church in Germany at Stuttgart. The new Council stated, in the clearest terms possible, the consciousness of guilt felt by the German people in what has come to be known as the "Stuttgart Declaration." The question of war guilt had poisoned ecumenical activities for a decade after the first

[27]Leonard Hodgson, ed., *The Second World Conference on Faith and Order Held at Edinburgh, August 3-18, 1937* (London, 1938), 270-4.

World War, but after the second it actually became a source of greater mutual confidence as a result of the attitude of the German Church leaders. According to Halfdan Hoegsbro, the Stuttgart Declaration is the "greatest ecumenical deed of our generation," for it was through this "narrow portal alone that the Christians of the nations which had been torn asunder could come to each other."[28]

In the February, 1946, meeting of the provisional committee, two important decisions were made. The time and place of the first General Assembly were fixed for Amsterdam, in the summer of 1948. An Ecumenical Institute, made possible by a grant from John D. Rockefeller, Jr., was also created.

In September of the same year the Ecumenical Institute was officially opened at Chateau de Bossey, twelve miles from Geneva. This institute has grown increasingly important since its foundation, serving as a co-ordinating center of the many ecumenical activities that have sprung up all over the world since the War. Research on ecumenical subjects seminars and lecture series are centered there, the Institute even offers a degree in ecumenical theology.

On August 22, 1948, 351 official delegates from 147 Churches in 44 countries met in Amsterdam for the first General Assembly of the World Council of Churches. Delegates from the smaller Eastern Churches were present, but the Orthodox Church of Russia and the Orthodox Churches of the satellite countries did not send delegates. Nor did the Roman Catholic Church.

There have been two ecumenical conferences since the Amsterdam Conference of 1948. The movement for Faith and Order, even after it joined the World Council of Churches, maintained its own separate identity until 1952 when, on the occasion of its third and final world conference in Lund,

---

[28]Halfdan Hoegsbro, "Oekumene in Deutschland," in *Bekennende Kirche* (Munich, 1952), 273.

Sweden, it dissolved itself into a commission within the studies department of the World Council of Churches. One interesting novelty of the Lund Conference was the presence of a Roman Catholic delegation as "observers," with the acknowledgment of the Holy Office via the Vicar Apostolic for Sweden, Bishop Mueller. The World Council of Churches held its second General Assembly in August, 1954, at Northwestern University, Evanston, Illinois, and its third in New Delhi, November, 1961.

ROME AND THE WORLD COUNCIL

The Roman Catholic Church was approached and invited to take part in each of the ecumenical conferences held in the second quarter of the twentieth century. It's answer was always courteous and sympathetic, but negative. In March, 1918, the three Primates of Scandinavia sent a letter to Pope Benedict XV, inviting him to send a representative to the world conference scheduled for that September. Cardinal Secretary of State Gasparri returned a very sympathetic reply but mentioned nothing about sending a representation.[29] The group of Protestant clergymen who visited the Pope in 1919 invited him to the formation meeting of the Faith and Order movement to be held in Geneva in the following year. They were received in a very friendly manner, but the refusal to participate was definite. The report of the Lausanne Conference (1927) noted: "in Rome, through the great courtesy of Archbishop Cerretti, a formal invitation and statement about the Conference were presented to his Holiness the Pope through Cardinal Gasparri; and the official refusal of the invitation was balanced by the personal friendliness and benevolence of the Pope."[30]

On the feast of Epiphany, 1928, Pope Pius XI issued the encyclical *Mortalium Animos* on "fostering the true religious

---

[29]Nils Karlstroem, *Rom und die Stockholmer Bewegung* (Uppsala, 1931), 4-9.

[30]Bate, *Faith and Order,* ix.

union." The time of issuance was judiciously chosen since the two great conferences of Stockholm and Lausanne had just been completed, and the Malines Conversations had come to an end because of the death of Cardinal Mercier.[31] The Pope's own words made it extremely clear that he had no intention of participating in ecumenical organizations. "Therefore, worthy brethren, it is clear why this Apostolic See never allows its own members to take part in the conferences of non-Catholic Christians. One may foster the reunion of Christians only insofar as one fosters the return of those standing outside to the one true Church from which they once unfortunately separated themselves."[32] He went on, however, to voice his own ecumenical desires. "May we however in good fortune attain what so many of our predecessors have not accomplished, that is to embrace with fatherly love that son whose fateful separation from us we mourn."[33]

The pattern was continued when, in 1936, the Anglican Archbishop of York, Dr. Temple, in preparation for the Edinburgh Conference of 1937, wrote Catholic Archbishop MacDonald of Edinburgh, inviting him to the Conference. In February, 1937, Archbishop MacDonald replied: "I have considered the position very carefully and have come to the conclusion that it will be better for me not to cooperate actively in the Conference which is to take place in Edinburgh next August."[34] However, this stand was somewhat altered so that four Catholic priests and one layman were admitted to the Conference as observers.

There was a good deal of hope that Rome would participate in the first General Assembly of the World Council of

---

[31]Paul Simon, "Zum päpstlichen Rundschreiben 'Mortalium Animos,'" *Die Friedenstadt,* II (1928), 62.

[32]Papst Pius XI, "Ueber die Förderung der wahren Religionseinheit," *Die Friedenstadt,* II (1928), 58.

[33]*Ibid.,* 59.

[34]Visser 't Hooft, "The Genesis," 685.

Churches in Amsterdam in 1948. During the winter of 1947-8 the Central Office of the Ecumenical Council in Geneva received a large number of letters from Catholic priests and laity asking for permission to attend the Amsterdam Conference as unofficial observers. Quite a few of these petitioners already had permission from their own religious superiors, bishops or cardinals. The Central Office with considerable care then prepared a list of twelve Catholics who were invited to attend the Conference as unofficial observers. In April, 1848, Cardinal de Jong, Archbishop of Utrecht wrote to Geneva that he reserved his *placet* concerning those Catholics who were to attend the Conference. He was given the list of names, and those Catholics who had been invited were advised to seek the Cardinal's permission. Cardinal de Jong replied that the list was not completely satisfactory and that a new one would be suggested. This list was never forthcoming. The Holy Office in Rome issued a *Monitum* in June of 1948, recalling that permission to attend an inter-faith meeting on an international level must come from Rome. None came.[35]

After this time, however, there were evidences of a more benign attitude in Rome toward the ecumenical movement. The somewhat severe wording in the *Monitum* of June, 1948, was followed by an *Instructio* from the Holy Office which was considerably milder in tone and encouraged Catholics to participate in inter-confessional work under the jurisdiction of the bishops. Although no Catholic representatives attended the Amsterdam Conference of 1948, there had been Catholic "observers" at the Edinburgh Conference of 1937, and there were to be such observers at the Lund Conference of 1952, and at the New Delhi Conference of 1961. Observers at both of these latter conferences had the ap-

[35]K. Hartenstein, "Oekumene und katholische Kirche," lecture delivered in Stuttgart, April 26, 1949. Mimeographed copy in "Haus der Begegnung" library, Niederaltaich Abtei, Niederbayern, Germany.

proval of the Holy Office; however, this was not true at the Evanston Conference of 1954.

In 1952 an international circle of Catholic theologians was set up "which handles from the Catholic side acute problems and questions of ecumenical nature and informs the Ecumenical Council of Churches what the Catholic doctrine in reference to these vital questions is."[36] In the fall of 1958, Msgr. Willebrands of the Netherlands became the first Catholic theologian to teach at the Ecumenical Institute at Bossey.[37] It was the same Msgr. Willebrands who, with three other Catholic priests, attended the meeting of the Central Committee of the World Council of Churches in St. Andrews, Scotland, in 1960 as observers. It may have been Willebrands who arranged the meeting between the Archbishop of Canterbury and Pope John XXIII later the same year.[38]

The crowning example of the growing interest of Rome in ecumenical matters was the calling of the Second Vatican Council, at which the problem of Christian unity was to be of major though indirect importance. According to Pope John XXIII, the Catholic Church cannot just stand unchanging and wait for the return of the non-Catholic Christians; it must renew itself to prepare for the reunion of the separated brethren. In June, 1959, John XXIII said:

> ". . . that there may be only one flock and one shepherd." (John 10-16) This inner hope had already led us and powerfully spurred us on to announce publicly our intention to call an ecumenical council. . . . The main goal of the council lies in fostering the growth of the Catholic faith and the true renewal of the morals of the Christian people, that the structure of the Church might be better adapted to the needs and conditions of our time. The council will certainly be a spectacle

---

[36]Thomas Sartory, "Besteht Hoffnung auf Ueberwindung der Glaubensspaltung?" *Oekumenische Rundschau,* VII (1958), 67.

[37]Interview with Msgr. J.G.M. Willebrands, August, 1958.

[38]*Time,* LXXVI (November 14, 1960), 63.

> of truth, unity and love, a spectacle which, we trust, when seen by those separated from this apostolic see, will be a gentle invitation to seek and find that unity which Jesus Christ so passionately besought from the heavenly Father.[39]

Thus from the beginning, the reunion of the separated brethren was closely connected to the inner renewal of the Catholic Church which was the announced aim of the Council. Perhaps the first single most important effect of the Council —at least for the immediate future—was the creation of the Secretariat for Christian Unity. This Secretariat, which during the Council was elevated to the rank of a full Commission, had for its president Augustin Cardinal Bea, a German Jesuit. Secretary of the Commission was Msgr. Willebrands, now bishop, who had also served as secretary of the international circle of Catholic theologians working with the World Council of Churches. The Secretariat, although it drew its members from all over the world, reflected the particular involvement of Germany in Protestant-Catholic affairs by the relatively large number of Germans who were original members. These included Archbishop Jaeger of Paderborn, the bishop officially in charge of German Una Sancta affairs.

The fruitful presence of observer-delegates officially deputed to the Council by such a large number of non-Catholic Churches was a testimony to the patience, skill and dedication of the Secretariat, as well as to the developing good will among the Churches. It was the Secretariat that was responsible for drawing up the constitution on ecumenism and getting it through the stormy waters of the Council. Most recently it inaugurated official discussions with the World Council of Churches.

It is against this background of an extremely intensified interest on the part of both Catholics and Protestants in the

---

[39]Encyclical *Ad Petri cathedram* from June 29, 1959, quoted in Hans Küng, *Konzil und Wiedervereinigung* (Vienna, 1960), 9-10.

ecumenical movement that the growth of the Una Sanca Movement in Germany must be seen. It is not very difficult to discern how those persons who became interested in the ecumenical movement were drawn into the work of the Una Sancta Movement as it developed just before, during and especially after World War II. In Germany the leaders of the ecumenical movement were very often active at the same time in the Una Sancta Movement.

Chapter Four

The Liturgical Movement

At the beginning of the nineteenth century, romanticism had deposed the rationalism of the Enlightenment. By the second half of the century positivism and scientism had become dominant, and the non-rational elements of man's nature were once again driven into the background. This new rationalism ceded in turn to a neo-romantic rebuttal around the turn of the century. This neo-romanticism manifested itself in almost all fields; in the shift from impressionism to expressionism in painting; in the appearance of such philosophers as Henri Bergson, with his emphasis on the non-rational faculty of intuition, and of Gabriel Marcel, Martin Heidegger and the anti-rationalistic existentialist school. It was marked by the spontaneous German youth movement, with its interest in nature and the history- and tradition-laden countryside. And only a little later, this same neo-romanticism made itself felt in Protestant theology, as the anti-rationalist school began its fight against all forms of the *analogia entis*.

Out of this background there came the liturgical movement, which insisted that religion and especially its worship must make an aesthetic appeal to all of man's senses and faculties. Not that the liturgical renewal was ever merely an exaltation of the non-rational side of man—it insisted on the essential duality of man's being and in this way avoided the extremes of either rationalism or romanticism.

It is not difficult to see the way in which the liturgical movement helped prepare the way for the Una Sancta Movement. In Germany, the very commonness of the liturgical renaissance in both the Catholic and Protestant Churches tended to draw the two Churches closer together. Also many of the aspects stressed by the Catholic liturgical movement found a sympathetic echo in Protestantism—the new emphasis on the role of the layman in worship, for example, and the introduction of the vernacular in liturgical celebrations. Such attitudes had long been thought distinguishing marks of Protestantism, and an earlier generation of Catholics might have denounced them as Protestantizing tendencies.[1]

Likewise in the Protestant Churches the parallel liturgical movement has led to a rediscovery of many things formerly considered strictly Catholic: the stressing of the sacramental aspect of the divine service rather than the sermon, the revival of private confession, the use of Gregorian chant and the Roman Catholic Breviary.

CATHOLIC LITURGICAL MOVEMENT: AIMS AND MEANS

The Catholic liturgical movement has been watched and applauded by Protestant theologians for a long time. Already quite early in the history of the movement, the Protestant theologian Friedrich Heiler said, "The liturgical movement in the Catholic Church is the most significant and most hopeful tendency in the contemporary Western World Church."[2] About the same time another German Protestant theologian, Rudolf Günther, voiced an opinion equally as strong: "Among all the movements which appear in the Catholic Church today, the liturgical movement is the most immanent, and yet at the same time it is directed toward all members. It deals with piety itself, and not only that of the religious but of all the faithful."[3] More recently, Ernest

[1]Quoted in Ernest Koenker, *The Liturgical Renaissance in the Roman Catholic Church* (Chicago, 1954), 69.

[2]Friedrich Heiler, *Der Katholizismus, seine Idee und seine Erscheinung* (Munich, 1923), 429.

[3]Rudolf Günther, "Die liturgische Bewegung in der katholischen Kirche," *Monatscrift für Gottesdienst und kirchliche Kunst,* XXVIII (1923), 81-82.

Koenker, a Protestant theologian and student of German and liturgical matters, declared that today we are witnessing in the Catholic Church profound changes which are probably more important than anything since the fateful sixteenth century, for they bid "fair to reshape the whole face of the Roman Catholic Church."[4] If the liturgical revival is able to proceed unhindered now that it has gained considerable momentum, "it will be more significant than any of the movements in the Roman Catholic Church during modern times."[5] The aim of the liturgical movement is not merely the revival of a number of rubrical practices, although in some cases this may be the practical consequence of some of the principles of the movement. The central aim of the movement is to make the liturgy of the Church the integrating force, the center, of the Catholic's whole life. To paraphrase Pius X's famous statement on the matter, the active participation of the Christian in the liturgy of the Church is the primary and indispensable source of the true Christian spirit.[6] But if the liturgy is to become this dynamic force, the layman must be encouraged to take a more intelligent and active part in worship. And this emphasis on the position of the layman cannot help but encourage a better understanding of the position of the Protestant Churches. Indeed, many of the elements in the renewed liturgy designed to achieve this lay participation are the most cherished practices of Protestantism.

The central concern of the liturgical movement is the celebration of the Mass and the making of the layman's part in it more meaningful and active. To accomplish this many different approaches have been used, one of the most important being the placing of the missal in the hands of the layman. In 1855 the ban on translating the missal into the vernacular

---

[4]Koenker, *Liturgical Renaissance,* 2.
[5]*Ibid.*, 1.
[6]Pius X, *Motu Proprio on Sacred Music* (Conception, Mo., 1945), 3.

was lifted;[7] in 1884 Pater Anselm Schott, O.S.B., of Beuron Abbey, Germany, published his *Messbuch der heiligen Kirche,* a translation and explanation of the *Missale Romanum.* This Latin-German missal has since become the most famous of the translations of the Mass prayers into German, over six and a half million copies in thirteen editions having been printed.[8]

However, the use of the missal was never considered a final goal by the leaders of the liturgical movement, for even with the missal the people are still mere spectators at the Mass. To bring the layman to a more active participation in the Mass the Dialogue Mass, or *Missa Recitata* was inaugurated. At a Dialogue Mass, which anticipated many of the reforms of Vatican II, the entire congregation recited the responses otherwise made by the server alone and sometimes recited along with the priest those parts of the Mass which would be sung by the choir at a High Mass, i.e. the *Gloria, Credo, Sanctaus* and *Agnus Dei.* Often the epistle, gospel and other parts of the Mass which change from day to day were read aloud by a layman in the vernacular, and sometimes other prayers from the ordinary of the Mass were recited by the congregation in its own language while the priest said them in Latin. This manner of celebrating the Mass, first used to a great extent by chaplains in World War I, spread more and more extensively:[9] in Germany by the end of World War II seventy-five per cent of the parishes used the Dialogue Mass.[10]

---

[7]Klemens Tilmann, "Die Liturgie missionarisch gesehen," *Stimmen der Zeit,* CXLIII (1948), 169.

[8]*Beuron* (Beuron/Hohenzollern, 1956), 86.

[9]Gerald Ellard, S.J., *Men at Work and Worship* (New York, 1940), 131.

[10]Alphonse Heitz, "Dernières étapes du renouveau liturgique allemand," *La Maison-Dieu,* VII (1946), 66.

But the Dialogue Mass too, in its turn was considered by many leaders to be only a half-way point in the direction of the ideal, the Congregational Sung Mass, or *Missa Cantata.* Since the Low Mass is only a comparatively late Western development the High Mass has usually been considered the ideal. The leaders of the liturgical movement wished to reinstate the position of the congregation in the High Mass, so that they once again would sing those parts of the Mass which the choir now sings only because of the default of the congregation: the *Kyrie, Gloria, Credo, Sanctus* and *Agnes Die.* The choir would then be free to practice the more difficult proper parts of the Mass, the Introit, Gradual, Alleluia, Offertory, and Communion verses for each Sunday.[11] Although apparently not as popular in the beginning as the Dialogue Mass, the Congregational High Mass in Germany has come into its own since World War II.[12] Vatican II, of course, has crowned all this liturgical reform and has furnished it vast additional impetuses.

Since the liturgical movement aims at intelligent lay participation in the liturgy, the leaders of the movement have long advocated a much greater—if not complete—use of the vernacular. They argued that this was the case during the first two and a half centuries of the Western Church when the language of the liturgy was the generally understood *koiné* Greek. Later, Latin became the vernacular and was then substituted for the Greek. A second "vernacularization" of the Western liturgy failed to materialize at the end of the Middle Ages. At that time the use of a vernacular liturgy

---

[11]Cf. H. A. Reinhold, "Choir and/or People," *Orate Fratres,* XVIII (1943-44), 73-76.

[12]Herman Sasse, "Liturgy and Lutheranism," *Una Sancta,* VIII (1948), 9.

became the hall mark of the Protestant groups and the Catholic Church reacted by insisting on a Latin liturgy.[13]

In Germany, however, the use of German hymns during the Mass developed particularly after the Thirty Years War because of the widespread lack of singers who could master the Latin liturgy. Rather than be forced always to hear a Low Mass German Catholics had the choir parts translated into their mother tongue, or substituted hymns for them; a number of these hymns, which are still in use, were written by Protestants.[14] This use of German hymns, of course, really only reactivated a trend begun before the Reformation but which, no doubt, was abetted by the predominant use of vernacular hymns in the Lutheran liturgy.[15] This tradition was carried on until the Constitution on the Liturgy of Vatican II by the "Pray and Sing Mass" which combined both Latin and German. The congregation answered the prayers in Latin as in a dialogue Mass. While the Priest recited the *Gloria, Credo,* and other prayers in Latin paraphrased hymns were sung in German. In 1958 the Holy See urged all the faithful to say the *Pater Noster* and the *Domino non sum dignus,* among other prayers, with the priest in Latin.[16] Before then, however, German congregations already had been in the habit of saying the "Our Father" and "Lord I am not worthy" together with the priest *in German,* and continued to do so afterward. In addition many sacraments and sacramentals such as marriages, funerals and vespers have long been celebrated mostly or entirely in German.[17]

---

[13]Cf. Henry Jenner, "An Historical Accident," *Orate Fratres,* XXI (1946-47), 84-85.

[14]Ludwig Andreas Veit and Ludwig Lenhart, *Kirche und Volksfrömmigkeit im Zeitalter des Barock* (Freiburg, 1956), 184.

[15]*Ibid.,* 187.

[16]*Acta apostolica sedis* 50 (1958), 630-663.

[17]Koenker, *Liturgical Renaissance,* 149.

The new stress on the layman's active participation in the liturgy has re-emphasized a line of thought which is similar to the Lutheran doctrine of the priesthood of all believers, that of the general priesthood of the laity. This concept goes back to the early years of the Church when there was not the definite line of demarcation between the laity and clergy there is today.[18] The confessions, however, do differ on this point. Luther taught that all Christians are priests unto each other through their faith and downgraded sacramental Holy Orders. The Catholic liturgical movement, however, stresses that the layman should fulfill his functions within the priesthood of Christ, in which he participates through Baptism and Confirmation, but, at the same time, describes Holy Orders as a more complete participation of this priesthood of Christ; thus Baptism, Confirmation, Holy Orders and finally episcopal consecration are the four ascending stages in the Christian priesthood. The importance of the first two has been neglected by Catholics until recently.[19] Despite the important differences, however, the similarity of the Lutheran and this Catholic concept is great.

By such means the liturgical movement hopes to revive the vitality of the Catholic Church today. Thus it will lead the laity to find the source of their religious life in an intelligent and active participation in the Mass, reception of the sacraments, use of sacramentals, praying of parts of the Breviary—and all this within the rhythm of the liturgical year. But this is only the necessary first step; the layman is expected to integrate his life into this pattern. It is because of this "follow through" that men like Ernest Koenker can say, "'If the renaissance can continue unhindered, there may be a 'Liturgical Springtime' of the Roman Catholic

---

[18]Ibid., 201.
[19]Pius X, *Motu Proprio,* 3.

Church—an awakening, the importance of which many would not now dream."[18]

HISTORICAL DEVELOPMENTS IN GERMAN COUNTRIES

Although the liturgical revival had its first beginnings in 1840, at the end of the earlier romantic period, when Abbot Prosper Gueranger started his monumental *L'Année liturgique,* and was given papal approval in Pope Pius X's *Motu Proprio,*[19] it reached maturity in Germany at the first Liturgical Week held for laymen at the Benedictine abbey Maria Laach during Holy Week of 1914. Thus, although started before the first World War, the liturgical movement was affected by that war. As is often the case in great calamities, many people turned toward religion after the war to find the answers to needs they now felt were unfulfilled by the materialistic, rationalistic society which had led them to this great debacle; many also became admirers of that renewed, vital aspect of religion which rejected a one-sided rationalistic approach, the liturgical renaissance. The postwar period also was a time of the "monastic revival" in the Catholic Church; many of the monasteries that had been secularized under Napoleon were now returned to religious hands.

Abbot Ildefons Herwegen and Dom Odo Casel were the leading spirits of the liturgical movement at Maria Laach, and it was due largely to their efforts and those at other Benedictine abbeys, particularly Beuron in southwestern Germany, that the intellectuals' understanding of the liturgy was revolutionized. The abbeys, which were visited and studied, became not only research centers but also living examples of a vital liturgical life.[20]

About the same time two men, Romano Guardini and Josef Jungmann, S.J., were becoming influential, both in a

[20]Juan C. Ruta and Johannes Straubinger, *Die katholische Kirche in Deutschland und ihre Probleme* (Stuttgart, 1954), 29-30.

scholarly and, Guardini particularly, a practical manner. Guardini published his now classic *The Spirit of the Liturgy* on Easter, 1918, opening the Maria Laach publication series *Ecclesia orans.* Guardini also took a leading part in the *Quickborn* and other groups of the Catholic youth movement and began to infuse into them the ideals of the liturgical movement. Throughout the 1920's these ideals spread through the whole Catholic youth movement, and at the end of the decade "the stream began to flow into the people."[21]

Father Gerald Ellard, S.J., who studied in Germany in the early 1930's, has a fascinating description of an experience with one of the Catholic youth groups, the *Neudeutschland.* A group of about thirty university students who belonged to the *Neudeutschland* invited Father Ellard to go with them on a week-end mountain climbing trip. Most of the outing was typical of German youth groups with intellectual discussions and singing of folksongs, in this case around a St. John the Baptist bonfire honoring the summer solstice. But on Sunday morning they walked an hour to a mountain chapel where a dialogue Mass, complete with hymns, recitation of prayers and offertory procession was celebrated—much to the astonishment and edification of the mountain folk attending Mass who were used to thinking of university students as a rather religiously negligent lot. Father Ellard was told that this sort of thing had been going on since the end of the war, affecting millions of Catholics who passed through the youth groups into adulthood in the German parishes at large.[22]

The Catholic liturgical movement has used many means to promote its ideals, such as publications, liturgical institutes,

---

[21] *Ibid.*

[22] Gerald Ellard, "Tiptoe on a Misty Mountain Top," *Orate Fratres* IV (1929-30), 394 ff.

liturgical congresses, and ecclesiastical liturgical commissions. Since the first World War there has been an overwhelming amount of written material, both scholarly and popular. Two of the more important publications are *Liturgiegeschichtliche Quellen und Forschungen,* which has been edited by the Benedictine monks of the abbeys of Maria Laach, Beuron, Emmaus, St. Joseph at Coesfeld, and Seckau since 1918, and the *Jahrbuch für Liturgiewissenschaft,* which was first published in 1921 under the leadership of Dom Odo Casel and continued through 1941, then reappeared in 1950 under the title *Archiv für Liturgiewissenschaft.* The list of liturgical institutes, which are often centers of both research and teaching, continues to grow: the Abbot Herwegen Institute at Maria Laach, the Institute of Christian Antiquity and Liturgy at Salzburg, and the Liturgical Institute at Trier which is under the supervision of the German hierarchy. In 1940 the hierarchy took liturgical matters more directly under its care by appointing a liturgical commission made up of some of the outstanding leaders of the liturgical movement.[23] It was the institute at Trier that was responsible for initiating the first Liturgical Congress of Germany, which met in June of 1950 at Frankfurt.[24]

By the time of the second World War former students of Guardini and Jungmann, who for decades taught in various German and Austrian universities, began to take over parishes of their own and started to combine liturgical and pastoral theology in practice. Some of them, along with the Oratorian Fathers in Leipzig, founded an institute for the study of pastoral liturgics.[25]

Another major center of the liturgical apostolate in German-speaking lands was Klosterneuburg, near Vienna. In

[23]Koenker, *Liturgical Renaissance,* 19-20.

[24]Theodor Bogler, *Liturgische Erneuerung in aller Welt* (Maria Laach, 1950), 24-25.

[25]Ruta and Straubinger, *Katholische Kirche,* 31.

some ways the work done from here by Father Pius Parsch was just as important and influential as the work of Maria Laach. Dr. Parsch was a man of amazing organizational ability, capacity for work, eye for detail and insight into what would most effectively reach the people. At the same time he was a person both of great scholarship and concern for individual people. After the first World War he turned the little parish at Klosterneuburg into a model liturgical parish and an experimental station. From there he spread his work to Vienna itself, conducting or inspiring some twenty liturgical weeks in various churches and parishes within a three year period. This work was so effective that by 1930 he was able to say that there were few parishes in and around Vienna, a huge Catholic metropolis, that remained uninfluenced by his popular liturgical activity. But even more phenomenal and widespread was the extraordinary amount of material produced by Dr. Parsch's Popular Liturgical Apostolate press which he began in 1922. Before the decade was over one hundred people were engaged in this work; the press distributed fifteen million Mass-texts throughout German-speaking lands, 200,000 copies of another liturgical pamphlet series, two periodicals—one a weekly—and books. All this was only a good beginning; Dr. Parsch's work and influence continued to grow throughout the 1930's at a fantastic rate.[26]

PROTESTANT LITURGICAL MOVEMENT

Paralleling and to some extent stemming from the Catholic liturgical revival is the liturgical renaissance in the Protestant Churches, more especially the Lutheran, in Germany. The Lutheran Churches of the Reformation period retained an amazing number of the liturgical practices of the Catholic

---

[26]Pius Parsch, "From Other Lands," *Orate Fratres* V (1930-31), 127-130.

Church. A comparison of the Lutheran Mass of 1578 with the Catholic will show that the entire foremass, the consecration and the communion are almost identical; only the offertory and canon are missing from the Lutheran Mass. Moreover, Matins, Lauds, Vespers and Compline were retained by the Lutherans in a form very similar to the Catholic.[27] It was only where Calvinism, or crypto-Calvinism, with its sermon-centered services gained the upper hand in Germany that the Lutheran's Catholic-like liturgy was driven out. (Actually, the down-grading of the eucharistic liturgy in Reformed Christianity is to be laid at the feet of Zwingli rather than Calvin.) Even in those areas where Lutheranism did not succumb to Calvinism its liturgy was eventually affected by it and later by the anti-liturgical *Aufkläung*. Hence, by the beginning of the twentieth century,[28] there was ample ground for a liturgical revival in the Lutheran Church.

This revival has been directed mainly by three groups: the High Church Union of the Augsburg Confession, the Berneuchner Circle-Michaels Brotherhood, and the Alpirsbacher Circle. The High Church Union, the first of these to be organized, arose like the Catholic liturgical revival, during the first World War. Its inspiration was the printing in 1917 of ninety-five theses by Lutheran Pastor Heinrich Hansen for the four hundredth anniversary of the publication of Luther's theses.[29] The target of Hansen's theses, however, was quite different from that of Luther's; it was the state of the Protestant Church about which he bitterly complained. "The mark of contemporary Protestantism is mass defection and isolated believing groups and individuals, general death and scattered

---

[27]Veit and Lenhart, *Volksfrömmigkeit,* 182-183.

[28]*Ibid.,* 8-9.

[29]Hans Heuer, *Die liturgische Bewegung in unserer Kirche,* Jahrebuch des Martin Luther-Bundes, (Munich, 1946), 91.

sparks of life."[30] He believed that the only spiritual force influencing the life of the people in Germany then was "the Roman Church, because it is catholic. . . . If Protestantism is again to gain an influence in the public life of the people it must recall once more that it is catholic."[31] To realize these ideas a group of laymen and clergymen founded the High Church Union in October of 1918.[32]

In the first issue of the new Union's periodical Siegfried Graf von Lüttichau asked, "Does our Protestant service fulfill its religious task?"[33] In an attempt to answer the question in the affirmative the High Church Union set up as its goals a number of liturgical reforms. A new awareness of the significance and objective character of the sacraments was to replace the stress on the sermon, and the liturgy was to be enriched by such things as music, church and altar decoration. The Union hoped to reintroduce private confession and to encourage practices like church visits, recitations of hours of the Office, and the monastic life within the Protestant Church. The Union also took upon itself the task of making a Breviary for Protestants. And, what is patently very important to Catholic-Protestant reunion efforts, the High Church Union stressed the notion of ecumenism: "The awareness must be awakened and strengthened in Protestant Christianity that it belongs to the one all-inclusive Church of Christ."[34]

Although this ecumenism was an essential element of the Union, a number of the members thought it was not given

---

[30]Heinrich Hansen, "Spiesse und Nägel," *Die Hochkirche,* I (1921), 116.
[31]*Ibid.*
[32]P. Siegfried Graf von Lüttichau, "Die hochkirchliche Verinigung," *Die Hochkirche,* I (1921), 145.
[33]*Ibid.,* 146.
[34]"Was will die hochkirchliche Vereinigung?" *Die Hochkirche,* II (1922), 1.

its rightful importance; consequently they broke off in 1924 and formed the High Church Ecumenical Federation, which for several years included Catholic members. They also published their own periodical, *Una Sancta,* for four years under the editorship of Professor Alfred von Martin. However, the split between the Union and the newly formed Federation was healed after the original rupture, and ecumenical thought was given a much stronger stress.[35] Ecumenism continued to grow so much in importance, especially under the pressure of the persecution of the Nazis, that after the war the first general convention, which took place at Marburg on May 7, 1947, changed the name of the Union to the Evangelical-Ecumenical Union. Also interesting, in the light of the Una Sancta Movement, is the Union's incorporation of the following into the new statement of its goals: "The Evangelical Union . . . works together with the ecumenical groups and the Una Sancta circles."[36]

Although the High Church Union along with its successor is not large numerically, it has had an important influence. One Catholic, Max Pribilla, S.J., said that it is indeed a "small flock . . . but a high Christian idealism and a spirit of reconciliation born of love permeates its members."[37] The Protestant theologian Otto Urbach wrote that Friedrich Heiler (who became the leader of the Union some years after its founding) and the High Church Union have led Evangelical Christendom to the immeasurable religious values of the early Church. Moreover, "almost an entire generation of Protestant theologians and laymen were led for the first time to the living sources of Catholicism by the for-

---

[35]Friedrich Heiler, "Evangelisch-ökumenische Vereinigung," *Oekumenische Einheit,* I (1948), 165.

[36]*Ibid.,* 168.

[37]Max Pribilla, *Um die Wiedervereinigung im Glauben* (Freiburg, 1926), 14.

mer Catholic Heiler. His pupils are deeply indebted to him for this."[38] This has been accomplished mainly through periodicals, books, national conferences and teaching at university posts by members of the Union.[39]

The second group, which grew from completely different roots, was led by Bishop Wilhelm Stählin and Pastor Karl Bernhard Ritter and called itself the Berneuchner Circle. The name came about quite accidentally; Berneuchen is the name of a manor in Neumark where, since 1923, this group met annually. Having experienced the inspiration of the youth movement, these men more and more clearly tried to throw off the influence of liberal theology and find some other basis for ordering their spiritual life. They concluded that the great issue in the Church today was not moral corruption or even the infidelity to Holy Scriptures of four hundred years ago, but rather an over-intellectualization and over-abstraction; therefore all efforts should be directed toward giving the spiritual life a greater and more perfect concrete form.[40]

The Berneuchner Circle has made its influence felt in two areas, largely through the printed word. It has provided material helpful to the Protestant's spiritual life: its *Das Stundengebet* (Divine Office) and the *Gebete für das Jahr der Kirche* (Prayers for the Church Year) are very like the Roman Catholic Breviary in structure, and often use identical prayers, psalms and music. The Circle also developed a Bible reading plan which follows the church year, along with a hymn for each week and a Collect prayer for each Sunday.[41]

---

[38]Otto Urbach, "Ist der Gegensatz von Katholizismus and Protestantismus unüberbrückbar?" *Theologie und Glaube* XXXIII (1941), 3.

[39]Two outstanding examples are Heiler who is still professor of comparative religion at the University of Marburg, and von Martin who retired from the Technische Hochschule in Munich in 1958.

[40]"Berneuchnen," *Evangelisches Kirchenlexikon*, Vol. I (1956).

[41]Heuer, *Liturgische Bewegung*, 92.

A second part of its effort went into such works as the volumes of *Leiturgia, Handbuch des evangelisches Gottesdienstes,* which has been coming out since 1952, and their quarterly, *Quatember,* both of which are devoted to doctrinal and practical discussions of liturgical and pastoral problems.[42]

Growing out of the Berneuchner Circle in 1931 was a broader group of laymen and clergy, the Michael's Brotherhood, which published its aims in a declaration called *Credo ecclesiam.* After an indictment of the influence which prevents the Church from being what it should be, it repeats that what is needed today is not an elimination of moral corruption, but rather a service in society, *diakonia;* an effective witness for Christ, *martyria;* and a renewal of personal and corporate piety, a sacramental worship, *leiturgia.* The members try to put these aims into practice mainly in their congregations.[43]

The results of the Berneuchner Circle and Michael's Brotherhood have been recognized by Catholic as well as Protestant theologians and laity. A Catholic, J. P. Michael, in writing of the advancing work of Protestants in regard to private confession said, "It has become apparent that the preparatory work of the Michael's Brotherhood in that field was really the seed which has since sprouted."[44]

The third group that has been a leader of the liturgical revival in Protestant Germany is the Alpirsbach Circle. Alpirsbach was at one time a Benedictine cloister with a romanesque basilica located near Freudenstadt in the Black Forest. The Circle takes its name from this cloister where, under the influence of the theology of Karl Barth, a group of Protestant theologians led by Wilhelm Gohl (later missing in Russia) and Richard Goelz gathered regularly for theo-

---

[42]Berneuchnen." *Evangelisches Kirchenlexikon,* Vol. I, (1956).

[43]J. Robert Nelson, "Six Approaches to the Church," *The Ecumenical Review,* VIII (1956), 341.

[44]J. P. Michael, *Christen suchen eine Kirche* (Freiburg, 1958), 94.

logical recollection and work. During Alpirsbach weeks there were Eucharistic services and a careful use of psalmody and Gregorian chant in the Benedictine tradition.[45] It is particularly in this area of chant that the Alpirsbach Circle has done its work of creation, instruction, and research such as that evident in the publication of an *Antiphonale* and Masses;[46] in the present German Lutheran liturgy the *Kyrie, Gloria, Credo,* responses, psalmody and many hymns are sung to many of the same Gregorian Chant melodies as those used in the Catholic liturgy—in German however.[47] Hans Heuer says of them: "The Alpirsbachers have again made accessible to our congregations many worthwhile church hymns which had been forgotten in our churches, and have developed valuable new liturgical practices."[48]

As a result of the work of these organizations the Churches themselves officially began to take part in the liturgical movement. In the Lutheran Churches of both Hanover and Bavaria liturgical conferences have been working to improve the Church within their own areas by such means as the forming of new *Agende,* regulations and prayers of religious service for the feasts of the year, similar to the Catholic Missal. In order to coordinate their work the two Churches formed a joint liturgical commission.[49] This led to liturgical renewal on a much broader scale. In 1948 the United Evangelical-Lutheran Church of Germany (VELKD) was founded; it encompassed ten of the thirteen Lutheran State Churches in Germany, about twenty million persons or well over half the German Protestants. Already in 1949 the VELKD, synthesizing the previous liturgical research and practical experimentation, put out a *Church Hymn Boook,*

---

[45]"Alpirsbacher Kreis," *Evangelisches Kirchenlexikon,* Vol. I (1956).
[46]Roger Schutz, "Sakrament-Liturgie-Ordensgemeinschaften," *Dokumente,* XIII (1957), 206.
[47]*Evangelisches Kirchengesangbuch* (Munich, 1959).
[48]Heuer, *Liturgische Bewegung,* 92.
[49]*Ibid.,* 92-93.

which includes the renewed liturgy, and a Lectionary, the readings of the epistles and gospels in the liturgy. The latter is very obviously similar to the Roman Missal not only in the readings for the Sundays of the year but also for such days as the Marian feasts of February 2 and March 25, and All Saints on November 1. Since most Lutheran Churches kept the Catholic liturgical calendar almost intact for many decades after the Reformation, this revival of early Lutheran liturgical practices again draws present-day Lutheranism closer to Catholicism.[50] In 1952 the first part of an *Agende* was issued.[51] Although the use of these formularies cannot be made obligatory but can only be suggested, one Lutheran liturgist, Ludwig Weck of Munich, believes their use in Germany will be almost universal by 1970.[52]

CONFESSION, "KIRCHENTAG" AND CLOISTERS

For the most part private confession has long been considered a prime distinguishing factor between the Protestant and Catholic Churches. Luther, however, and the Lutheran Church after him, not only permitted the continuance of private confession but even warmly encouraged it, calling it "that all-healing thing"; it was only the ecclesiastical obligation of periodic private confession that was objected to.[53] Luther said that he would not for the world deprive any man of the same benefit he had received from it. "I would have long ago been overcome and strangled by the devil had not this confession preserved me."[54] The Augsburg Confession also stated "Concerning confession it is taught that one should retain private absolution . . . and not let it fall away. Likewise it is not necessary in confession to enumerate all sins and misdeeds, for it is not even possible."[55]

[50]Veit and Lenhart, *Volksfrömmigkeit,* 6.
[51]Michael, *Christen suchen,* 85-86.
[52]Interview with Ludwig Weck, June, 1960.
[53]Veit and Lenhardt, *Volksfrömmigkeit,* 25.
[54]*Luthers Werke* (Weimarer Ausgabe, 1883 ff.), XIII, 62.
[55]*Evangelisches Kirchengesangbuch,* 709.

It was only in the latter part of the seventeenth century, with the rise of Pietism, which saw private confession as a danger in the direction of over-externalization, that private confession began to be considered a Catholic institution that had no place in the Protestant Church.[56] This situation continued until the Protestant theologian Wilhelm Loehe attempted to revive private confession in the middle of the nineteenth century. Although his efforts were not successful, the situation today is different. Particularly in Germany, feelings of disillusionment and guilt set the stage for a reintroduction of private confession, and today private confession for Protestants is becoming a much more common thing. There has even been a form for confession in the Lutheran Church issued by the VELKD in 1953 in which, after the penitent confesses his sins, the pastor pronounces the following absolution: "In the power of the command which the Lord gave his Church I pronounce you free: your sins are forgiven. In the name of the Father. . . . "[57] The Protestant *Kirchentagen*, annual religious rallies attended by hundreds of thousands of Protestants, have been the scenes of thousands of private confessions. At the seventh *Kirchentag* at Frankfurt, in 1956, under the general theme of "Reconcile yourself with God!" the closing assembly of 500,000 heard this statement: "We seek men to whom we can tell everything, everything about us. Are there such men in the Protestant Church? Who has time for us? Who can listen, listen without thinking about his own problems and without turning away when there are hard things? Who can help us? You pastors, can you hear confession? Do it finally, we beg you, for Christ's sake!"[58]

Protestants have also of late been looking on saints and the value of their veneration with a more kindly eye. Walther

[56]Hans Schomerus, "Wiedereinführung der Beichte?" *Christ und Welt* (Stuttgart), June 20, 1948, p. 24.
[57]*Evangelisches Kirchengesangbuch*, 647.
[58]Michael, *Christen suchen*, 95.

Nigg's book *Grosse Heiligen,* the best written example of this changing attitude, has drawn high praise since its publication in 1946 from both Protetsants and Catholics. Here the lives of several saints such as St. Francis Assisi and St. Theresa of Avila are described for inspiration and held up for imitation.

Still more striking is the growing, new appreciation of monasticism among Protestants. Walther Nigg also published in 1953 a book called *Vom Geheinmis der Mönche* in which he praised monasticism as a great Christian good, the loss of which Protestantism sorely feels.[59] The Protestant Walther von Loewenich echoed his idea. "One can't sum up this powerful manifestation of a heroic Christianity simply under the heading of a 'false emphasis on works' . . . Monasticism is the spring at which Catholic piety has ever renewed itself."[60]

There has been not only a change in attitude toward monasticism but also a change in practice; Protestant religious orders have sprung up. A number of organizations either are called or are similar to Third Orders; the members do not live in monasteries but, with the help of their rule, follow their particular vocations "in the world." Some of these groups are the Sydower Brotherhood, the Christus Brotherhood, the Third Order of St. Francis, the Johannes Brotherhood and the Michael Brotherhood: the last three are the most important.[61] The Third Order of St. Francis, which grew out of the high church movement, was founded in 1927 by Friedrich Heiler. Most of the members were Lutherans, often members of the High Church Union who saw a particular value in the spirit of St. Francis, but some members were Roman Catholics, Anglicans or members of

[59]Walther Nigg, *Vom Geheimnis der Mönche* (Zurich, 1953). *Warriors of God* (New York, 1959).

[60]Walther von Loewenich, *Der moderne Katholizismus,* (Witten, 1956), 410-411.

[61]"Bruderschaft," *Evangelisches Kirchenlexikon,* Vol. I (1956).

other denominations. While the High Church Union had theological and ecclesiastical goals, the Third Order of St. Francis aimed at a more personal Christianization of life; nevertheless, the Third Order is strongly directed toward both the liturgical and ecumenical movements.[62]

Also associated with the high church movement was the Evangelical-Catholic Johannes Brotherhood, founded in the fall of 1929 as a successor to the Evangelical-Catholic Eucharistic Association.[63] Because of the great value placed on having "genuine sacraments," the leader of the Brotherhood, Friedrich Heiler, arranged to receive the episcopal consecration from a bishop of the Gallican Church which traces its spiritual family tree back to the Syrian-Jacobite Patriarchate in Antioch, thereby giving Heiler "Apostolic succession," though not in union with Rome. On August 25, 1930, Friedrich Heiler received from the hands of the Gallican Bishop Petrus Gaston Vigue, using the Roman ritual, all the Holy Orders including the episcopate. Consequently he is in a position, probably, to give valid orders to Protestant ministers, a power he has not infrequently used.[64] The Johannes Brotherhood's rule is particularly interesting because of its special emphasis on liturgical activities: the members are to participate regularly in prayer, and whenever at all possible, in common with others; members are to take part zealously in parish life, especially the Lord's Supper at least every Sunday and private confession at least once a year; every member should also make an annual retreat with daily prayer, reception of sacraments and meditation.[65]

---

[62]Elizabeth Hempel, "Die evangelischen Franziskanertertiaren," in *Vierzig Jahre Hochkirchliche Bewegung. Eine heilige Kirche Sonderheft* (Munich/Basel, 1957/58), 83-87.

[63]Albrecht Volkmann, "Die Evangelisch-ökumenische Johannesbruderschaft," in *Vierzig Jahre hochkirchliche Bewegung,* 75-76.

[64]Gottfried Hoffmann, "Protestantismus und Kirche," *Die Anregung,* VII (1955), 13.

[65]Volkmann, Johannesbruderschaft," 75-76.

There are also actual religious orders such as the Brethren of the Common Life in Nuremberg and Augsburg. But most interesting are two Protestant orders which were founded mainly for ecumenical and contemplative reasons. One is a group of several dozen men, mostly of Reformed background, who established *Communauté de Taizé-les-Cluny* in France near Switzerland; since a number of the men are German, quite close relations with Germany are maintained. Here the members live a life very similar to that of Benedictines, including vows, habit and chanting of a breviary.[66] The other group is the Ecumenical Marian Sisterhood in Darmstadt, Germany, which began its common life in 1947 with nine sisters. At present there are about sixty sisters; their life is centered about prayer, private and liturgical, including partial recitation in choir of the Divine Office in German (according to the Benedictine rite) and the singing of the *Deutsche Messe.* They include publishing and catechetical and retreat work among their activities, and consequently have become well known, being visited by thousands each year. As their name implies, they were founded to pray and work for the *Una Sancta Ecclesia.*[67]

A brief word should also be said about the renewed Protestant interest in the Roman Breviary. Already, as mentioned above, parts of it are recited by many Protestants both in common and private. Walther von Loewenich said that the Protestants need something like the Breviary. "Whoever is acquainted with the Roman Breviary knows what a wonderful treasure it contains. The Breviary is one of the most beautiful books of prayer I know."[68] After briefly

---

[66]Thomas Sartory, "Gedanken von Regel von Taize," *Una Sancta,* XIV (1959), 242-261.

[67]Basilea Schlink, *The Oecumenical Sisterhood of Mary in Darmstadt –Its Origin and Purpose* (Darmstadt, 1957), 3-6.

[68]Walther von Loewenich, "Der Katholizismus und wir," *Zeitwende,* XIX (1948), 722.

reviewing the contents of the Roman Breviary Loewenich continued: "I personally see nothing in it which could not also be a gain for Protestantism. So great a Protestant as Loehe felt it a definite lack that we possess no Breviary."[69]

Without any doubt the liturgical movement in the Protestant Church has made and continues to make tremendous progress. Hans Asmussen, a Lutheran theologian, stated: "We stride forward at such a pace that one can only be amazed . . . . What passes today as matter-of-fact was unthinkable thirty years ago."[70] And as the liturgical movement in the two Churches grows stronger, so does the bond between the two Churches. In fact, the Protestant theologian Heinrich Hermelink held that the liturgical movement was the most powerful cause of the conversations between the Churches.[71]

Moreover, the liturgical movement is very intimately connected with another movement of ecumenical importance within the Catholic Church, the Bible movement. Since the liturgy is made up mostly of the Scriptures, a liturgical revival would be associated naturally with a scriptural revival, something very dear to the Protestant's heart.

---

[69]*Ibid.*

[70]Hans Asmussen, *Zur gegenwärtigen Lage der evangelischen Kirche in Deutschland* (Berlin, 1952), 12-13.

[71]Heinrich Hermelink, *Katholizismus und Protestantismus* (Stuttgart, 1949), 9.

Chapter Five

The Bible Movement

THE movement in present-day Catholicism which most closely corresponds to the aims and aspirations of the Protestant Church is the Bible movement. The Bible was the foundation stone upon which the Churches of the Reformation raised their ecclesiastical structures; by putting more stress on a broader use of the Bible by both the clergy and laity, the Catholic Church is championing a cause that is often thought to be characteristically Protestant. According to the *Lexikon für Theologie und Kirche,* the Catholic Bible movement includes the various undertakings and organizations which attempt to bring the Holy Scriptures closer to all members of the Church by means of texts and reference material, lectures, conferences, Bible study groups and the like. Thus the Bible movement is in reality only a part of the much larger religious revival since the first World War; for the most part it has been closely allied to the liturgical movement and transmitted by Catholic Action.

From the time of Reformation, the Catholic Church, in its effort to combat the Protestant stress on the free interpretation of the Bible by every layman, had felt itself forced into placing stringent limitations on the reading of the Bible. Conditions had so changed, however, that by the time of Leo XIII there was an increasing emphasis on the use of the Bible. In his Encyclical *Providentissimus Deus* of 1893, Leo XIII encouraged Catholic biblical scholarship, insisted on a strengthening of the biblical training of the clergy, and granted an indulgence for regular reading of Scriptures.[1] In the *Con-*

---

[1]"Bibelverbreitung im modernen Katholizismus," *Die Religion in Geschichte und Gegenwart,* Vol. I (1957).

stitutio Officiorum ac Munerum of January 25, 1897, the publishing of the original texts of the old catholic translations of the Eastern Church was approved, and all limitations on possessing and reading approved translations of the Scriptures were set aside; from this document the canons on Scripture reading were developed.[2] Then in 1902 Leo XIII founded the St. Jerome Society which distributed 180,000 Italian copies of the New Testament in its first year.[3] Pope Pius X, when he was still the Patriarch of Venice, had also distributed free copies of the New Testament in Italian,[4] and after becoming pope recommended in 1907 that the laity possess and read the gospels in the vernacular.[5]

This stimulation from the highest office of the Church soon had its effect in German-speaking lands. In 1908 Norbert Peters started Bible study hours, worked for the reading of scriptural selections at student Masses, formed young student Bible-Circles and distributed German editions of the Scriptures in Germany.[6] In Austria the Bible and liturgical movements came together in one person, Pius Parsch, who, after returning from the first World War, began to hold Bible study hours in Klosterneuburg near Vienna. Out of this biblical renewal there grew the "volksliturgische Apostolat" with its periodical *Bibel und Liturgie.*[7]

After the first World War Bible study hours grew popular, particularly among the youth, both at school and even more in their youth groups; the Catholic youth movement was an important vehicle for the spread of the Bible movement. The Bible study hours usually followed a pattern. The first part of the meeting was devoted to a detailed study of a

---

[2]*Codex juris canonici* (Vatican, 1917),canons 1385, 1391, 1399, 1400.
[3]"Bibellesung," *Lexikon für Theologie und Kirche* Vol. I, (1957).
[4]Anselm Rüd, "Pius X. und die Bibelbewegung," *Bibel und Kirche,* IX (1954), 73.
[5]"Bibellesung."
[6]"Bibelverbreitung."
[7]"Pius Parsch," *Bibel und Kirche,* IX (1954), 67.

chosen section of Scripture: a reading aloud of the text, a period of silent meditation and re-reading and then questions on the meaning of individual words and phrases. This was followed by a discussion and evaluation of the message of the text read, a comparison with other statements of the same author, and the spelling out of the dogmatic and spiritual implications of the text and its connections with the liturgy.[8]

Revewed Catholic concern for the Bible received an organizational imprint in Germany on September 22, 1933. At that time Dr. Johann Straubinger, with seven others, founded the society called the "Catholic Bible Movement" in Stuttgart. The aims of the Bible Movement were "to distribute the Holy Scriptures among Catholic people" and "to open up to the people in every conceivable way the 'Book of Books.' "[9] The means used to achieve these ends were various; a regular distribution of the Bible in families and homes, the making available of biblical excerpts at very little cost, the furtherance of textual unity among translations for liturgical use, the printing of study helps for organizations like Bible study groups, and the distribution of study aids such as films and slides. The society publishes its own quarterly, *Bibel und Kirche,* "which discusses Biblical matters in interesting essays and gives many practical and worthwhile suggestions for pastoral work and for life."[10] It also maintains its own publishing house for the printing of books, pamphlets and maps concerned with the Bible. One of the more important works published by the *Bibelwerk Verlag* is a biblical concordance in German—of which 16,000 copies have been published so far—which was compiled by Dr. Straubinger

---

[8]"Bibelstunde," *Lexikon für Theologie und Kirche,* Vol. I (1957).

[9]Wilhelm Auer, *Das katholische Bibelwerk Stuttgart* (Stuttgart, (1957), 2.

[10]*Ibid.,* 3. Cf. Wilhelm Auer, "Bibel und Kirche, die Geschichte unserer Zeitschrift," *Bibel und Kirche,* XI (1956), 17-18.

and his successor Josef Bärtle.[11] It is particularly useful, for it is the only one available for the German Catholic Bible.

The Bible Work (the name was forcibly changes from Bible Movement since nothing outside the Nazi party could have the name movement) is now spread over all dioceses of West Germany, and has over five thousand members. Each diocese has its diocesan director and every seminary has its student representative.[12] Typical of the attitude of the German hierarchy toward the efforts of the Bible Work is a statement of Bishop Karl Joseph Leiprecht: "Through its periodical, *Bibel und Kirche,* and the scholarly and popular publications of the publishing hourse, through the Bible Weeks and Bible Conferences, meetings and exhibitions and through so many necessary menial tasks, an attempt has been made 'to place the light on the candle stick that it may give light to all who are in the house.' "[13]

Scholarly Biblical Developments

Various causes led to the sudden growth of a Bible movement at just this time. "The first reason was that liturgical spring which had already begun to flourish at the beginning of the century among the German youth, for what could be more conducive to cherishing Sacred Scripture than the Catholic liturgy?"[14] The second cause is the great mass of scholarly work which has been produced by Catholic theologians during the last decades in the field of scriptural research, particularly exegesis. Although the sixteenth and seventeenth centuries were a "second Golden Age" of exegesis, the eighteenth century and first part of the nineteenth century

---

[11]Wilhelm Auer, "Zur Geschichte unseres Bibelhandbuches," *Bibel und Kirche,* XIII (1958), 53.

[12]Letter from Dr. Wilhelm Auer (director of the Catholic Bible Work) to Leonard Swidler, July 30, 1958.

[13]Karl Joseph Leiprecht, "Bischofswort zum Jubilaeum des katholischen Bibelwerks," *Bibel und Kirche,* XIII (1958), 2.

[14]Wilhelm Auer, "De activitate Biblica," *Verbum Domini,* XXXI (1953), 178.

was a period of virtual stagnation. Then came the "higher critics," many of whom maintained that the Israelite religion was nothing other than the natural development from the beginnings of religion in animism, fetishism and totemism through polythesism to monothesism; all this, they maintained, could be shown by subjecting the Bible to a literary criticism, to an analysis of the various writing styles found in the several book of the Bible. One result of this literary criticism, particularly under the hand of Julius Wellhausen, was that many of the Old Testament books were divided into different layers, each of which was attributed to a separate author who reflected the religious view of his time. This of course called into question the historical authority of the various books.

The impact of the school of literary criticism was so powerful that by the turn of the century it dominated almost the entire field of non-Catholic Scripture scholarship. Catholic scholars were thrown on the defensive; they saw their task as one of proving the genuineness and credibility of the scriptural books. In exegesis they were not so much interested in the theological and religious content as they were in language, style, sources and layers.

But even as Julius Wellhausen published his fundamental work, Prolegomena zur Geschichte Israels, in 1878, a new science, which was to counteract much of the work of the school of literary criticism and put the spur to a more positive Catholic biblical scholarship, was just starting to come into its own, the science of archeology. The deciphering of the Babylonian cuneiform begun in 1802 by Grotefend was finally completed in the last decade of the nineteenth century; only thereafter could the most ancient texts in this script, the Sumerian, be slowly decoded and understood. Still it was some decades before this and other discoveries could be fully developed, before archeology completely understood its task and worked out its technique. Then slowly ancient biblical cities such as Jericho, Sichem, Samaria and Silo were excavated. Even more important than the discovery of the houses, tools, religious statues and pictures of the ancient Israelites and other Eastern peoples was the uncovering of ancient writings. Among these were things such as the Assyrian-Babylonian royal annals, the Elephantine papyri, the code of laws of Hammurabi and unnumbered papyrus documents and fragments in Hebrew, Aramaic and Greek;[15] the recently discovered "Dead Sea Scrolls" show that work in this field is still far from exhausted.

In Protestant ranks the result of these developments was a growing tendency away from the "evolution-historical" schema of the school of literary criticism which had held the upper hand at the turn of the century. In 1924 the Protestant Old Testament scholar Hugo Gressmann wrote that "in our science we need not *more,* but rather fewer investigations of the literary criticism type."[16] By 1935 literary criticism played a very modest role in the international Conference of Old Testament Scholars in Göttingen, a conference attended by both Catholic and Protestant theologians. Johannes Lindblom said: "The Old Testament science has experienced in the last fifteen years a type of self-consciousness. One has become a bit tired of the old set of questions. The individual investigations, the religious-historical and philological minute researches, the genetic and analytical specialized research, the purely humanistic viewpoints and problems alone no longer satisfy us in our research."[17] Scholars now became less concerned with the form and more with the *content* of Scripture and that research which led one

---

[15]Augustin Bea, S. J., "Der heutige Stand der Bibelwissenschaft," *Stimmen der Zeit,* CLIII (1953-54), 91-94.

[16]Hugo Gressmann, "Die Aufgaben der alttestamentlichen Forschung," *Zeitschrift für die alttestamentliche Wissenschaft,* XLII (1924), 8.

[17]Johannes Lindblom, "Zur Frage der Eigenart der alttestamentlichen Religion," in *Werden und Wesen der alten Testaments* (Beihefte zur *Zeitschrift für die alttestamentliche Wissenschaft,* LXVI) (Berlin, 1936), 128.

to understand the content: archeology, oriental literary history and religious history, and Jewish religious history. Coupled with this was the decline of the liberal theology and the advent of Barthian theology in 1919 with its special emphasis on the theological, the religious meaning of the Bible. As a result of these changes, Catholic and Protestant biblical scholarship, like Catholic and Protestant theology in general, found themselves no longer in a relation of almost complete opposition, but in one of at least possible cooperation.

Perhaps the greatest single result of this new attitude in Protestant theology is the *Wörterbuch zum Neuen Testament* founded by Gerhard Kittel and continued by Gerhard Friedrich after Kittel's death in 1948. Cardinal Bea, one of the foremost Catholic biblical scholars, said of this work: "The Theological Dictionary is an extremely significant step forward for the New Testament exegesis and in a certain sense also Old Testament exegesis. The Catholic exegete of today can no longer ignore its opinions and explanations."[18] This extraordinary work is an excellent example of the biblical projects in which Catholic scholars have participated with Protestant, for, in late years, partly because of the new Protestant attitude in biblical matters, there has been a gradually growing cooperation between Protestant and Catholic theologians in the field of biblical research.[19]

---

[18]Bea, "Der heutige Stand," 96.

[19]One example of inter-confessional cooperation of Scripture scholars in America is particularly interesting: The Anchor Bible, being published in honor of W. F. Albright, will be a translation of all the books of the Bible by the best available experts who studied under Professor Albright. The scholars include Protestants, Catholics and Jews—the two Jewish scholars are translating St. Paul's Epistle to the Hebrews! It is hoped that this will at least be the first step in the direction of attaining an English translation of the Bible common to all faiths. See: David Noel Freedman, "Toward a Common Bible?" in *Scripture and Ecumenism*, ed. by Leonard Swidler, (Pittsburgh: Duquesne University Press, 1965), 133-150.

CHANGING CATHOLIC ATTITUDES

Papal encouragement of Catholic biblical scholarship took a strong upswing in 1893 with Leo XIII's encyclical *Providentissimus Deus.* It sketched on a grand scale a carefully worked out plan which was not to be merely defensive and apologetic, but to gain all possible positive values from the recent research. In 1902 Leo XIII set up the Papal Biblical Commission as an official papal organ to foster biblical studies by encouragement and advice, but which, unfortunately, under Pius X became a restrictive instrument. Leo also laid plans for the founding of an institute for biblical studies in Rome; the project was only carried out, however, by his successor Pius X in 1909, when the Papal Bible institute was founded.

Intensive work with the new archeological discoveries had already begun with the work of Rudolf Cornely, S.J., (1830-1908) who in 1884 began to edit the *Cursus Scripturae Sacrae*, a biblical commentary aimed at drawing everything of positive value from the archeology and literary documents of the Old Testament and assimilating it into the body of Catholic theology. He was soon followed by the Dominicans under the energetic leadership of M. J. Lagrange (1855-1938), who in 1890 founded in Jerusalem the "Ecole pratique d'études bibliques," which school published the results of its work in the *Revue Biblique* and the commentary collection, *Etudes Bibliques.*

A temporary set-back resulted from the "modernist" condemnation in 1907. The condemnation of Alfred Loisy, the leading modernist and a renowned biblical scholar tended to put all "progressive" biblical research under a cloud. Even Father Lagrange was forbidden to work on the Old Testament for a time. The ultra-conservative element dominant during the rest of Pius X's pontificate resulted in "unjustified deletions" and "heresy-hunting."[20] However, the modernist

[20]Jean Steinmann, *Biblical Criticism* (New York, 1958), 61-71.

issue was swallowed up by the catastrophe of the first World War, and Catholic biblical research, finding encouragement in Benedict XV's encyclical *Spiritus Paraclitus* which was written on the fifteen hundredth anniversary of St. Jerome's death (1920), continued apace. Afterward it absorbed such German Protestant Scripture techniques as form criticism, which in some ways was like the literary criticism approach; it tended, however, to counteract the earlier biblical criticism by eliminating the apparent scriptural historical contradictions that the literary critics unearthed. In form criticism the different parts of Scripture are analyzed and compared to other oriental literature so as to determine the literary form of the scriptural passage, which could be either a factual report, a poetical commemoration, an epic, a parable taken from life or any of the other literary genres of oriental literature. It is only when the literary form of a piece of writing is determined that the real meaning of what the author wanted to say becomes apparent. "This is true for all times. If, for instance, we are unaware that a certain text is really a telegram, we might conclude that the author must have been angry when he wrote it. Without knowing the literary form of a passage, it is impossible to get at its meaning."[21]

From this point the work broadened out tremendously. In the field of translations alone the increase in activity has been amazing; in 1800 there were 71 translations of the Bible; today there are over 1100.[22] In Germany before 1920 the only Catholic German translations were from the Latin Vulgate, but since then there has been a constant stream of modern German translations from the original texts. This change alone has tended to bring the Protestant and Catholic

---

[21]Gregory Baum, "Approaches to Scripture," *The Commonweal,* LXXIV (April 14, 1961), 71-72.

[22]"Bibelübersetzugen," *Lexikon für Theologie und Kirche,* Vol. I (1957).

translations closer together since both are made from the original languages.[23] It has also fostered Protestant-Catholic cooperation. For example, in the foreword of the 1959 edition of his New Testament translation Father Otto Karrer acknowledged the help of several "scholarly friends of Protestant faith who through their selfless cooperation made an excellent contribution of Christian brotherliness." In addition a number of Bible commentaries have been appearing in the past few decades in Germany: *Exegetische Handbuch zum Alten Testament* (1912), the "Bonner Bibel" (1918) and (1923), the "Regensburger Bibel" (1938), the "Echter Bibel" (1947) and the *Herders theologischer Kommentar zum Neuen Testament* in fourteen volumes, of which only the "Epistles of St. John" by R. Schnackenburg in 1953 has appeared. The last four were especially chosen by the Protestant encyclopedia, *Religion in Geschichte und Gegenwart,* as worthy of mention.[24] Since the war there has also appeared a Bible atlas in Dutch, English, French and German edited by L. H. Grollenberg, O.P., an unusually excellent piece of work. There is the new Latin translation of the psalms by the

---

[23]Very popular was the so-called "Grünwald-Bibel" translated by Riessler and Storr in 1924-6, which by 1956 had gone through seven editions, and the Henne-Rösch translation (1921) which reached its twelfth edition by 1954. In 1947, a Family Bible came out in Zurich, and the "Keppler-Bibel" which was begun by P. von Keppler in 1915 and completed by von Schweitzer and Ketter passed the one million copies mark in 1950; after the second World War the Herder Publishing Company published its "*Herder-Familien-Bibel*" which was translated by the convert Karl Thieme while in voluntary exile in Switzerland during the Hitler Period. A New Testament translation which the Protestant encyclopedia, *Religion in Geschichte und Gegenwart,* describes as "outstandingly well-written" was finished by Otto Karrer in 1950. "Bibelübersetzung IV," *Die Religion in Geschichte und Gegenwart,* Vol. I (1957).

[24]*Ibid.* Cf. also "Bibelkommentare," *Lexikon für Theologie und Kirche,* Vol I (1957).

[25]L. W. Grollenberg, OP, *Atlas of the Bible* (London, 1957).

Biblical Institute under the direction of the Holy See.[26] The Benedictines of Beuron Abbey, famous in the liturgical movement, are working on a monumental edition of the *Vetus Latina,* the Latin translations of the Scriptures before the time of Jerome. The text, with all variations, is being culled from the works of the Fathers of the Church and when finished will be an invaluable aid to textual critics.

The climax, in one sense, of all this biblical research is the tremendous development experienced in the newly-emphasized science of "biblical theology." According to Cardinal Bea, Catholic exegetes had too long emphasized apologetics and allowed positive theological evaluations to slip much too far into the background in their science.[27] It was also for this reason that Pope Pius XII stressed the need for Catholic exegesis to take care "to show what the theological doctrinal content of the individual books and writings is."[28] Biblical theology however is not a mere listing of scriptural proofs, of "loci probantes," for theses in the new predominating systems of theology. "Biblical theology as we understand it today is the systematic presentation of the origin and the stepwise unfolding of the teaching of the Old or New Testament religion according to the different periods of revelation. It is just this unified and encompassing manner of viewing the truths of the faith that is particularly suited to show the unity and inner connectedness of Catholic teaching. Biblical theology thus understood is the completion and crowning of the minute work of the entire exegetical field."[29]

---

[26]Professorum Pontifici instituti Biblici (eds.)., *Liber psalmorum cum canticis breviarii Romani* (New York, 1945).

[27]Bea, "Der heutge Stand," 101.

[28]*Acta apostolica sedis* 35 (1943), 310.

[29]Bea, "Der heutige Stand," 101. Some of the outstanding works in the field of biblical theology are *Theology of the Old Testament* by P. Heinisch, *The Theology of St. Paul* by F. Prat, *Theology of the New Testament* by Meinertz, the periodical *Biblica* with its supplement volumes, and the *Biblische Zeitschrift* by Schnackenburg and Hamp.

This continually increasing activity in the field of Catholic Biblical scholarship also received continued papal support in addition to the encouragement of Leo XIII and Benedict XV already mentioned, for on September 30, 1943, Pope Pius XII issued an encyclical, *Divino afflante Spiritu,* in which he stressed the need for fundamental criticism of the original texts and the establishment of the literal translation or meanings as primary; only later could allegorical and spiritual meanings from the Fathers and the liturgy be correctly elaborated. Pius XII re-emphasized this same point in the later encyclical "Humani generis" (1951).

Thus in the years following the pioneering encyclical, *Providentissimus Deus,* in 1893, there has grown up a Bible movement that has encompassed both the theologians and biblical scholars and the faithful of the Catholic Church. The Protestant Danish theologian Kristen Skydsgaard noted the significant difference in the situation when Leo XIII wrote the *Providentissimus Deus* and when Pius XII on its fiftieth anniversary in 1943 wrote *Divino afflante Spiritu.* Skydsgaard noted that in his time Leo XIII felt the historical-critical research needed to be de-emphasized, and moreover the occasion for writing the 1893 encyclical was a "too progressive-minded" article by a highly-placed theologian. (Skydsgaard is here referring to the much-maligned Loisy) "In the encyclical '*Divino afflante Spiritu*' the tone is completely different. With a rare clarity, if also in certain points with great caution, the Pope declared himself an advocate of a historical, scientific study of the Bible. What in 1893 was 'allowed' with great restraint, is here 'requested' and recommended."[30] Pius XII approved the Bible movement and ended with the words of Jerome: "Not to know the Scriptures means not to know Christ."[31]

---

[30]Kristen Skydsgaard, "Römischer Katholizismus und evangelisches Luthertum," in *Welt-Luthertum von heute* (Stockholdm, 1950), 310.
[31]*Acta apostolica sedis* 35 (1943), 326.

That this renewed emphasis on the Bible has had strong repercussions in the interconfessional field is a fact recognized by both Catholics and Protestants. Abbot Heufelder said, "The Bible movement among us Catholics is not just a sort of hobby, but rather contributes essentially toward Catholics and Protestants finding each other again on the common ground of Holy Scriptures. . . . The Priests who work with this attitude in the Bible movement prepare the way for reunion."[32] The Protestant Georg Donatus expressed a similar view: "A Catholic who is seen by a Protestant brother with the Holy Scriptures in his hand and heart is a more solid pillar of the yearned-for Church structure than the most brilliant theological discussion."[33]

In turn the Una Sancta Movement has itself fostered the Bible movement. In an article on the Bible movement, Franz Hillig, S.J., commented: "Certainly the Una Sancta work has also had a fruitful effect on Catholic Bible work. The conversations between the confessions lead automatically to the Scriptures . . . And it is significant that in the work of the Society of Christ the King, Meitingen bei Augsburg, the two, Bible and Una Sancta, stand together in the foreground."[34]

---

[32]Quoted in Juan C. Ruta and Johannes Straubinger, *Die katholische Kirche in Deutschland und ihre Probleme* (Stuttgart, 1954), 207.

[33]Georg Donatus, *Es gibt kein Züruck* (Stuttgart, 1953), 177.

[34]Franz Hillig, S.J., "Wo steht die katholische Bibelarbeit?" *Stimmen der Zeit, CLI* (1952-53), 206.

Chapter Six

Lay Movements

ONE of the strongest movements in present-day Catholicism, the Lay Apostolate, along with its Protestant counterpart, is of special importance to the Una Sancta Movement. Its very basis, the emphasis on the importance of the layman in the Church, brings the Catholic position closer to that of the Protestant Churches with their doctrine of the general priesthood of the faithful. Although this is not a new concept, but goes back to the early years of the Church when the modern, definite line of demarcation betweeen the laity and clergy did not exist, there is a specific distinction between the Catholic and Protestant positions.

Luther said, "Clergy and laity are distinguished from each other, apparently, only by the fact that the former have the commission to administer the Sacraments and the Word of God. Otherwise they are utterly alike. And Peter and John say it right out: All are priests. I am astonished that ordination was ever able to become a sacrament."[1] Here is at least a de-emphasis of the directly divine character of the hierarchy, although certainly the hierarchy did not cease to exist in some form in Lutheranism. Still, especially since the Enlightenment, the hierarchy gradually lost its authoritative character in doctrinal matters, until this century, when the tendency is being reversed. Other reform groups in varying degrees went much further than Lutheranism in placing the layman on the level with the cleric. It is in the abandoning of sacramental character and apostolic succession that the essential separation between the Catholic and

---

[1]Quoted in Franklin Littell, *The German Phoenix* (New York, 1960), 153.

Protestant doctrines of the general priesthood of the faithful lies, and not in the raising up of the layman to a position of significance.

In reaction to their weaknesses in face of the Nazi onslaught, the Protestant Churches since the end of the war have been emphasizing the need for greater authority, and in doing so are drawing closer to the Catholic position. Yet, paradoxically, the Protestant Churches have also been experiencing a revival of the importance of the laymen in the Church. And so, with the rise of the lay movements in both Churches more and more laymen are taking a more vital interest in religion and are given a greater voice within their Churches; and because these same laymen have a much greater contact with Christians of other denominations throughout their lives than do most clergymen, the Una Sancta Movement has found an especially favorable soil in the Catholic and Protestant lay movements.

THE LAITY IN CATHOLICISM

Until recently the Catholic laity have been considered almost entirely from a negative point of view, as non-clerics or non-religious. The Catholic theologian Karl Hermann wrote: "It seems as if the Church more and more looked upon itself as a religious order and a Church of the clergy . . ."[2] The words of Eduard LeRoy are even more biting: "The simple faithful play only the role of little sheep on Candlemas. One blesses them and shears them."[3] This great cleft between the cleric and the simple layman, which did not exist in the early centuries of the Church, developed only after the time of Constantine when the position of the cleric became continually more isolated from the rest of the Church. In the sixteenth century the Reformers attempted to counter

[2]Konrad Algermissen, *Konfessionskunde* (Paderborn, 1957), 291.
[3]Yves Congar, *Jalons pour une théologie du laicat* (Paris, 1953), quoted in *ibid.*

this trend by stressing the importance of the faithful rather than that of the clergy, and in reaction the Catholic Church stressed even more on the importance of the clergy.

The episcopacy and papacy are of the essence in the Catholic Church, but they are not complete in themselves. They are quite obviously so formed as to pass on the good news, the *eu angellion* of Christ, and dispense the sacraments he instituted. The laymen are the hierarchy's *raison d'être*. But unfortunately many believe, or at least act as if they believed, that this passive role of the laymen was the most correct and most desirable role for the faithful. This is certainly not the case, as is borne out most vividly by the statements of the recent popes. They have been calling for the laity to take an active role in the Church. St. Pius X, when he was still the Patriarch of Venice, said in a speech: "Catholic Action will not please certain timid souls, who though good living, are so attached to their habitual quiet and so afraid of every innovation that they believe that it is quite sufficient to pray, because God knows best how to defend the faith and humiliate His enemies, and make the Church triumphant. But these good people, whom I would call optimists, will wait in vain for society to rechristianize itself simply by the prayers of the good. Prayer is absolutely necessary because in the ordinary economy of salvation God does not concede graces except to him who prays, but India and Japan would never have been converted by the prayers alone of Xavier, the Apostles would never have conquered the world, if they had not done the work of heroes and martyrs. It is necessary therefore, to join prayer with action."[4]

Pius XI was even more insistent that the layman fulfill his function in the Church. He wrote: "It is absolutely necessary that in this our age all should be apostles: it is absolutely necessary that the laity should not sit idly by. . . . The crisis we are experiencing is unique in history. It is a

---

[4]*Program of Action* (Grailville, Loveland, Ohio, 1946), 43.

new world that must burst out of a crucible in which so many different energies are boiling. Let us thank God that He makes us live among the present problems. It is no longer permitted to anyone to be mediocre. Everyone has the imperative duty to remember that he has a mission to fulfill, that of doing the impossible, each within the limits of his activity, to bring the world back to Christ."[5]

Although it is to the pontificate of Pius IX that the beginning of Catholic Action and the Lay Apostolate is usually attributed, it is Pope Pius XI who is given the title "Pope of Catholic Action." It was in his encyclical *Non Abbiamo Bisogno* (1931) that he gave what became the classical definition of Catholic Action: it is "the participation and cooperation of laity in the apostolate of the hierarchy."[6] The growth of Catholic Action under the direction of Pius XI's successor, Pius XII, continued at an even greater rate. During his pontificate two world congresses of the Lay Apostolate took place in Rome, one in 1951 and the other in 1957, and a Permanent Committee for International Congresses of the Lay Apostolate was established with his approbation after the 1951 Congress.

Almost every Catholic theologian of significance in the past few decades has written about the place of the laity in the Church. One of the most stimulating German theologians writing on this subject is Karl Rahner, S.J., who published, among other things, a provocative article on "Free Speech in the Church." He says that in continuing to bring Christ's teaching and saving grace to men the Church leaders, the hierarchy, must make decisions based on the existing conditions. Wherever these decisions are not directly concerned with the essentials of faith and morals but are questions of methods and discipline, as for example the liturgy, the way people, the lay people, actually feel about

[5]*Ibid.*, 45.
[6]Carlo Carbone, *Das Apostolat der Laien* (Feldkirch, 1956), 21.

such things must be taken into account as the "conditions" amidst which the official Church must take her appropriate action. Public opinion is one of the very important ways the hierarchy, which also needs human help, can get to know something about the actual situation in which they have to lead their people.

Therefore, individual expression of opinion needs to be encouraged. And if this is to be a genuine expression it will naturally have to include the possibility of lay criticism of clerical decisions, or lack of decisions. This should in no way raise the fear of irreverence or rebellion. Karl Rahner described the situation thus: "The position here is like that in different families: in one the children are allowed to criticize things openly and to express their own desires and complaints, and yet at the same time are most devoted and obedient children, whereas in another this freedom might undermine the parents' authority absolutely and in practice be a real threat to their ultimate right of decision. Obviously this depends on the way the children have been brought up. When they have been encouraged from their earliest days to voice their own desires and wishes quite frankly and yet at the same time have been brought up in a proper spirit of obedience, a frank exchange of views between them and their parents can do nothing but good and will never be regarded by either side as being impertinence or destructive criticism. But if they have been brought up to listen and obey, on the assumption that their parents' word is law; if, even when they are grown-up, they have to behave as though they could never have any views of their own; then any sudden permission to criticize will in fact undermine the authority of their parents. People in the Church (young men in Holy Orders, the laity and so on) must be brought up in a responsible spirit of obedience and be able to make proper use of their right to express their opinions."[7] These insights

[7]Karl Rahner, S.J., *Free Speech in the Church* (New York, 1960), 35 ff.

and those of other theologians have since been incorporated into the documents of Vatican II. The notions of the freedom and responsibility of the layman is now beginning to come into its own.

The Lay Apostolate in Germany has taken many forms, of which the Catholic youth movement was the most important for the Una Sancta Movement. Among Catholic youth groups there were 27 separate organizations in 1933 with a total of one and a half million members.[8] Although with the rise of Naziism the Catholic youth movement in Germany was practically annihilated, by 1953 the membership of Catholic youth organizations had risen again to above the half million mark, and they were publishing over a dozen periodicals with a total of 638,300 copies. These Catholic youth groups varied from groups of young farmers to groups of students and sport clubs. Like other German youth groups they included folk singing, folk dancing, hiking and working together. What differentiated the Catholic youth groups from the non-Catholic were their apostolic and liturgical elements. Although emphasis on the study of and participation in the liturgy varied from organization to organization, it was an essential element of all Catholic groups. The groups regularly studied a portion of the liturgy and Scriptures at their meetings, and whenever possible made a *Missa cantata* or *Missa recitata* or some other form of participation in the liturgy the focal point of their group activities, as for example, the week-long *Quickborn* conferences held at Burg Rothenfels. Sometimes the "Jocist" method started by Abbé Cardijn of Belgium was adapted; each meeting was divided into three parts: Scripture study, liturgy study and study of a practical problem which should issue in some concerted action to improve the situation. In this latter part the system of

---

[8]Juan C. Ruta and Johannes Straubinger, *Die katholische Kirche in Deutschland und ihre Probleme* (Stuttgart, 1954), 116.

"observe, judge and act," was often used, thereby giving the groups their special apostolic element.[9]

The Protestant reaction to the growth of the Lay Apostolate in the Roman Catholic Church supports the contention that the Lay Apostolate with its emphasis on the layman is a source of closer and more friendly contact between the two confessions. One Protestant theologian, for example, says: "There are spiritual movements in the Catholic Church of our day in which we can greatly rejoice. . . There is the lay movement where the universal priesthood is taken seriously. . . ."[10] Hans Rudi Weber, director of the department of the laity of the World Council of Churches, attended the world congress of the Lay Apostolate in Rome in the fall of 1957, and later wrote a commendatory report in the *Ecumenical Review* on the Lay Apostolate movement in general. In referring to the power of the Holy Spirit, he said: "There is no doubt that this renewing power is at present at work in the Roman Catholic Church, and especially in her lay movements."[11]

LAY MOVEMENTS IN PROTESTANTISM

There are also movements among the laity of the Protestant Church which have contributed to the Una Sancta Movement. The first is that of the growth of the study fellowship of the Evangelical Academies, which, though not entirely lay organizations, give the laity an extremely important place. The academies are centers of study where Protestant laymen of all interests and occupations gather together for conferences varying in length from one to several days. These conferences, on all possible subjects of interest to the modern layman, are directed from a Christian perspective. The first

---

[9]*Ibid.*, 162-166.

[10]Wilfred Lempp, *Oekumenisch oder katholisch?* (Tübingen, 1948), 25.

[11]Hans Rudi Weber, "Rome and the Lay Apostolate," *Ecumenical Review,* X (1958), 384.

of these Evangelical Academies was founded after the war at Bad Boll, and some twenty more have been established since then throughout Germany.[12]

The Evangelical Academies have established for Protestants several contacts with various aspects of the Catholic Church. Shortly before the declaration of the dogma of the assumption of the Blessed Virgin into heaven by Pope Pius XII in 1950, the Evangelical Academy at Tutzing am Starnbergersee devoted a conference entirely to the study of Mariology.[13] A more direct contact has been established by the academies in holding conferences which were in effect Una Sancta conferences. One of several such conferences took place when Lutheran, Catholic and Orthodox theologians met together for ten days in 1953 under the sponsorship of the Evangelical Academy of Schleswig.[14] Even more striking was the announcement in 1957 by the *Una Sancta* that in lieu of a German National Una Sancta Conference there would again be a common conference during Pentecost week between the Evangelical Academy at Bad Boll and the Catholic Academy Hohenheim.[15] At the opening of another Evangelical Academy, Rettwig-Ruhr, the opening address was delivered by a Catholic bishop, Dr. Stockums.[16] In addition, the Evangelical Academies have fostered inter-confessional contact by means of such publications as the booklet *Oekumenisch oder katholisch?* by Wilfrid Lempp.

Another movement of the Protestant laity which is working vigorously for the unity of Christian Churches is the *Evan-*

---

[12]Nils Ehrenstroem, "International Religious Cooperation in Relation to International Problems," January 13, 1951. Mimeographed. Submitted to Religious Affairs Branch, Office of the United States High Commissioner of Germany.

[13]Algermissen, *Konfessionskunde,* 871.

[14]D.T.S. and D.N.E., "Oekumenische Begegnung in Schleswig," *Una Sancta,* IX (1954), 17-18.

[15]*Una Sancta,* XII (1957), 62.

[16]Kurt Hutten, "Das Gespräch zwischen den Konfessionen," *Für Arbeit und Besinnung,* I (1947), 230.

gelische Kirchentag. These conferences on timely themes in a different German city each year attract hundreds of thousands of Protestants. The *Evangelische Kirchentage* grew out of the Evangelical Weeks of the years 1935-1937. When in the midst of the *Kirchenkampf* the Protestant Church of Germany was being split into the *"Bekennende Kirche," "Lutherrat," "Neutrale,"* and other groups, Dr. von Thadden-Trieglaff brought together a lay convention to foster the unity of the Church. This lay convention sponsored the Evangelical Weeks. With this experience and the added inspiration he received at the founding of the World Council of Churches in 1948 at Amsterdam, Dr. von Thadden founded the movement of the annual *Evangelische Kirchentag,* a primarily lay movement with strong ecumenical aims.[17] Following the spirit of this ecumenism the Protestant *Kirchentag* and the much older *Katholikentag* have developed the custom of exchanging official greetings with each other. "Dear brothers and sisters! It has become a heart-warming custom that in past years whenever Evangelical or Catholic Christians gather in their German "Church Conferences" they have sent each other a greeting."[18] Not infrequently Catholics participate in Protestant *Kirchentage.* "The deep impression your 1951 *Kirchentag* made on us Berlin Catholics remains unforgettable. Many of us have taken part in your meetings, but also those who have only met you on the streets of Berlin were gripped by your composure of deep faith."[19] The reverse also took place in a very dramatic manner when thousands of Protestants from the Eastern Zone of Germany on their way to the Protestant *Kirchentag* in Stuttgart were refused passage by the communists and decided

---

[17]J.P. Michael, *Christen suchen eine Kirche* (Freiburg, 1958), 93.
[18]Hedwig Klausener, "Wir grüssen alle, die Christus, unsern Herrn, lieben," *Una Sancta,* IX (1954), 33.
[19]*Ibid.,* 34.

instead of going home to participate in the 75th German *Katholikentag* which was taking place in Berlin.

Thus because of the growth of the lay movement in both Churches, an atmosphere has arisen which is conducive to the Una Sancta Movement. The situation was well described by the words of the 1948 *Katholikentag* which were addressed to the "separated brethren": "A new atmosphere of living together has thus arisen. The aims of the theological discussion between Catholics and non-Catholics have reached a new stage in that it no longer concerns a polemic exchange or an irenic bridging-over but rather its subject has become strictly the question of truth."[20]

---

[20]Heinrich Hermelink, *Katholizismus und Protestantismus* (Stuttgart, 1949), 35.

Chapter Seven

The Forerunners of the Una Sancta Movement

The High Church Movement

The Una Sancta Movement, characterized by a large number of groups of Catholics and Protestants meeting periodically, did not come into existence until after 1934. It was not until 1938 that Dr. Max Metzger founded his "Una Sancta Brotherhood" and only still later, after 1945, that the Una Sancta Movement surged out of the catacombs. Even so, there were already groping attempts toward a Catholic-Protestant *rapprochement* at the time of the first World War. The earliest movements came from within the Protestant *Hochkirchliche Vereinigung*, founded in 1918, which has been so important in the Protestant liturgical movement.[1]

There were for some time two currents of thought, within the ranks of the *Hochkirchliche Vereinigung*, one consciously German-Protestant and the other definitely ecumenical in aim. Those members of the ecumenical train of thought long considered it possible and valuable for the two groups to cooperate and remain together. On the other hand, the more rigidly Protestant group began more and more to draw distinctions between evangelical and non-evangelical values, thus contradicting the position of the ecumenical party, whose purpose was not to separate but to build bridges, to emphasize the "general," the "catholic."[2]

A paper on the confessional question read at a *Hochkirchliche* workshop in January of 1924 began to bring the matter

[1]Friedrich Heiler, "Evangelisch-ökumenische Vereinigung," *Oekumenische Einheit,* I (1948), 165.

[2]"Mitteilungen des Hochkirchlich-ökumenischen Bundes," *Una Sancta,* I (1925), 13.

to a head. The conflict mounted and the crisis was finally reached on July 1, 1924, when a *Hochkirchliche Vereinigung* conference passed the "Eberhard proposal"; in this proposal adherence to the *Confessio Augustana* was made obligatory in order that a "sharp dividing line against Rome" would be drawn and so that the *Hochkirchliche Vereinigung* would be given official confessional Protestant character.[3]

The situation had become impossible for those members with an ecumenical outlook: ten of them met on September 30 in Berlin and announced their common withdrawal from the *Hochkirchliche Vereinigung* and their founding of the *Hochkirchlich-ökumenische Bund.* Pastor E. Herzog was elected chairman, and Professor Alfred von Martin became vice-chairman and editor of their organ, the *Una Sancta.*[4]

The calling of the founding meeting of the *Bund* drew a response far beyond the ten men present. Dean A. E. Burn of Salisbury, "an outstanding representative of the Anglo-Catholics," expressed his intention to take part. Although at the last minute he was unable to attend, he sent the conference assurance of his and others' support. "In the name of the 'Literature Committee of the English Church Union' I wish to give to all members of the *Hochkirchlich-ökumenische Bund* the assurance that the progress of your movement will be attentively followed by numberless friends in England. We cherish the desire to remain in touch with you that we may pray for the guidance and grace of the Holy Spirit for you with full understanding."[5] Pastor H. Hansen, whose *95 Theses toward a Reformation of Protestantism,* published for the Reformation Jubilee in 1917, had been the original stimulus for the organization of the High-Church movement in Germany, enlisted himself as an honor-

---

[3]*Ibid.*
[4]*Ibid.,* 14.
[5]*Ibid.*

ary member of the *Hochkirchlich-ökumenische Bund.*[6]

A few months after the founding of the *Bund,* its relation with the *Hochkirchliche Vereinigung* was improved by a change of leadership in the *Vereinigung.* As a result, at the December 18, 1924, meeting in Berlin, the *Hochkirchlich-ökumenische Bund* decided to eliminate its requirement that all its own members automatically drop their membership in the *Vereinigung.*[7] The meeting defined the *Hochkirchlich-ökumenische Bund* as an association of believing Christians wishing to unite in joint action with all Christians who were "driven by the same zeal for the 'one, holy, catholic (i.e. universal) and apostolic church' to participate in the building up of the Kingdom of God on Earth."[8]

The *Bund* therefore declared its adherence to the Church as a divine institution of salvation, to Scriptures, and to the ecumenical symbols; where the practices of the ancient church had fallen into disuse, it favored their reinstitution. It sought:

> 1. for the re-establishment of the authority assigned by Christ to the holy Office of the Church and the episcopal constitution with apostolic succession,
> 2. for the acknowledgment of the objective character of the holy sacraments and the solicitous education for their salutary use,
> 3. for the re-establishment of the old Church liturgy, in particular the Holy Eucharist as the most important part and center of the Christian service,
> 4. for the renewal of the ecclesiastical customs in connection with the seasons of the Church year,
> 5. for the revival of the religious vocation including the later developed lay orders and their fostering of spiritual practices.

---

[6]"Aus Pastor Hansens 95 Thesen zur Reformation des Protestantismus," *Una Sancta,* I (1925), 10.

[7]"Mitteilungen des Bundes," 14.

[8]"Grundsätze des Hochkirchlich-ökumenischen Bundes," *Una Sancta,* I (1925), 3.

> With faith in the promise of our Lord (John 17:21), the *Bund* strives for a close contact and as intimate a union as possible with all Christians who stand on this common position without regard to the boundaries of confessions. It invites all who favor the ecumenicity and catholicity of the Church of Christ in the sense of these principles to join.[9]

The first goal, in stressing the need for a more effective and independent episcopacy, was also besides the stress on the sacramental, a reflection of the new political situation of the Lutheran Churches. Without their prince to act as *summus episcopus* after 1918, some sought to fill the power vacuum by building up the juridical power of the bishop or superintendent (which is merely the Latin translation of the Greek *episkopos*).[10]

These principles, with their heavy stress on the importance of the Church and the liturgy, were quite obviously strongly "High-Church." But the ecumenical characteristics were also notable, especially in the concluding paragraph. Both of these elements, but more especially the ecumenical, were repeated in the opening article, "*Was Wir Wollen*," of the first issue of the *Una Sancta.*

> . . . We naturally expect no one to deny those additional things which bind him personally to his confession; however, in our *Bund* we do wish in principle to de-emphasize everything that is confessionally dividing in order to work together on that ground which we have in common with adherents to all confessions, and, as far as in us, to serve in humility the coming of the kingdom according to the promise of our Lord in John 17:21.
>
> . . . And we turn on the other hand to all those, and not least to our Roman Catholic fellow-Christians, who, penetrated with a truly world-wide ecumenical conviction, wish to work

---

[9] *Ibid.*

[10] Cf. Andrew Drummond, *German Protestantism since Luther* (London, 1951), 258 ff.

> with us to free the Christian spirit everywhere from confessionalistic narrowness and particular seclusion and attain the breadth of real "catholicity."[11]

Several projects of the *Hochkirchlich-ökumenische Bund* show its leanings toward ecumenism. For one thing, it talked of forming an "Una Sancta Community, i.e., a circle of spiritually and intellectually united men."[12] The *Bund* also developed affiliations with the Barth-Gogarten school of theologians and with both the Protestant and the Catholic youth movements, particularly the *Quickborn,* seeing in them kindred spirits.[13] As both the Barthian theology and the lay movements in the Churches helped prepare the way for the way for the later Una Sancta Movement, it is significant to find both of them already in contact with this forerunner of the Una Sancta Movement. A third effort toward ecumenism was the publishing on the seven hundredth anniversary of his death of a special edition of the *Una Sancta* devoted entirely to St. Francis of Assisi,[14] one saint loved and admired by all Christians. Throughout its first year the *Una Sancta* used as the opening article of each issue a meditation on a liturgical feast or season common to the two Churches, such as Advent, Lent or Epiphany. The underlying concern for attracting Catholics was particularly pointed up by an article in the second issue, "After Epiphany (a Chapter from the Cult of the Saints)." A footnote to the title read, "In the face of the hateful and hate-bearing polemic which the *Evangelische Sonntagsblatt aus Bayern* recently saw fit again to direct against the Catholic cult of Mary and the saints, we are especially happy to be able to publish this discussion by our highly-esteemed co-worker."[15]

---

[11]"Was Wir Wollen," *Una Sancta,* I (1925), 1-2.
[12]Cover of *Una Sancta,* II, I (1926).
[13]"Mitteilungen des Bundes," 64.
[14]*Franz von Assisi* (Sonderheft der *Una Sancta*), (1926).
[15]*Una Sancta,* I (1925), 21.

CATHOLICS AND THE HIGH CHURCH MOVEMENT

The hope of bringing Catholics into the project was soon fulfilled: an article by a Catholic theologian, Johannes Albani, appeared in the second issue of the *Una Sancta.*[16] The editor remarked, "It is a joy for us to be able to present for the first time, with this contribution, the words of a Roman Catholic member; and so much the more since this man is no unknown in the High-Church movement and because the decided ecumenical direction of our circle has made it possible for him, a convert, to return now to the High-Church arena."[17] Several other Catholic theologians followed Albani in contributing to the *Una Sancta.* Among these was Joseph Wittig,[18] some of whose works, unfortunately for him and the *Bund,* were later placed on the *Index Librorum Prohibitorum.*[19] By its second year the *Una Sancta* was also publishing the work of Franz Müller,[20] one writer whose work would carry over to the successor of the *Una Sancta.* There likewise appeared an article by Arnold Rademacher,[21] who later, as a Catholic theology professor at the University of Bonn, exerted considerable influence on the ecumenical trend in the Catholic Church. Robert Grosche, later the founder of the periodical for "Kontroverstheologie," *Catholica,* also wrote for the *Una Sancta.*[22] In the same year another Catholic, Hermann Platz, became a member of the editorial committee.

---

[16]Johannes Albani, "Alleinseligmachend," *Una Sancta,* I (1925), 27.

[17]*Una Sancta,* I (1925), 27.

[18]Joseph Wittig, "Natur und Uebernatur," *Una Sancta,* I (1925), 137; and Joseph Wittig, "Der Heilige Troubadour," in *Franz von Assisi,* 8.

[19]Hedwig Brey, "Non evacuetur crux Christi zur Indizierung Wittigs," *Una Sancta,* II (1926), 179.

[20]Franz Müller, "Aus dem geistigen Leben des deutschen Katholizismus," *Una Sancta,* II (1926), 85.

[21]Arnold Rademacher, "Kirche und Bildung," *Una Sancta,* II (1926), 213.

[22]Robert Grosche, "Franz von Assisi und Benedikt," in *Franz von Assisi,* 71; and book reviews in *Una Sancta,* III (1927), 114 ff. and 118 ff.

The following year, 1927, saw Catholics taking an even more prominent part editorially in the *Una Sancta*: for the first two issues of that year one of the two co-editors working under editor von Martin was Heinrich Getzing, a Catholic.

After two and a half years of existence, the *Hochkirchlich-ökumenische Bund,* whose vigor was indicated by the fact that it held seven general conferences in slightly over two years,[23] was able to heal the breach between itself and the *Hochkirchliche Vereinigung.* The leaders of the two organizations met on January 19, 1927, in Berlin, after a common celebration of the eucharistic liturgy, to draw up and discuss the reunion proposals; these proposals were then presented to the two general conference meetings on March 1 and 2, 1927, in Berlin. As the editor of the *Una Sancta,* Alfred von Martin, explained, the *Hochkirchlich-ökumenische Bund* started with the intention of carrying out High-Church work with an ecumenical conviction. But it soon became clear to the members that it was the ecumenical work itself which was most important, and nothing would foster this ecumenical understanding as quickly as would the High-Church work within the Protestant Churches. The *Bund* decided therefore not to dissolve but to maintain its existence within the *Vereinigung,* keeping as its own task the promoting of ecumenical work. The *Hochkirchlich-ökumenische Bund* was then renamed *Oekumenischer Bund.* All Protestant members of the *Oekumenischer Bund* were urged to become members of the *Hochkirchliche Vereinigung* and *vice versa.* In addition the now combined organizations agreed to have their general conferences on successive days in the same area; this was already the case on March 1 and 2, 1927, in Berlin.[24]

---

[23]*Una Sancta,* I (1925), 110 and 170; II (1926), 221 and 339; III (1927), 139 and 247.

[24]Alfred von Martin, "Oekumenische Chronik," *Una Sancta,* III (1927), 248-250.

A REJECTION BY ROME

Into the midst of this rapidly developing cooperation between Protestants and Catholics there fell a bombshell in the form of a decree from Rome. On the last page of the third issue of the *Una Sancta* of 1927, the two Catholic members of the editorial staff declared that they and other Catholic authors would no longer be able to work with the *Una Sancta.*[25] The reason for their withdrawal was the decree of the Holy Office of April 11, 1927, which prohibited Catholics from both belonging to the *Hochkirchlich-ökumenische Bund* and contributing to the *Una Sancta.*

The next issue of the *Una Sancta* contained an article by the editor, Alfred von Martin, discussing the reason for the Roman decree; although he explained that he believed it was based on false information, he said nothing about the possible sources of this information.[26] However, in an interview years later he revealed what he believed to have been the source. A conference of the *Hochkirchlich-ökumenische Bund* (probably in November, 1926)[27] had included a lecture by Friedrich Heiler, a former Catholic who had become a Protestant theology professor at Marburg University. A Jesuit present at the conference apparently received the impression that Heiler was antagonistic to the Catholic Church and could be a great corrupting influence on Catholics coming in contact with him. The priest also seemed to think that Heiler was the leading spirit of the *Hochkirchlich-ökumenische Bund* and that it would therefore be dangerous for Catholics to maintain a membership in the *Bund.* The ensuing report to Rome by this Jesuit theologian apparently bore fruit in the decree.[28]

---

[25]*Una Sancta,* III (1927), 396.

[26]Alfred von Martin, "Katastrophe oder—Krisis?" *Una Sancta,* III (1927), 527 ff.

[27]Cf. *Una Sancta,* III (1927), 132.

[28]Interview with Alfred von Martin, March 10, 1959.

Von Martin contended that the whole affair was really a case of "mistaken identity." "For Heiler . . . at that time (1926) still was not a member of the *Hochkirchlich-ökumenische Bund* (founded 1924)—in which indeed he never did play any leading or significant role—and . . . in the *Una Sancta* was always only a co-worker as every other. . . . Insofar as one can speak *at all* of a leading theologian of the *Bund* and a spiritual mentor of the *Una Sancta* . . . it was under no circumstances Heiler, but rather at most Glinz."[29] Professor von Martin's point is corroborated in that Heiler's name appeared nowhere on the masthead, though by 1927 there were thirteen men from eight nations acting in an editorial capacity; it was not until the thirteenth issue that an article of Heiler's was published.[30]

In the end von Martin said, "The magazine *Una Sancta* is dead. It is impossible always to stand there with the hand outstretched while the other is admonished to persist in stiff reserve. A new periodical that is likewise ecumenical but no longer on a High-church basis must carry on on a new path."[31] The last issue of the *Una Sancta* already contained an advertisement for its successor, *Religiöse Besinnung*.[32] Although Alfred von Martin became a convert to the Catholic Church in 1940, he claims that his conversion was in no direct way connected with his interconfessional activities, for he no longer took an active part in ecumenical work after the dissolution of the *Una Sancta*.[33]

After the April 11th decree of the Holy Office a new basis for future action was necessary. Although the *Hochkirchlich-ökumenische Bund* had been dissolved and the *Oekumenischer Bund* formed in its place only on March 2, 1927,

---

[29]Von Martin, "Katastrophe?" 529.

[30]Friedrich Heiler, "Evangelisches Hochkirchentum," *Una Sancta*, II (1926), 37.

[31]Von Martin, "Katastrophe?" 538.

[32]*Una Sancta*, III (1927), 540.

[33]Interview with Alfred von Martin, March 10, 1959.

the *Oekumenischer Bund* convened again on October 25. The members of the Bund decided that it was absolutely essential to their ecumenical work that their organization be open to all Christian groups and that it was particularly imperative that Catholics take an active part. Consequently an entirely new organization, one with no ties to any other organization, was founded; it was called *"Oekumenische Arbeitsgemeinschaft."*[34]

Underlying the *Arbeitsgemeinschaft* was the assumption that some truths and practices were common to both Churches; these certainly formed a basis for conversations. These conversations were not to be seen as challenges but as exercises in Christian brotherliness, penance, humility and the recognition of common guilt. The whole undertaking was to be looked upon as merely a preparation for a future union of Christians. "Thus the solution, 'an ecumenicity that embraced all or none at all,' brought the former *Oekumenischer Bund* to an end in one form and immediately to a new beginning in another."[35]

In January of 1928, just a few months after the forming of the new *Oekumenische Arbeitsgemeinschaft,* Pope Pius XI issued the encyclical *Mortalium Animos* with rather chilling effect in ecumenically oriented circles, particularly in Germany. The *Oekumenische Arbeitsgemeinschaft* was thrown a state of suspended animation. Some decision had to be made, however, and a first conference was called for in Berlin on June 27, 1928. Alfred von Martin said he went to the conference in a mood of "absolute pessimism." He was, however, completely overwhelmed by the optimistic keynote address delivered by the Catholic theologian Johannes Albani in which he demonstrated that the latest encyclical had not shut all possible doors to future ecumenical coopera-

---

[34]G. A. Glinz, "Oekumenische Chronik," *Una Sancta,* III (1927), 525-526.
[35]*Ibid.*

tion with Catholics. The decision of the conference was to continue on; this decision had a special significance since they were "the sole ecumenical organization in which Roman Catholics participated."[36] Furthermore, as a result of Pfarrer Glinz's resignation of the chairmanship of the *Gemeinschaft* for private reasons, it was decided that there should be dual chairmanship in the future with one Protestant and one Catholic presiding.[37] The first such chairman elected, though not until December 5, 1928, were the Protestant Karl Buchheim and the Catholic Franz Müller.[38]

The *Gemeinschaft* continued to flourish for a time, for the following June 14 another considerably larger conference took place with the Catholic Peter Wust delivering the main address;[39] a somewhat smaller conference was reported for January 17, 1930.[40] And then nothing—until the appearance in the late fall of 1932 of an article in the periodical *Religiöse Besinnung* signed by five people: the two chairmen of the *Gemeinschaft,* the secretary, and W. Froböse and Karl Thieme, then the editor of the *Religöse Besinnung.*[41] The unfavorable conditions of the time—the depression and the political unrest in Germany preceding Hitler's rise to power—had caused, according to the authors, the weakening of the earlier energy of the *Gemeinschaft;* a conference planned for the spring of 1932 had had to be cancelled for lack of response. They were therefore forming an *"Arbeitsgemeinschaft des Austausches über ökumenische Fragen"* to take the place of the defunct *Arbeitsgemeinschaft,* and all interested former members or

[36]Alfred von Martin, "Oekumenische Arbeitsgemeinschaft," *Religiöse Besinnung,* I (1928), 187.
[37]*Ibid.,* 183-188.
[38]Karl Buchheim, "Oekumenische Arbeit," *Religiöse Besinnung.* II (1929), 95.
[39]*Ibid.,* 96.
[40]Karl Buchheim, "Wintertagung der 'Oekumenischen Arbeitsgemeinschaft,'" *Religiöse Besinnung,* II (1929), 234.
[41]"Oekumenische Arbeitsgemeinschaft, "*Religiöse Besinnung,* IV (1931-2), 206.

readers of the *Religiöse Besinnung* were invited to contact them by letter.

THE SUCCESSORS TO THE "UNA SANCTA"

In its final issue the *Una Sancta* had already mentioned its successor periodical. It was to be edited by the Protestant Georg Boss under the title of *Religöse Besinnung.* But this magazine was definitely not to be an organ of the *Oekumenische Arbeitsgemeinschaft* as the *Una Sancta* had been for the *Hochkirchlich-ökumenische Bund.* The new editor insisted strongly that this was not another circle or group—neither an old nor a new one; it rejected any official connection with an organization or Church. The *Religiöse Besinnung* wanted only to be a means for all Christian groups to learn to know themselves and other better.[42] What is more, a "pure 'Protestant' ecumenicity was rejected. It was founded on the basis of both a Catholic and Evangelical participation."[43]

The articles appearing for the first three years in the *Religiöse Besinnung,* very much like those of the *Una Sancta,* always dealt with ecumenical matters and were written by Catholics, Protestants and Orthodox. Catholics who were to become very important in the Una Sancta Movement, such as Max Pribilla, Anton Fischer, Johannes Pinsk, and Arnold Rademacher, published major articles;[44] either an article by Max Joseph Metzger, the future founder of the Una Sancta Brotherhood, or a long quotation from his newspaper the

[42]*Religiöse Besinnung,* I (1928), 108.

[43]*Religiöse Besinnung,* III (1930), 48.

[44]Max Pribilla, "Sichtbare und unsichtbare Kirche," *Religiöse Besinnung,* III (1930), 65; Anton Fischer, "Der Prüfstein," *Religiöse Besinnung,* I (1928), 315; Anton Fischer, "Der Katholizismus und die Einheit der Kirche," *Religiöse Besinnung,* II (1929). 192; Anton Fischer, "Die wichtigste katholische Aktion," *Religiöse Besinnung,* III (1930), 29; Johannes Pinsk, "Die Einheit der Kirche," *Religiöse Besinnung,* I (1928), 45; Arnold Rademacher, "Um Ercheinung und Wesen der Kirche," *Religiöse Besinnung,* III (1930), 31.

Katholischer Missionsruf appeared in almost every issue of the *Religiöse Besinnung* in its first three years.[45] Metzger's successor as leader of the Una Sancta Movement, Matthias Laros, was also quoted at length; even then Laros was using the phrase which was later to become his motto and the title of his book on the Una Sancta Movement—"*Schöpferische Friede.*"[46] (Creative Peace) Among the ranks of the Protestant contributors also were men who would loom large in the future development of the Una Sancta Movement, men such as Otto Dibelius, Wilhelm Stählin, and Friedrich Heiler; even the founder of the ecumenical movement of Life and Work, Archbishop Nathan Soederblom, wrote an article on "Christian Unity."[47]

The reception of the work of the *Religiöse Besinnung* apparently was increasingly warm. By the fall issue of the second year the editor had received a large number of commendatory letters, and apparently there had been no unfavorable reviews. Boss quoted briefly or listed five different newspapers or books containing favorable comments; at the same time he described the skeptical silence of so many other leading Protestant and Catholic periodicals.[48] A year and a half later he was able to give a much more formidable listing of favorable reviews—seventeen German periodicals, including most of the leading Catholic and Protestant magazines and newspapers; he still had seen no unfavorable reviews.[49]

After three years Georg Boss decided that he could no longer carry the burden of the *Religiöse Besinnung's* editorial

---

[45]*Religiöse Besinnung,* I (1928), 60, 171, 272 and 366; II (1929), 122 and 157; III (1930), 99, 123 and 200.

[46]Georg Boss, "Was heisst ökumenisch?" *Religiöse Besinnung,* I (1928), 171.

[47]Nathan Soederblom, "Christliche Einheit," *Religiöse Besinnung,* II (1929), 185.

[48]*Religiöse Besinnung* II (1929), 122.

[49]Georg Boss, "Zum Beschluss des 3. Jahrgangs," *Religiöse Besinnung,* III (1930), 200.

work and handed the task over to the Protestant Karl Thieme. In his final editorial Boss announced that each future issue would be devoted to a single theme, not necessarily so specifically ecumenical as in the past.[50] The next several issues were devoted mainly to such questions as communism, marriage, education, and Kierkegaard, with articles on ecumenical matters appearing here and there. Then, shortly after the rise of Hitler, *Religiöse Besinnung* ceased entirely.

On July 11, 1933, the semi-pagan *"Deutsche Christen"* party, an instrument of the Nazis, seemed to triumph within the Protestant Church of Germany; at the same time the *"Deutsche Evangelische Kirche"* was forcibly given a new constitution by Hitler which put the Protestant Churches very largely under the control of government-appointed leaders. It was several months before any organized resistance began to show itself as it eventually did in the form of the anti-government "Confessing Church" (*"Bekennende Kirche"*).[51] As noted by Karl Thieme on August 10, 1933, the Evangelical Church as such "no longer existed." There were those who were still loyal to her and defended her, "but these were merely individual pastors and congregations, no longer a Church."[52] For this reason the *Religiöse Besinnung* would no longer appear.

Thieme ended his final editorial with an extraordinary question. "Here, then, is the question which we now put to the Roman Catholic Church. There are German Evangelical Christians, there are Christian families, there are also probably whole believing congregations with their shepherds, all of whom are forced by their consciences to ask for admittance into the one, eternal Church. But they are compelled by those same consciences, by their understanding of

---

[50]*Ibid.*

[51]J.P. Michael, *Christen suchen eine Kirche* (Freiburg, 1958), 35-36.

[52]Karl Thieme, "Una Sancta Catholica," *Religiöse Besinnung,* V (1932-3), 55.

the welfare of the Church, and by the anxiety with which their brethren watch the course they are now taking, to insist upon conditions already accorded Slavic Christians—to request that under the guidance of their own shepherds they may, in their own beloved language, render God service and worship according to the ordinances of the Catholic Church. Will this plea be granted or repudiated?[53]"

This plea was received with much sympathy and gratitude in Rome, but it was nevertheless in essence rejected. Rome was very hesitant, at a time when the situation of the Protestant Church in Germany was extremely confused, to make any moves that might look like proselytising or might disturb the relations between the two Churches in Germany—especially since only a small group of Protestants was supporting the plea. The Vatican, having just a few weeks before signed a concordat with Germany, was very reluctant to disturb things in any way, for fear of giving the Nazis an excuse to break the concordat. There were, however, a number of Catholics who were disillusioned with the action of the Holy See.[54]

Several months before the final issue of the *Religiöse Besinnung*, a similar plan for a reuniting of the Christian churches had been published by the Protestant theologian J. Lortzing in the Catholic periodical *Die schönere Zukunft.*[55] Lortzing submitted that the same procedure used by the Catholic Church in receiving the Eastern Uniate Churches could be employed with Protestantism; groups of "Uniate Protestants" could be formed which would serve as starting points for a growing return to Rome. For these groups he asked only three things: vernacular in the liturgy, comunion

---

[53]*Ibid.*, 58.

[54]Joseph Meurers, *Begegnung der Konfessionen* (Cologne, 1947), 42-43.

[55]J. Lortzing, "Für die Wiedervereinigung der Protestanten mit Rom," *Schönere Zukunft, VIII* (1933), 449-451.

under both species, and married clergy, at least for those converted ministers already married.[56]

Lortzing, a Lutheran minister and son of a minister, who could trace his family back to Gustavus Adolphus' Chancellor Oxenstierna, had written a large number of books and articles on Catholicism, discussing both the needs for and the means toward reunion.[57] He appeared however, never to have been connected with any ecumenical group or organization, although he was a very frequent contributor to the *Schönere Zukunft.*[58]

A year before the end of the *Religöse Besinnung* another periodical with an ecumenical purpose was founded by the Catholic theologian Robert Grosche, who had been a contributor to the *Una Sancta.* The inspiration to found the periodical, he said, came from a lecture by Karl Barth in 1928.[59] The periodical was named *Catholica Vierteljahrschrift für Kontroverstheologie;* it attempted "to speak to the Evangelical Christians of today: not in order to arrive at an abstract or 'superchurch' Una Sancta via illegitimate compromises, but simply to present to Evangelical Christians the teachings of the *Ecclesia Catholica* in these days which are so demanding of Catholics and Protestants."[60] One writer explained that *Kontroverstheologie* has a three-fold purpose: it wishes to develop a discussion between Catholic and Protestant theology in which both the binding and dividing factors are brought out clearly; it also should make it possible for Catholic theologians to direct specific questions to

[56]*Ibid.* Cf. the favorable answer to Lortzing's article, Hans Eibl, "Um die Union der protestantischen Christen mit Rom," *Schönere Zukunft,* VIII (1933), 785-786.

[57]Bernhard Seiller, "Pastor Lortzing—ein Vorkämpfer der Wiedervereinigung der Protestanten mit Rom", *Schönere Zukunft,* X (1935), 879-880.

[58]Michael Buchberger, *Aufbruch zur Einheit und Einigheit im Glauben* (Freiburg, 1948), 20.

[59]Interview with Robert Grosche, August 3, 1958.

[60]Cover of *Catholica.*

Protestant theologians; and it should enable the Protestants to do the same.[61] In practice this exchange was accomplished in a manner other than that attempted in the *Una Sancta* and *Religiöse Besinnung.* There, both Protestant and Catholic theologians contributed articles, whereas in the *Catholica* the authors were almost always Catholic theologians presenting their own doctrine while at the same time comparing it with a Protestant position on the matter. Thus, particularly in the first several issues, there was a series of articles dealing with Catholic theology and the dialectical theology of Karl Barth.[62]

The *Catholica* brought forth echoes from other periodicals; the *Evangelische Theologie* remarked that the "anti-theses" of Karl Barth against Catholicism were, after a genuine discussion with *Catholica,* beginning to bear fruit.[63] The *Neue Züriche Nachrichten* wrote: "Grosche's organ has shown itself to be the place where all the questions of contemporary Protestant theology are extraordinarily well presented and answered from the Catholic viewpoint. Even worthwhile contributions to Catholic theology itself have resulted."[64] That the *Catholica* made this good impression on Protestants mainly was due to its avoiding the "all too material and political points of dispute of the Reformation period,"[65] and concerning itself strictly with religious and theological matters in a non-polemic manner.[66] The *Catholica,* like so many

---

[61]Bernhard Rosenmöller, "Katholische Kontroverstheologie," *Catholica,* II (1933), 48.

[62]Robert Grosche, "Die dialektische Theologie und der Katholizismus," *Catholica,* I (1933), I ff; Robert Grosche, "Karl Barth und die analogia entis," *Catholica,* IV (1936), 185 ff. Gottlieb Söhngen, "Analogia entis I," *Catholica,* III (1935), 113 ff. Gottlieb Söhngen, "Analogia entis II," *Catholica,* III (1935), 176 ff.

[63]Back cover of *Catholica,* IV, 4 (1936).

[64]*Ibid.*

[65]Wernor Koch, "Die evangelische Kirche und die zweite Reformation," *Frankfurter Hefte* (June, 1947), 560.

[66]*Ibid.* Cf. Buchberger, *Aufbruch zur Einheit,* 19-20.

other Catholic and Protestant periodicals and newspapers, was banned in 1939 by the Nazis in their increasing oppression of the Christians.

One other periodical attempted to some extent to carry on the religious and theological discussions between Protestants and Catholics in Germany. In January, 1919, *Die Hochkirche* was started under the editorship of Pfarrer Heinrich Mosel, one of the founders of the "*Hochkirchliche Vereinigung.*" The ecumenical character of the periodical became somewhat stronger when a new editor, Paul Bronische, took over in 1923. In 1928, a year after the *Una Sancta's* failure, Friedrich Heiler became editor of *Die Hochkirche* and changed it from "a mouthpiece of a specific group to an ecumenical organ, thereby allowing theologians and laity from the different Christian Churches and lands to work together."[67] In 1934 the title was changed to *Eine heilige Kirche;* on the cover appeared, "The successor of 'Die Hochkirche' and 'Religiöse Besinnung'." However, Catholic participation in Heiler's periodical was much more limited than in the *Una Sancta* and *Religiöse Bessinnung.* After 1937 the *Eine heilige Kirche* was suppressed by the Nazis, then allowed to publish again, but only twice a year and only on a "purely scholarly" basis; the war brought it to a complete halt. Not until three years after the war did Heiler pick up this work again, combining his former periodical with the old *Eiche* of Friedrich Siegmund-Schultze which had been founded in the second decade of this century and also been stopped by the Nazis in the 1930's. The *Eiche* was not directed toward Catholic-Protestant relations but rather toward the rapidly growing Ecumenical movement among the Protestant and some Orthodox Churches. The new combined magazine, first called *Oekumenische Einheit* and later renamed *Eine heilige Kirche,* maintained the policy of having practically all

[67]Friedrich Heiler, "Geleitworth der Herausgeber," *Oekumenische Einheit,* I (1948), 2.

non-Catholic contributors, just as *Catholica* had almost all Catholic writers.[68]

SCATTERED ECUMENICAL PUBLICATIONS

In 1934 the Catholic Bishop Maurice Besson of Fribourg, Switzerland, published in French a book entitled *After Four Hundred Years* (the German version came out a year later) which gave a considerable additional impulse to the growing concern about ecumenical matters. This was the same Bishop Besson who had a few years earlier granted permission to Dr. Max Metzger, the future founder of the Una Sancta Movement, and a few other priests to attend the first council for Faith and Order in Lausanne, Switzerland. The book took the form of an imaginary series of letters exchanged between a Catholic and a Reformed pastor who discussed the problem of the division of faith and the various approaches and obstacles to reunion.[69] The positions of both sides were treated sympathetically; the whole book was irenic in tone.[70] *After Four Hundred Years* was apparently widely read and widely applauded by both Catholics and Protestants.[71]

About the same time Besson's book was causing a stir in Germany, a co-editor of the *Deutsche Rundschau*, the Protestant Paul Fechter, added another voice to the waxing ecumenical discussion with his article "Die Fremdheit." (The Alienation).[72] Fechter maintained that the vast majority of Germans, Protestant and Catholic, misunderstood one an-

---

[68]*Ibid.*, 2-5. Cf. Heiler, "Evangelisch-ökumenische Vereinigung," 165 ff.

[69]Buchberger, *Aufbruch zur Einheit*, 7.

[70]Max Pribilla, "Nach vierhundert Jahren," *Stimmen der Zeit*, LXV (1935), 156.

[71]Cf. *ibid.* 155 ff.; Buchberger, *Aufbruch zur Einheit*, 7; Paul Fechter, "Was kann man gegen die Fremdheit tun?" *Deutsche Rundschau*, LXII (1936), 113 ff.

[72]Paul Fechter, "Die Fremdheit," *Deutsche Rundschau*, LXI (1935), 18-25.

other's positions, and that the time was ripe for beginning a process of mutual enlightenment. This article drew a whole series of answers in other periodicals, for the most part agreeing with his description of the lamentable situation and adding their own suggestions for remedies.[73] Fechter himself wrote another article some months later on "Was kann man gegen die Fremdheit tun?" (What can one do about the Alienation?) in which he said the first contacts should be made on strictly non-religious levels such as sport and singing societies.

The discussion with Fechter was continued after the appearance of Fechter's second article by the Catholic Ernst Michel in a particularly good article in *Hochland*.[74] Although Michel seconded Fechter's general thesis, he believed that not only had Fechter underestimated the dogmatic and practical differences between Catholics and Protestants and their importance, but he had also overlooked the important work toward a *rapprochement* already begun. Michel later spoke of the "Alienation" beginning to thaw, outside of the still frozen north and middle German states, which would of course include Leipzig where the *Deutsche Rundschau* is published. One sign of improvement of the situation was that the *"Evangelischer Bund"* and the *"Gustav-Adolf-Verein,"* specifically anti-Catholic societies from the *Kulturkampf* era, had declined greatly in members and influence;[75] later under

---

[73]Cf. "Die Ueberwindung der konfessionellen Fremdheit," *Zeit im Querschnitt,* (October 1, 1936), 276 ff; Aronld Rademacher, *Die Wiedervereinigung der christlichen Kirchen* (Bonn, 1937), 48-49; Karlheinz Schmidthüs, "Was kann man gegen die Fremdheit tun?" *Die Schildgenossen,* XV (1936), 292-296; Ludwig Winterswyl, "Katholisch-protestantische Aussprache," *Die Schildgenossen,* XV (1935),) 88-90; Ernst Michel, "Was kann man gegen die Fremdheit tun?" *Hochland,* XXXIII (April, 1936), 41-50. Max Pribilla, "Die Ueberwindung der konfessionellen Fremdheit," *Stimmen der Zeit,* LXVI (1936), 528-540.

[74]Michel, "Was kann man gegen die Fremdheit tun?" 41-50.

[75]*Ibid.,* 45. Heinrich Hermelink, *Die katholische Kirche unter den Pius-Päpsten des 20. Jahrhunderts* (Zurich, 1949).

the new leadership of Heinrich Bornkamm the *Bund* changed completely and became much more irenic in purpose.[76] At the same time the strongly confessional, defensive apologetics had begun to disappear on the Catholic side.

When Michel spoke of the "strong beginnings of the different confessions towards understanding each other and towards learning to know themselves better which already exist in other areas of Germany and which especially in the past fifteen years have developed with great promise," he doubtless was referring to such developments as the "*Hochkirchlich-ökumenische Bund*" and the "*Religiöse Besinnung.*" And although Michel does not mention Pius XI's *Mortalium Animos* specifically, he was obviously referring to it when he said a "setback" suffered by the movement toward the "Reunion of the Confessions" led the different confessions to drink more deeply from the sources of their own faith and come up with a reinvigorated view of life; it provided a stronger foundation for the "discussion between the confessions."[77] This is the way to overcome the "Alienation," insisted Michel; members of both sides, especially the laity, must integrate their lives ever more completely with their religious principles; then a proportionately intensive and fruitful exchange will grow, such as has been the experience of the youth movements and circles of leading Protestants and Catholics.[78] However, much sooner than either Fechter or Michel anticipated, inter-confessional organizations developed on a religious basis.

Another development of the 1930's favoring the rise of the Una Sancta Movement was the appearance of the two *Konfessionskunde*, or *Dictionaries of the Christian Faiths,* both highly praised by Protestants and Catholics alike; these studies attempted "to give a picture of the inner life,

[76]"Evangelischer Bund," *Evangelisches Kirchenlexikon,* 1956.
[77]Michel, "Was kann man?" 46-47.
[78]*Ibid.,* 44.

the history, organization and piety of all Christian Churches and sects."[79] Although the two books cover almost the same material, they were written independently of each other, one by a Protestant, Hermann Mulert, and the other by a Catholic, Konrad Algermissen. These *Konfessionskunde* were important because they attempted to present the positions of the various Christian Churches as objectively as possible. Max Pribilla, S.J., a sympathetic but sharp critic of ecumenical matters, commented, "Great gaps of the past are here filled in and mountains of prejudices which an unfortunate and loveless polemic has built up over the centuries, are torn down in patient and painstaking work."[80]

TWO CATHOLIC ECUMENISTS

"On the Catholic side of the inter-confessional discussions there is one man, Arnold Rademacher, who has put forth an unusual effort to meet the Protestants on their own ground"; such was the judgment of the Protestant church historian, Heinrich Hermelink.[81] Rademacher, one of the authors publishing in the *Religiöse Besinnung*, was professor of Catholic theology at the University of Bonn in the 1930's until his death in 1939.[82] In addition to his various articles[83] and lectures,[84] Rademacher spread his ecumenical ideas through four books published a short time before his death.

79Max Pribilla, "Konfessionskunde und konfessionelle Verständigung," *Zeit im Querschnitt*, (March 1, 1940), 74.

80*Ibid.*

81Heinrich Hermelink, *Katholizismus und Protestantismus* (Stuttgart, 1943), 24. Cf. also the similar appraisal by the Protestants J. Lortzing, "Professor Rademachers 'Schwanengesang,'" *Schönere Zukunft*, XIV (1939), 1062-1063, and Otto Urbach, "Zum Gespräch zwischen den Konfessionen," *Hochland*, XXXVI (1939), 354-367.

82Buchberger, *Aufbruch zur Einheit*, 19.

83Cf. "Beobachtung und Bemerkungen," *Schönere Zukunft*, XIV (1939), 182-183.

84Cf. some of Rademacher's published lectures, *Der religiöse Sinn unserer Zeit und der ökumenische Gedanke* (Bonn, 1939).

The first of the four works, *Die Wiedervereinigung der christliche Kirchen* (The Reunion of the Christian Churches), was intended "to help to awaken the concern for the reunion of the Christian Churches where it still slumbers and to strengthen it where it is already awake."[85] First Rademacher discussed the oneness of the Church as a prerequisite for reunion in faith; then he outlined the various hindrances to a reunion of the Christian Churches: religious indifference, mutual prejudices, chauvinistic overemphasis of national consciousness, the stressing of form in the Roman Church, the defensive attitude toward other-believing Christians, and a lack of personal responsibility. The several possible approaches to reunion such as state interference, negotiations among the denominations. or theological conferences were all set aside as either unacceptable or insufficient; the only really possible way to union is God's grace. "It will be a miracle of grace and to some extent a repetition of the Pentecostal miracle."[86] Nevertheless, Rademacher saw hopeful signs in the rise of the ecumenical movement and the various movements within the Churches such as the Catholic liturgical movement, the biblical movement, the Lay Apostolate movement and the Protestant High Church movement and *Berneuchner Kreis*.[87] His final chapter concerned the Catholic task in preparing for reunion: he prescribed an openness of mind and heart toward the question of union, an irenic disposition, and a conscious fostering of an ecumenical perspective.

In the next two books,[88] intended as sequels to the first, Rademacher tried to develop "a concept of faith which does not depend on scientific thought or philosophical, theological knowledge, but rather is an approach to the Reformation

---

[85]Rademacher, *Die Wiedervereiningung*, lv.
[86]*Ibid.*, 85.
[87]*Ibid.*, 115-117.
[88]Arnold Rademacher, *Die Innere Einheit des Glaubens* (Bonn, 1937), and *Der Glaube als einheitliche Lebensform* (Bonn, 1937).

notion of *Sola Fides Salvificans*. This faith is thought of as a kind of wager in which the total giving over to God must constantly be conquered or won by the continual grace of God and one's obedience to it."[89] His last book *Der religiöse Sinn unserer Zeit und der ökumenische Gedanke* (The Religious Meaning of our Time and the Ecumenical Idea), was, as the title itself suggests, pointed toward the phenomenal rise of the ecumenical movement with its profound significance for all religious men of this age.

A circle of followers who grew up around Rademacher continued to work together even after his death. Matthias Laros, later the Catholic leader of the Una Sancta Movement, was also a student of Rademacher and a member of the so-called "Rhine-circle" gathered around him.[90]

One other Catholic theologian did a great deal during the years between the wars to foster the ecumenism; Max Pribilla, S.J., published an almost constant stream of articles and books on ecumenical matters. In 1926 Pribilla wrote a small book favorably commenting on the Ecumenical Council for Life and Work at Stockholm in 1925.[91] After the Ecumenical Council for Faith and Order at Lausanne in 1927 Pribilla published a much larger book about the whole ecumenical movement and Rome's relation to it;[92] this book soon attained the reputation of being the best thing written on the movement.[93] A Protestant theologian commented, "It is written not only with an unusual knowledge of the subject but also with a great sensitivity and reveals an ecumenical tact from which we also can learn a great deal."[94] One result of the book was the growth of a close friendship between Archbishop Soederblom and Father Pribilla; the

---

[89]Hermelink, *Katholizismus und Protestantismus*, 24.

[90]Rademacher, *Der religiöse Sinn*, 25.

[91]Max Pribilla, *Um die Wiedervereinigung Im Glauben* (Freiburg, 1926).

[92]Max Pribilla, *Um kirchliche Einheit*, (Freiburg, 1929).

[93]Adolf Deissman, *Una Sancta* (Gütersloh, 1936), 55.

[94]*Ibid.*

two men exchanged letters[95] and Father Pribilla was even invited to make a lecture tour through Lutheran Sweden.[96] This friendship also doubtless played a part in a meeting of Protestant and Catholic theologians at Berlin in 1934.

HITLER AND THE CHURCHES

1933, the year of the rise of Hitler, was a momentous year for Germany. Although the *Reichskonkordat* which Rome obtained from Hitler seemed to augur a favorable future, in view of the plight of the Protestant Church, many Catholics felt they were merely in a calm before the storm: this was true.[97]

Of the two Churches the Catholic Church was in a better position to meet the attacks of the Nazi government, not only because it had a more unified organization than the Protestant Church, but also because it could depend on a more solidly organized support outside of Germany, support that was led by Pope Pius XI and his encyclical aimed at National Socialism, *Mit brennender Sorge,* (1937). But the Catholic Church also felt the ever-increasing pressure from the government. Many Catholics, priests and laymen, went to prison, concentration camps and even death for standing by Christian principles, and beside them were many Protestants suffering for similar principles.[98] These common experiences forged bonds of personal friendships between

---

[95]Pribilla, "Nach vierhundert Jahren," 168.

[96]Deissmann, *Una Sancta,* 56.

[97]Franz Ranft, *Zur Begegnung von Katholiken und Protestanten* (Fulda, 1947), 4-5.

[98]Most recently there has been a series of articles, plays and books which have indicated that the Catholic Church's resistance to Nazism was somewhat less glorious than the picture previously painted had it. For example: Ernst-Wolfgang Böckenförde, "German Catholicism in 1933," *Cross Currents,* XI (1961); Gordon Zahn, *German Catholics and Hitler's Wars* (New York: Sheed and Ward, 1962); Carl Amery, *Die Kapitulation* (Reinbek bei Hamburg: Rowohlt, 1963); the play *Der Stellvertreter* by Rolf Hochhuth; Guenther Lewy, *The Catholic Church and Nazi Germany* (New York: McGraw Hill, 1964).

Catholics and Protestants which since have done a great deal to further the work of the Una Sancta Movement. In general it can be said that the cooperation of the two Churches in the face of the common enemy was never so close.[99]

Another result of the Nazi government's attacks on religion was a powerful push within the Protestant Church toward a greater inner unity and the placing of a stronger stress on the "Church." Since the seventeenth century efforts had been made to bring all Protestant Christians in the Germanies into one Church. A specific plan was initiated at the *Wittenberger Kirchentag* of 1848 but was soon defeated by political reaction. A German Evangelical Churches Committee was formed in 1903; but it was only after the collapse of the individual established state churches in 1918 that an *Evangelischer Kirchenbund* came into existence in 1922. A national church was finally formed in 1933 when the *Deutsche Evangelische Kirche* was founded with a constitution given it by Adolf Hitler. But the price was high: it meant accepting the Nazi *Weltanschauung* advocated by the so-called "*Deutsche Christen*" with their anti-Semitism, state supremacy and "*Führerprinzip*." This last involved acknowledging as their lawful leader a "*Reichsbischof*" who was a member of the Nazi government.[100] The Protestant Church was even more absorbed into the state when in 1935 a Reich's Ministry for Church Matters was formed.[101]

To the everlasting credit of the Protestant Church in Germany, hundreds of the Protestant pastors and parishes from all three main branches of German Protestantism, the Lutheran Churches, the Reformed Churches and the United Churches, joined the so-called *Bekennende Kirche* under the leadership of Karl Barth, Hans Asmussen, Martin Neimöller

---

[99]Walther Hofer (ed.), *Der National sozialismus Dokumente 1933-1945* (Frankfurt, 1960), 119-166.

[100]"Kirche," in *Christliche Religion*, ed. by Oskar Simmel and Rudolf Stählin (Frankfurt, 1957), 162-163.

[101]Hofer, *Nationalsozialismus*, 123.

and others.[102] A meeting was held at Barmen in 1934 where the rising consciousness of church was given expression in the *Barmer theologische Erklärung*,[103] a direct rebuttal of several of the tenets of the Nazi supported *"Deutsche Christen."*[104] The stress on the notion of the Church already growing through the liturgical movement, the ecumenical movement, and dialectical theology was given a dramatic emphasis at Barmen. "The '*Bekennende Kirche*' thought... in a real sense to set up a Church. It wished to attack the evil at the root; the separation of faith and the order of the Church should be rejected as a four-hundred-year error, not that one wishes after observing the Catholic Church to eliminate the here [Protestant Church] dominating heresy, but rather because the Church should stand up to the state."[105]

Although it was under this anti-Christian pressure of the Nazis that what came to be called Una Sancta Circles were first formed, the Nazi oppression served only as a catalytic agent speeding up and expanding a reaction that would have taken place in any case because of the cumulative effect of the liturgical, biblical, ecumenical and other movements.

A KEY CONFERENCE IN BERLIN

The key meeting took place Pentecost week 1934 at the seminary of Hermsdorf near Berlin, the result of the late Archbishop Soederblom's wish.[106] The meeting was held under the patronage of Berlin's Catholic bishop Nicolaus

[102]Ernst Zeeden, "Ueber die innere Entwicklungsgeschichte des Protestantismus seit der Reformation," *Theologie und Glaube,* XLI (1951), 218-242.

[103]J.P. Michael, *Christen suchen eine Kirche* (Freiburg, 1958), 161.

[104]"Kirche," in *Christliche Religion,* 163.

[105]Michael, *Christen suchen,* 36.

[106]August Rehbach, "Brückenschlag zwischen den Konfessionen," *Bayerische Rundschau,* III (1948), 154; Friedrich Heiler, "Utopie oder Wirklichkeit der Una-Sancta-Arbeit?" *Oekumenische Einheit,* I (1948), 10; Hermelink, *Katholizismus und Protestantismus,* 27.

Bares; the cathedral dean Paul Simon presided.[107] It was the same Bishop Bares, who died a short while after the 1934 meeting, that had earlier sent an outstanding young theologian to take an active part in and give literary assistance to the preparatory discussions before the second Lausanne ecumenical conference.[108] The Protestant participants in the Berlin meeting were members of the *Hochkirchliche Vereinigung* or like-minded theologians; they included Stählin, Ritter, Heiler and the Swedish Lutheran Nygren;[109] even Anglicans took part. The men from the Catholic side, theologians of equal note, included Pietryga, Pribilla and Guardini.[110]

The themes of the conference were grace and justification, grace and Church, grace and sacraments.[111] One participant reported that the conference "clearly showed that there existed between the representatives of the *Hochkirchliche Vereinigung* and the Catholic theologians no points of dispute, and that there was a surprisingly far-reaching agreement even between the representatives of other Protestant schools of theology and the Catholic theologians; therefore a continuation of this discussion should take place in smaller circles so as gradually to attain complete agreement with Catholic dogma."[112] The unidentified reporter went on to say that for those Protestants close to the Catholic Church the obstacles to reunion were not so much matters of dogma as of disci-

---

[107]Cf. Paul Simon, Karl Meissinger and Otto Urbach, *Zum Gespräch zwischen den Konfessionen* (Munich, 1939).

[108]Deissman, *Una Sancta*, 56.

[109]Heiler, "Utopie oder Wirklichkeit," 10.

[110]Hermelink, *Katholizismus und Protestantismus*, 27.

[111]Heiler, "Utopie oder Wirklichkeit," 10.

[112]Typewritten anonymous document with the title, "Denkschrift betreffend die Wiedervereinigung deutscher Evangelischer mit der römisch-katholischen Kirche." It must have been written in 1934, for it refers to the Berlin meeting as having taken place "this year." The author was obviously a member of the *Hochkirchliche Vereinigung*, possibly Friedrich Heiler.

pline and liturgy. He asked whether the Holy See could not grant the *Hochkirchliche Vereinigung* the following five requests: 1. The use of the mother tongue in the celebration of Mass; 2. the basic retention of the centuries-old Lutheran form of the liturgy with adjustments and enlargements being made to correspond to dogma; 3. the use of a simplified ceremonial for at least a transitional period; 4. the reception of Communion under both forms; 5. the retention of a married clergy at least for converted Protestant clergy. The author felt that if these simple requests were granted it would give a concrete example to other Protestants that joining the Catholic Church would not entail the giving up of all their worthwhile traditions and customs, but rather their preservation and completion. The writer even gave detailed suggestions as to how this might actually be accomplished and believed that the reception of such groups and congregations of Protestants into the Catholic Church would prepare the way for the complete reunion of the Protestant and Catholic Churches.[113] This appeal actually sounds quite similar to the ones made by Karl Thieme and J. Lortzing in 1933; later, in 1947, the Catholic theologian Karl Adam strongly suggested that most of these concessions could and should be made,[114] and in 1960 an Evangelical-Catholic League was founded by the Lutheran Max Lackmann to carry the plan out.

UNA SANCTA CIRCLES SPREAD

It appears that this Berlin meeting was the spark that started the flame throughout the rest of a very inflammable Germany. Heiler, who was at the meeting, said that the discussion was continued in circles in individual cities, particularly Berlin, Paderborn, Kassel and Munich;[115] there

[113]*Ibid.*
[114]Karl Adam, *One and Holy* (New York, 1951), 120-125.
[115]Heiler, "Utopie oder Wirklichkeit," 10.

were reports of monthly meetings between Catholic and Protestant pastors in central Germany in Bornstadt, Sangershausen, Eisleben, Nordhausen and Erfurt.[116] Apparently the circle at Kassel quickly took a leading position, attaining a membership of two to three hundred in a short time, and it in turn gave impetus to the founding of more circles in other cities; still other circles arose independently.[117] Even a partial list of the cities and towns in which there existed such circles of Protestant and Catholic laity and clergy is impressively long.[118]

An interesting description of one Una Sancta circle which flourished in Berlin for several years during the war was related by the writer and lecturer August Winnig. Shortly after the beginning of the war he met a Jesuit, Pater Georg, "the oldest son of the last king of Saxony," who introduced him, a Lutheran, to a circle of about thirty Catholic and Protestant laymen and clerics which met monthly in the home of Frau Kracker von Schwarzenfels. The group included Hans Lilje, later Lutheran bishop of Hanover and an outstanding figure in the ecumenical movement, and Hans Asmussen, a leader of the *Bekennende Kirche* and after the war a pioneer in public theological discussion within the Una Sancta Movement. This group broke up when in 1943 Pater Georg died accidently and shortly afterwards Frau

---

[116]Edgar Grüber, "Im Zeichen des 'Schöpferischen Friedens,'" *Zeitwende,* XXI (1949), 295; Kurt Hutten, "Das Gespräch zwischen den Konfessionen," *Für Arbeit und Besinnung,* I (1947), 205.

[117]Franz Ranft, "Katholiken und Protestanten sprechen sich aus," *Schönere Zukunft,* XIII (1938), 998-1000; Franz Ranft, "Die ökumenische Aufgabe und der Laie," *Schönere Zukunft,* XV (1940), 174-175; Ranft, *Zur Begegnung,* 4-5.

[118]Some cities having Protestant-Catholic circles were: Bielefeld, Berlin, Mainz, Frankfurt, Kassel, Hannover, Hamm, Leipzig, Hamburg, Munich, Stuttgart, Jena, Krefeld, Naumburg, Erfurt, Bornstedt, Sangershausen, Eisleben, Paderborn, Passau, Bamberg, Alpirsbach, Niederalteich, Metten, Beuron, and Weingarten. Buchberger, *Aufbruch zur Einheit,* 18-19; Hutten, "Das Gespräch," 205; Heiler, "Utopie oder Wirklichkeit," 10.

von Schwarzenfels' house was destroyed in an air raid.[119] Father Max Metzger, who founded the Una Sancta Brotherhood in 1938, was also a close friend of Pater Georg and doubtless visited this particular Una Sancta circle since he made Berlin his headquarters in the 1940's. It was Metzger who delivered the eulogy for Pater Georg: "He would have offered his life for his Catholic faith which he carried deep in his heart . . . How he suffered over the tragic division in the Church of Jesus Christ which he so wished to see united, as a living testimony of the unifying Holy Ghost." This sermon was delivered June 18, 1943, just a few days before Metzger was arrested for the last time and executed by the Gestapo.[120]

Special ecumenical celebrations were also often held, such as one on May 8, 1940, in the Dominican church of St. Paul in Berlin, where prayers were said and hymns were sung in common, and representatives of both faiths spoke.[121] Often the meetings themselves were held in Catholic and Protestant churches and were disguised as liturgical ceremonies to avoid the police decree against public gatherings.[122]

Just exactly what role Dr. Max Metzger played in the growth of these different circles is difficult to determine. Hermelink, immediately after speaking of the 1934 discussions, wrote "There were, however, many other smaller discussions inspired by the work of Dr. Metzger. These took place in such towns and cities as Kassel, Cologne. Berlin, Dresden, Leipzig, Erfurt, Chemnitz, Augsburg, Munich and Stuttgart.[123]

---

[123]Hermelink, *Katholizismus und Protestantismus,* 27.

[119]August Winnig, *Aus Zwanzig Jahren* (Hamburg, 1951), 216-220.

[120]Max Josef Metzger, *Gefangenschaftsbriefe,* ed. by Hannes Bäcker (Meitingen, 1948), 120.

[121]Buchberger, *Aufbruch zur Einheit,* 18-19.

[122]Interview with Pastor August Rehbach (Prot.), one of the early leaders of the Una Sancta circle in Munich, on September 29, 1959.

This obviously was not an exhaustive list but a geographic sampling. Heiler, just after mentioning the 1934 Berlin meeting and the four cities in which that discussion was continued, stated, "Thanks to the zealous recruiting of the priest, Dr. Maximilian Metzger . . . more and more circles were caught up with the concern for the reunion of the Churches – above all among the laity."[124] It is certain that some groups arose without the influence of Metzger. In Munich, for instance, a group started in 1938 completely independently of Metzger;[125] the Wuppertal circle was founded by Rademacher, also in 1938.[126] Some like Stuttgart were originally started by Metzger[127] and others like Bornstedt were encouraged and influenced by him.[128] Eventually when he had contact with most of them, he formed the Una Sancta Brotherhood and began to draw the movement together. This was Metzger's great service to Una Sancta work: out of scattered individual efforts he made a unified movement which still maintained a high degree of spontaneity and individual independence.

[124]Heiler, "Utopie oder Wirklichkeit," 10.

[125]Interview with Abbot Hugo Lang of Munich, one of the initial members, on October 13, 1959.

[126]Arnold Schulte, "Wuppertal," *Una Sancta,* XII (1957), 58.

[127]"Stuttgart," *Una Sancta,* VII (1952), 7. Cf. Matthias Laros, "Una Sancta-Einigung," *Una Sancta Rundbrief,* No. 6 (1947), 8.

[128]"Aus Bornstedt bei Eisleben," *Una Sancta.* VII (Pfingsten, 1952), 12.

Chapter Eight

Max Metzger: Una Sancta Founder and Martyr

Early Life

The founder of the Una Sancta Brotherhood, Max Josef Metzger, was born of Catholic parents on the third of February, 1887, in Schopfheim in the Black Forest. After attending the Konstanzer Gymnasium on Lake Constance until 1905, Metzger began his theological studies at the University of Fribourg, Switzerland, later returning to the Black Forest to complete his studies in Freiburg im Breisgau. He was ordained there in 1911. While at the University of Freiburg in Breisgau Metzger devoted most of his time to church history studies under the direction of Professor Georg Pfeilschifter, who himself was interested in ecumenical affairs and in 1923 published a small book entitled *Die kirchlichen Wiedervereinigungsbestrebungen der Nachkriegszeit* (The Ecclesiastical Reunion Efforts of the Post-War Period). It was under this same professor that Metzger finished his work for a doctorate in theology; for his thesis he edited and compared the theological contents of two medieval *pontificales*.[1]

Metzger's later work in the Una Sancta Movement was only one of a number of crusades and reforms he actively supported throughout his life. Most of these interests can be traced to experiences in his early years as a student and young priest.

---

[1]Cf. Lilian Stevenson, *Max Joseph Metzger, Priest and Martyr, 1887-1944* (London, 1952), 3-4; and Walter Wilhelm Baumeister, *Max Josef Metzger, Ein Herold Christi des Königs* (Meitingen, 1951), 29-30.

In 1915 Metzger moved to Graz, Austria, to take up his work of combating alcoholism. In his student days at Fribourg he, with other members of the student St. Vincent de Paul Society, had tried to fight the effects of alcoholism by working with the children of the slum areas. He was so impressed with the futility of his work that he pledged himself to total abstinence and already before his move to Graz had published several articles and brochures on alcoholism. As general secretary of the *Katholische Kreuzbündnis gegen Alkoholismus für Oesterreich* (Catholic Crusade in Austria Against Alcoholism), Metzger's duties included both writing and editorial and supervisory work for two magazines, and lecturing even as far away as Freiburg and Berlin.[2] Although the audiences before which Dr. Metzger spoke were of a varied sort, he had a particularly close and personal relationship with the German *Kreuzbündnis* and the German *Quickborn,* the youth organization strongly influenced and led by Romano Guardini.[3] So great was Metzger's enthusiasm for the *Quickborn* movement with its strong liturgical stress that he gave lectures in Vienna, St. Poelten, Linz, Salzburg and Innsbruck to promote the movement in Austria.[4]

WORK FOR PEACE

Experience as an army chaplain with front line troops in the fall and winter of 1914-15 led Metzger to write an essay denouncing war, *Friedensruf an die Völker* (A Call to the Nations for Peace). Although the work was forbidden by the military censor, Metzger was able to publish it

---

[2]Max Josef Metzger, *Vaterländische Friedensarbeit* (Graz, 1916), 20-26; *Der Völkerbund und die katholische Internationale* (Bochum, 1920), 48; and cf. Max Metzger, *Der Kampf um die Nüchternheit in 19. und 20. Jahrhundert* (Heidhausen-Ruhr, n.d.), 25.

[3]Metzger, *Vaterländische Friedensarbeit,* 41-45.

[4]*Ibid.,* 20.

in Graz, upon his move there in 1915, under the title of *Rassenhass oder Völkerfriede* (Race Hatred or Peace of Nations). From that time until the rise of the Nazis, Metzger was deeply involved in several world peace organizations. He was himself a founder, along with Pater Wilhelm Impekovin, of the *Weltfriedensbund vom Weissen Kreuz* (World Peace League of the White Cross)—the name comes from the cross stamped on the altar breads used at Mass.[5] In this cause he published pamphlets, remembrance cards, and leaflets in "numberless" quantities; he gave lectures and led discussions promoting world peace;[6] he edited the periodical *Friedensherold;*[7] he worked with Esperanto.[8]

Already during this period Metzger began to cooperate with non-Catholic Christians, particularly in his peace work. He was especially active in the International Fellowship of Reconciliation (IFOR), "a movement uniting Christians, both Catholic and Protestant, in work for peace." In 1920 he attended one of the early council meetings, "a young Roman Catholic priest who had heard of this movement and felt it to be something after his own heart . . . . For some eight or ten years we had the benefit of close contact with him on our Council."[9] Father Metzger even invited the IFOR to send a delegate to a conference of his at Constance in 1923. This representative, Lilian Stevenson, the only non-Catholic present, referred to her experience as a "memorable week." Metzger remained active in the Fellowship at least until 1927 when he took part in a Fellowship-sponsored youth conference at Vaumarcus, Switzerland, centering

---

[5]Max Metzger, Prof. Arendsen, W. Baumeister, *Seelsorgshilfe durch Laiendiakonat* (Graz, 1922), 16.

[6]Metzger, *Der Völkerbund,* 30; and Max Josef Metzger, *Gefangenschaftsbriefe,* ed. by Hannes Bäcker (Meitingen, 1948), 24.

[7]Metzger, *Gefangenschaftsbriefe,* 24.

[8]Metzger, *Der Völkerbund,* 39.

[9]Stevenson, *Max Joseph Metzger,* 8.

around the 700th anniversary of St. Francis of Assisi. The Fellowship's songbook, *Eirene,* even contains a peace song written and set to music by Father Metzger during this period.[10]

Dr. Metzger was never a person who could be satisfied with operating on a limited scale; he always attempted to draw ultimate conclusions and organize things on a world-wide basis. Already in 1917 he represented the *Weltfriedensbund vom weissen Kreuz* at an international peace conference in Bern, and two years later he was again in Switzerland representing the *Bund* at the opening meeting of the League of Nations.[11] He also participated in similar international peace gatherings at the Hague in 1920 and at Graz in 1921; the same year he spoke at a large gathering in Paris —"He was the first German to speak there after the war."[12] The year 1922 found Metzger in Luxemburg, and in 1923 he was at Constance for the first conference of the *Friedensbund deutscher Katholiken,* which he helped to found;[13] in 1928 and 1929 he participated in congresses in the Hague.[14]

FOUNDER OF A RELIGIOUS SOCIETY

Spurred on by these and other interests, Father Metzger joined with Pater Wilhelm Impekovin on June 27, 1919, to form the *Missionsgesellschaft vom weissen Kreuz* (Mission Society of the White Cross) which was later to assume great importance in Una Sancta work; it was to be a "whole order with the openness and mobility of laymen," consisting of men and women, married and single, lay and clerical.[15]

---

[10]*Ibid.,* 8-9.
[11]Metzger, *Der Völkerbund,* 30.
[12]Stevenson, *Max Joseph Metzger,* 7-8.
[13]Interview with Sister Gertrudis, November 2, 1959.
[14]Metzger, *Gefangenschaftsbriefe,* 33-34.
[15]Baumeister, *Max Joseph Metzger,* 36.

The *Missionsgesellschaft vom weissen Kreuz,* whose name was changed in 1925 to *Gesellschaft Christi des Königs* (Society of Christ the King), had no specific field of work, but rather provided a common spirit and rule to be lived by; the work would be decided upon as the need arose. Rather than do work already handled by other orders, the Society wanted to fill the gaps caused by the rapidly changing social environment, pastoral work, spiritual work, works of mercy, the winning of lay apostles, work for peace and for the unity of the Church, efforts to promote wholesome and simple living and to provide help for those suffering under the un-Christian economic order of the day.[16]

In 1927 Father Metzger left Graz to look for a more benign clerical climate for his work. In 1938 the Caritas Society of Augsburg offered him some small housing facilities and the responsibility of conducting an inebriates' home in the little village of Meitingen, a dozen miles from Augsburg. The offer was accepted and proved to be a turning point in the growth of the Society of Christ the King.[17] The quantity and variety of projects the Society performed by the time of the death of the founder in 1944 was extraordinary: it included running alcohol-free restaurants, doing assistant pastoral work, and operating homes for the aged, epileptics, convalescents, young girls, and working girls.[18]

At the headquarters in Meitingen Father Metzger started a publishing and printing company, the *Christkönig-Verlag,* later renamed *Kyrios-Verlag* to circumvent the Nazi rule against using "King" in titles of organizations—the substitution of the Geek *Kyrios* for the German *König* went unnoticed by the Nazis. Through this publishing house he

---

[16]Stevenson, *Max Joseph Metzger,* 5.

[17]*Ibid.,* 7.

[18]Baumeister, *Max Joseph Metzger,* 42-43; and interview with Sister Gertrudis, November 2, 1959.

edited a successor to his earlier *Katholischer Missionsruf* which he had begun in 1918 and *Ruf zur Wahrheit, Gerechtigheit und Liebe* begun in 1920; this new periodical, *Christkönigsbote,* continued till its suppression by the Nazis in 1935. Besides these periodicals the *Kyrios-Verlag* turned out a stream of books, booklets, pamphlets, and cards; Metzger himself wrote many of them.[19]

METZGER AND THE LITURGICAL AND BIBLICAL MOVEMENTS

Both the liturgical and biblical movements did much to prepare the environment in which Metzger later founded the Una Sancta Movement. Metzger himself, and through him his Society of Christ the King, was deeply influenced by these movements. Already in the organization of the *Missionsgesellschaft vom weissen Kreuz* special groups were set up to work on things liturgical and biblical; the *Benediktus-Diakonat* devoted its efforts toward the fostering of the liturgical movement, and the *Hieronymus-Diakonat* contributed to the bible movement.[20] Writing from his prison cell in 1943, Mezger questioned himself about the Society. "Was it capable of becoming a movement, both biblical and liturgical . . . and finally, through it all, the realizaion of an 'Una Sancta' as the Lord would have it and as the world needs it?"[21] A visit to Meitingen today would no doubt produce an affirmative answer to the first part of the question, just as Metzger thought it would in the 1930's and 1940's. In a small pamphlet he invited Protestant ministers to visit Meitingen and take part in the daily liturgical celebrations, feeling confident that they, like many other Protestant ministers before them, would lose many of their preju-

[19]Friedrich Siegmund-Schultze, "Max Joseph Metzger," in *Oekumenische Profile* (Berlin-Hermsdorf, n.d.), 13.
[20]Bruder Paulus, *Das weisse Kreuz* (Graz, n.d.), 18-23.
[21]Metzger, *Gefangenschaftsbriefe,* 259-260.

dices. He described the manner of celebration of the Mass: a lector reads the instructional parts of the Mass aloud in German and the whole congregation answers the prayers and either recites or sings the *Gloria, Credo* and other prayers, one day in German and another day in Latin; at the offertory time the people bring in procession the hosts which the priest later consecrates and distributes. "Nothing here is 'unearnest' or pure 'ceremony': the whole community celebration breathes the spirit of the 'primitive Church.'"[22] All of this obviously was strongly in the spirit and letter of the liturgical movement.

Sister Gertrudis Reimann, Metzger's long-time co-worker, reported that the New Testament was a "rule of life" for him and that he was a "herald and prime-mover of the liturgical and biblical movements."[22] On December 1, 1939, Metzger, having been placed under arrest for suspicion of complicity in political activities, wrote to the police listing his publications of the previous months in order to show that his interests were not political. Of the four articles apppearing in periodicals, three were published in *Bibel und Liturgie.* While in prison he wrote to one of the Sisters asking for books, requesting specifically a Bible concordance, Greek New Testament and dictionary, and his Luther Bible.[24] Nor did this pattern change: during his final imprisonment Father Metzger was transferred from one prison to another and deprived temporarily of his few belongings. He wrote, "What a joy it was to get back my books today: my Breviary in Latin and German and my New Testament in Greek and German. So at once I took up my reading where I had had to leave off three weeks ago."[25]

---

[22]Max Metzger, *Was trennt uns Christen?* (Meitingen, n.d.), 3-4.
[23]Gertrudis Reimann, "In Memoriam Dr. M. J. Metzger," *Una Sancta,* IX (1954), 2.
[24]Metzger, *Gefangenschaftsbriefe,* 151.
[25]*Ibid.,* 234.

Fitting in well with his interest in practical liturgical matters was Father Metzger's musical ability. He apparently had a very pleasant voice and enjoyed composing the texts and medolies for hymns of all sorts. In the *Alleluia-Liederschatz* which was published while the Society was still centered in Graz, forty-one out of the ninety-one songs were written by Metzger. In the introductory section he wrote, "I fear somewhat the music critics who perhaps will look here for 'art.' But I don't know very much about that. Perhaps several charitable persons will nevertheless be pleased with the 'craftsmanship.' But that also means nothing to me; however, it is important to me when simple people sing with me because their heart is as full and as happy as mine is."[26] This pleasure in singing continued throughout his whole life.

Even after his sentence to death he wrote that he felt "a great desire to sing as a relief to my feelings, but of course this has to be carried out with due restraint."[27] Some two weeks later he complained of not having been able to say Mass for over six months, not even at Christmas, "but I joined in a Protestant Christmas service behind the door of my cell, and sang heartily with them. 'Una Sancta!' "[28] This was while his hands and feet were bound by chains. In this lull between the fall of the gavel and the fall of the executioner's axe Dr. Metzger occupied himself partly with writing music—sometimes on the flypages and margins of his Bible or Breviary.[29] "In spite of the loneliness, I am not bored. I study, read, and write: I compose music and write poems, even if the music can't all be put down on

---

[26]Bruder Paulus, *Alleluja Liederschatz des weissen Kreuzes* (Graz, n.d.), 1.
[27]Metzger, *Gefangenschaftsbriefe,* 249.
[28]*Ibid.,* 269.
[29]Stevenson, *Max Joseph Metzger,* 28.

paper . . . . I have written three People's Masses in German, one of which I have already sent you."[30]

THE ECUMENICAL MOVEMENT

Along with his interest in working for peace and unity among nations, Dr. Metzger took an active interest in the movement which worked for peace and unity among Churches, the ecumenical movement. Having received permission from Bishop Besson of Geneva along with sixteen other Catholic priests, Metzger attended the World Conference for Faith and Order in Lausanne in 1927 as an "observer." At the end of the conference he and another German priest, Hermann Hoffmann, approached the German Protestant theologian Friedrich Siegmund-Schultze, who was very active in the ecumenical movement, in order to obtain the permission of the conference leaders for the two priests to make a report to the Holy Father on the Conference. They were introduced to the Episcopal Bishop Brent of Chicago who gladly encouraged them; however, after their arrival in Rome the Vatican did not permit the delivery of their report.[31]

At the same conference Father Metzger composed a new melody for the so-called "Stockholm Song," "*O Saliga Dag*" by Nataneal Beskow, which had been sung a great deal at the World Conference for Life and Work at Stockholm in 1925. He showed the composition to Siegmund-Schultze who immediately took him to Archbishop Soederblom who graciously accepted the gift and immediately hummed through the notes. He then commented, "It would be very nice if we would be able to use this composition from a Catholic brother in our song book. However, first of all it wouldn't fit the character of the poet or the song to have this hope for the unity and peace of the Church in a minor key. And

---

[30]Metzger, *Gefangenschaftsbriefe,* 273-274.
[31]Siegmund-Schultze, *Max Josef Metzger,* 16-17.

secondly—he added smilingly—the melody we are now using comes from my predecessor in Uppsala, whose work I could not eliminate from our songbook."[32]

The Una Sancta Brotherhood

With the rise of the Nazi party Father Metzger's work in ecumenical circles was limited almost exclusively to Germany, as was that of other German churchmen. His peace work was also strongly curtailed. Doubtless these circumstances helped to concentrate Father Metzger's efforts on the betterment of Catholic-Protestant relations in Germany; to this end he founded in 1938 an "Una Sancta Brotherhood."[33] There had been, of course, various and increasingly friendly contacts between members of the two Churches, but Metzger's Una Sancta Brotherhood seems to have been the catalytic ascent to start the whole process moving rapidly and in the more organized manner which still continues today. Metzger travelled throughout Germany, making use of his wide circle of acquaintances among Protestants and Catholics to contact or start inter-confessional groups in dozens of the cities of Germany from Berlin through Marburg, Frankfurt, Heidelberg, Stuttgart, Munich and Nuremburg to Leipzig.[34]

The purpose of the "Ecumenical Meeting-Circle," or "Una Sancta Circles," as they were soon called, was to serve the *rapprochment* and mutual understanding between believing Christians of different confessions in view of "the last wish of the common Lord, '. . . that all may be one!' "[35] In a mimeographed circular Metzger suggested three different forms of such inter-confessional meetings. The first was

---

[32]*Ibid.*
[33]Metzger, *Gefangenschaftsbriefe,* 187.
[34]Stevenson, *Max Joseph Metzger,* 40-41.
[35]Max Metzger, "Oekumenische Begegnungskreise," leaflet hectographed at Meitingen, n.d., p. I.

merely a mutual exchange of visits on a friendship basis with discussions on themes of common religious interest: a situation where two clergymen of different confessions lived near each other would be considered particularly apt for this type of Una Sancta contact. The second form was a public lecture series. These he thought, would be best held in neutral locations, but alternating between halls belonging to the different confessions might also be successful. The series ought to consist of talks by members of both churches on the same questions and should take place regularly about every month. Material on a suggested series of themes covering the entire Christian doctrine systematically, or material just on controversial questions was available through the Una Sancta Brotherhood center at Meitingen. Metzger admonished those interested in this form of ecumenical work that they should not open the lectures to an unlimited audience since it was all too easy for argumentative persons to slip in and ruin everything being worked for; the same was even more true in the case of the lecturers, "who should be, as far as is possible, men who both know their subject well and are irenically inclined, who combine an earnest seeking of truth and a preparedness for understanding."[36]

The third form of Una Sancta circles was what Metzger considered possibly the most effective of the three types. This should be a discussion group of carefully chosen mature people of different confessions; the number should not exceed thirty so as not to destroy the intimacy of the discussion. He insisted that the choice of the location of the discussions was important, that it should be psychologically conducive to a friendly exchange of opinion; parliamentary forms were ruled out. He thought there should be two short simple talks by persons of different churches of twenty to forty minutes

---

[36] *Ibid.*, 2.

in toto on the theme to be discussed at some length afterwards by everyone. He highly recommended that the meetings be opened and closed with a common prayer or reading from Scripture; prayers such as the Apostles Creed and the Our Father were obvious choices; "Catholics ought not shy away from praying the ancient ecclesiastical doxology at the end"[37] of the Lord's Prayer.

In addition, meeting through common prayer was urged, especially during the Church Unity Octave from January 18 to 25 and the time between the Ascension and Pentecost; members should carry over their ecumenical work into their correspondence and to ecumenical-minded publications and cooperation in social work projects. Finally he advised that organizational character be kept down to a minimum, partly to keep a free spirit in the group and to avoid police observation as much as possible. Everything about Una Sancta work should be absolutely free from everything that smacks of convert making.[38]

The immediate results Metzger had hoped for from these exchanges were quite explicitly stated elsewhere by him.

> First, many differences are actually not very deep-seated—often they are only apparent contradictions—which are brought about by the different terminologies of the two camps. As soon as an earnest attempt is made to clearly present the whole truth to the other side in their own language, it often turns out that the one side's thinking on fundamentals is not essentially different from the other side's. Secondly, many differences are not of an exclusive character, but rather . . . come from the emphasis (often one-sided and overdone) of one truth, with which however the apparently opposing truth is perfectly compatible in a higher unity.[39]

---

[37]*Ibid.*

[38]*Ibid.*, 3.

[39]Max Metzger, "Aufbruch zur Una Sancta," *Theologie und Glaube,* II (1941), 3.

In the spring of 1939 Father Metzger sent a letter to all the Protestant ministers in Germany saying that as the Church of Christ was meant by Him to be one and as the divisions come from men, it is therefore the duty of all believing Christians to desire and work for the oneness of the Church–which is exactly the purpose of the Una Sancta Brotherhood. At the end of the letter–its tone gives the reader the impression of a straightforward sincerity and genuineness, as do all of Metzger's letters–he asked for an answer.[40] "A manifold echo came back. With a single exception the answers indicated throughout a strong concern also on the part of the Protestant brethren for a preparedness to cooperate in making the unity in Christ more visible and a more powerful witness in the view of the world than it is today."[41]

Apparently partly on the strength of these favorable reactions, Metzger held the first Una Sancta Conference at Meitingen during Pentecost week of 1939. The conference, which lasted three days and was attended by sixty Catholic and Protestant clergy and laymen,[42] was declared successful by Metzger and by the Protestants.[43] A little over a year later, in August of 1940, the second Una Sancta Conference at Meitingen took place.

The theme chosen for the conference was quite bold considering the circumstances; it was "the Church." About an equal number of lectures were delivered by theologians from each confession. In addition to the intellectual exchange provided by the lectures and discussions, all the conference

---

[40]A typewritten copy of the letter is at the Christkönighaus in Meitingen.

[41]Max Josef Metzger, *Vom meitinger ökumenischen Gespräch* (Meitingen, n.d.), I.

[42]Stevenson, *Max Joseph Metzger*, 9.

[43]Metzger, "Aufbruch zur Una Sancta," 4.

participants took part in the Mass liturgy, saying the prayers and singing the hymns as described earlier, and in the German form of the hours of the Divine Office. Again, the results of the conference were "harmonious"—to the point where Metzger could later say that for the ecumenical exchange Meitingen had already become a symbol.[44] At this conference there were eight Protestant clergymen, all Lutheran, indicating that even from the beginning the Una Sancta Movement drew its strongest Protestant support from Lutherans, for liturgically and otherwise they were closer to Catholicism. These clergymen represented different theological schools; the Berneuchner Circle even sent an official delegate. There were also fourteen Catholic non-local clergy present and a large number of local lay people—mostly Catholics, of course, because of the predominantly Catholic area. In addition "a large number of Protestant pastors (also a Protestant *Landesbischof*) had sent letters of well-wishing and regret that they were personally unable to participate because of the many demands on their time." On the Catholic side there were university professors and pastors who were members of the Society of Christ the King, Augustinians, Benedictines, Jesuits and Carmelites.[45] That the attendance was relatively small, and also that this was the last Meitingen conference, was largely due to the ominous presence of the Gestapo; there were at least two agents at the conference, including one disguised as a priest.[46] By this time the *Kirchenkampf* (Struggle over the Church) had been going on for several years and hundreds of priests and ministers were in concentration camps and prisons, including on three different occasions Father Metzger. Any un-

---

[44] *Ibid.*, 4-5.

[45] Metzger, *Meitinger Gespräch*, 2. Unfortunately the name of the "Landesbischof" is not ascertainable.

[46] Interview with Sister Gertrudis, February 10, 1958.

usual religious activity was considered suspect by the Nazis, and Dr. Metzger seemed to be under special suspicion as was indicated by his several arrests and the Gestapo house searches, doubtless because of his many foreign contacts and known pacifist tendencies. Nevertheless, on November 5 and 6 of the same year the discussion on the Church was continued in a conference in Berlin, where Metzger was then living, in which thirty-six Protestant clergymen and twenty-two Catholic priests and some sixty laymen took part and "carried on the discussion with the best of mutual understanding."[47]

LETTER TO PIUS XII

In Advent of 1939 Metzger, again in a Nazi prison, took the opportunity to write a letter to the Pope concerning the divisions within Christianity and included some suggestions as to how to overcome them. He may well have been influenced to write such a letter at that time not only because of the world situation—the false war after the fall of Poland was then in progress—but also because Pius XII, from whom much was expected and who had spent many years in Germany as papal Nuncio, had come to the throne only a few months before. Although there is no certain evidence that the letter ever reached its destination it is known that it was posted over the Swiss border.[48]

Metzger began the letter by speaking of the urgent need for peace and descried the impotence of a disunited Christianity to avoid the disaster of war: but the fault for these divisions in Christianity "has not been on one side only"—almost the same words Pope John XXIII later used.[49] "Holy Father! The need of our day . . . imperatively demands

[47]Metzger, "Aufbruch zur Una Sancta," 5.
[48]Interview with Sister Judith Maria, August, 1963.
[49]*New York Times* (Atlantic edition), January 31, 1959.

the utmost effort to heal the dismemberment of the Christian Church . . . I know that your Holiness grieves especially over the disunity of the Body of Christ . . . [and that] much has already been attempted in this direction during recent years. But the results have as yet been so meager. Why?"[50] Metzger went on to say that both the Church and humanity have too much at stake for the Holy Father to reject without a fair trial the suggestion of one even so insignificant as he; besides being a priest and doctor in theology he offered his wide personal acquaintance with many clergymen of the Anglican, Old Catholic and German, Swiss, Danish, Swedish and Dutch Reformed and Lutheran Churches, his work in the ecumenical movement and his founding of the Una Sancta Brotherhood as reasons to give his ideas on this problem a hearing.

In Metzger's opinion difficulties of a psychological nature were much more important in preventing a closer approach of other confessions to Rome than differences in dogma.

> The opinion of the best people among non-Catholic Christians is that a certain proud self-righteousness on our side prevents our acknowledging the faults and failings within our own Church, the sins and errors through which we share in the guilt of these divisions; it prevents that readiness to repent which, they say, we always exact from others. They deduce from this that the Holy Ghost is not the soul of the Church because, instead of putting her own house in order, she practices a too rigorous condemnation (I Cor. 11:3) only finally to be exercised by the Lord. They do not believe that our leader is utterly prepared to serve as the Master did in all humility (John 13:14; Matt. 18:2 and 20:26) but see in the claim to authority (which they consider as inconsistent with evangelical simplicity) a thirst for power and an all too human spirit of self-assertion. They consider that the exercise of their holy office in the Church is often incompatible with the apostolic exhortation in I Peter 5, 3, and therefore distrust the

[50]Metzger, *Gefangenschaftsbriefe,* 186.

> office itself. They believe that in discussions with "heretics" there is more desire for a victory for dogmatic and narrow orthodoxy than holy zeal for the truth of God, and are convinced that they have experienced among many, even among leading representatives of the Church, an overbearing spirit and a merciless severity.[51]

Metzger hastened to add that he did not agree with these criticisms, but they had to be seriously met and dealt with.

More specifically Father Metzger suggested that although to some the time might seem ill-suited to increase the efforts toward reunion of Christianity, he believed that the immense suffering of war would make people more open to such suggestions. In 1530 the last Germanic pope, Hadrian VI, had attempted to arrange for an ecumenical council to which the Protestants would be invited. "Unfortunately, this great plan, which undoubtedly would have achieved the best results, was not carried out. People's minds were still too heated . . . . But has not the time come today to repeat this experiment?"[52] The description of how he believed this experiment could be effectively carried out deserves special attention because in so many ways it has been since realized. He thought the council would not be possible without extensive preparation, but on the other hand it ought not to be postponed; twelve outstanding Catholic theologians from each country where the divisions exist most strongly could be commissioned to contact a similar number of outstanding persons in the other Christian Churches to arrange a series of confidential conversations. A report would then be submitted to a pontifical commission which would study it with a view to preparing for a General Council. Metzger then questioned:

---

[51]*Ibid.,* 188-189.
[52]*Ibid.,* 192.

> Is all this which I lay before Your Holiness too daring? I know that it goes far beyond what can be counted on to succeed. But it seems to me that only a great venture of faith, humility, and love can solve the problem of the fate of Christendom. Church history and world history alike will raise a memorial to that wearer of the triple crown who begins this work on a generous scale, and to the one who may perhaps finish it later.[53]

The post-war events have proved Metzger's suggestions to be practicable, for, since 1947, fourteen leading Catholic theologians under the leadership of Archbishop Jäger of Paderborn and a like number of leading Protestant theologians under the leadership of Bishop Wilhelm Stählin of Oldenburg have been meeting annually; reports of these meetings, of course, go to Rome. In addition, after the Secretariat for the Promotion of Christian Unity was set up by John XXIII to prepare for Vatican II it was in constant contact with non-Catholics and was responsible for bringing non-Catholic observers to the Council.

SKIRMISHES WITH THE NAZIS

The story of Metzger's skirmishes with the Nazis began very soon after their rise to power in 1933. Late in that year, after a private conversation with the Archbishop of Freiburg, Metzger wrote and published a pamphlet, *Die Kirche und das neue Deutschland* (The Church and the New Germany), in which he pointed out the strong objections the Catholic *Weltanschauung* raised against working with the National Socialist system, but stated that in the interest of peace and the continued preaching of the gospel he was prepared to accept some feasible *modus vivendi*.[54] These pamphlets, to be sent to all the deans of every chapter of Catholic priests throughout Germany, were to serve as

[53] *Ibid.*, 193.
[54] *Ibid.*, 98-99.

discussion material in clerical circles. However, they soon fell into the hands of the Gestapo, which was very quick to sense any opposition to the Nazi regime and was already checking the mail closely. Although Father Metzger had signed the pamphlet merely with "p" (for Bruder Paulus, as he was called within the Society), he was arrested—typewriters and mimeographing equipment were also confiscated—and imprisoned from January 23 to 26, 1934, in Augsburg.[55] Somewhat later, leaflets of an old pacifist article written by Metzger began turning up in the Rhineland.[56] The results of these and other brushes with the Party were attacks by Party organs and the suppressing of the Society's *Christkönigsbote* in 1935 and little *Alleluia-Rundbriefe*, which went to all the members of the Society, in 1937; at the same time, between 1934 and 1938, the police conducted several unsuccessful house searches at Meitingen in an attempt to find evidence of hoarding foreign currency or food.[57]

In 1939, shortly after the beginning of the second World War, Metzger was twice arrested by the Gestapo. The first charge was quite humorous; Metzger's Society of Christ the King was suspected of being a "front-organization" for a monarchist party in Bavaria. He was arrested and imprisoned for one day, September 5, 1939, and in October he was subjected to more questioning, and more of the Society's material and equipment was confiscated.[58] The following month he was arrested again and imprisoned for a much longer time—from November 9 to December 4—without charge. Two days after his arrest Father Metzger wrote to the State Police asking why he was arrested; he was told by the commissioner in Augsburg that he was arrested, along

---

[55]*Ibid.* No copies of the pamphlet seem to be extant.
[56]*Ibid.*, 100.
[57]Max Josef Metzger, *Gefangenschaftsbriefe*, ed. by Matthias Laros (Meitingen, 1947), 77.
[58]*Ibid.*

with 120 other men, in connection with the Munich Bürgerbräukeller attempt on Hitler's life and that his foreign correspondence made him suspect. Metzger's reaction to this accusation, in a letter to Meitingen, was, "'Das ist zu dumm."[59] On the first of December he again wrote to the State Police demanding to know why he was being held and insisting he had no interest in politics, as was borne out by his activities which he described.[60] Upon his release Metzger again asked of what he was accused; the answer was that he should be satisfied with being free again.[61]

Later, in the fall of 1942, when the tide of the war was turning against Germany, Metzger prepared to send a letter to the *Führer* persuading him to resign in favor of a government which could obtain a peace settlement. In the beginning of the next year he showed a draft of the letter to his friend Dr. Matthias Laros.

> Mr. Chancellor, if you really love our people and are prepared to give your life's blood, as you have always insisted, then you must step back and make room for another government which is still able to conclude an honorable peace since our armies on the borders of the empire still present a considerable force which will not be easily overrun. Since the enemy does not wish to and will not treat with you, there remains, as in every law-abiding nation, only your stepping back in order to save the nation, even if you must lose your life in the process; now still in honorable battle, later, however, in shame and degradation.[62]

Laros finally disabused Metzger of his naiveté and the letter was not sent, but Metzger eventually did send a memo-

---

[59]Metzger, *Gefangenschaftsbriefe* (1948), 138.
[60]*Ibid.*, 178.
[61]*Ibid.*, 137.
[62]Metzger, *Gefangenschaftsbriefe* (1947), 78-79. This doubtless is not an exact copy of Metzger's letter, but rather Laros's recollection of it. The original was burned when the Gestapo arrested Metzger. (Interview with Sister Gertrudis, November 2, 1959.)

randum with a similar final purpose to the Lutheran archbishop of Uppsala, Sweden, Archbishop Eidem.[63] A little later in 1943, when the battle of Stalingrad was taking the lives of hundreds of thousands, Metzger drew up a memorandum on the state of Germany after the war; this state was to be based on moral truth, social justice and guarantees of peace. He hoped to deliver this memorandum to Archbishop Eidem, whom he esteemed highly, that he might present it to the allied powers at the defeat of Germany and also use his influence with the English bishops to obtain a moderation of the peace conditions.[64]

Dr. Laros warned him not to endanger his religious mission by mixing in politics. But Metzger answered:

> I have at this time wide foreign contacts. Must I not use them? If the peace of the peoples can be prepared for through a servant of the Church, perhaps her least important officially, is that not worth the investment of a life, What that could mean for the standing of the Church in the world today Don't you realize that there is a crying need at this very moment when everything is hanging in the balance for someone to fight for an endurable peace for his own people and, if necessary, to die.[65]

Dr. Metzger arranged to have the memorandum delivered to the archbishop personally by Dagmar Imgart, apparently a Swedish convert who for years had shown an interest in Una Sancta affairs and had won the trust of Metzger; however, she turned out to be a spy in the service of the Gestapo.[66] Mrs. Imgart arranged to meet Metzger at the Society's home, Piusstift, in Berlin along with "some friends" on June 29, 1943. After Metzger had handed the memorandum over

[63]Stevenson, *Max Joseph Metzger*, 14.
[64]Metzger, *Gefangenschaftsbriefe* (1948), 116.
[65]Matthias Laros, *Dr. Max J. Metzger (Bruder Paulus) Ein Blutzeuge des Friedens der Konfessionen und Völker* (Meitingen, 1946), 4.
[66]*Ibid.*, 3.

to her, Gestapo agents broke in, searched everyone, and, having found the document, arrested the Swedish woman and Dr. Metzger; Sister Bernharda, one of the community, was also arrested for befriending Jews. It was only later that the truth about Mrs. Imgart was learned.[67] At the same time Gestapo agents invaded the Society's home in Meitingen and confiscated all correspondence, both public and private; they also arrested Sister Judith Maria, the Mother Superior of the Berlin community, who had just arrived from Berlin to make a retreat at the mother house. Sister Bernharda was released after nine days, while Sister Judith Maria's imprisonment lasted about a month.[68]

FINAL IMPRISONMENT AND DEATH

Father Metzger was at first imprisoned at the Prinz Albrecht Strasse prison of Berlin in a common cell with twenty other prisoners; he was later transferred to Moabit prison, also in Berlin.[69] During this time and throughout the rest of his imprisonment Metzger had the opportunity to meet men with varied backgrounds. The descriptions he gives of some of these contacts in his letters indicate again how Metzger by his broadness of attitude was so aptly fitted for inter-confessional peace work, Una Sancta work. During his first month of imprisonment Metzger's bed was next to that of the President of the German Freethinker's Union. "In spite of the gulf which in the eyes of the world divided us, we were nearer to one another than were others, because of our mutual respect. I could see that he was a man of noble character, and one who was a good friend. I could imagine that in him there survived subconsciously something of the Christian education which had come down

[67]Metzger, *Gefangenschaftsbriefe* (1948), 212.
[68]Metzger, *Gefangenschaftsbriefe* (1947), 180.
[69]Metzger, *Gefangenschaftsbriefe* (1948), 212.

through centuries of German history; I would count such a man as among Christ's company more than many a baptized person whose soul has remained untouched by the Spirit of Christ. I have no right to judge of the future fate of any man. It is, however, my belief that it is only those who have fought against their conscience and convictions who are 'lost' in the proper sense of the word, that is, condemned to hell. How many so-called Christians are much worse in this respect than the 'heathen'!"[70] A little later Metzger shared a cell with a radio technician from Vienna; "again, I imagine, without Church attachment, but a decent fellow and an idealist, so that we get on well together."[71]

On October 13, Metzger was led before the People's Court of Berlin under the directorship of President Dr. Roland Freisler; also present were Sister Gertrudis, Sister Judith Maria, Domkapitular Dr. Hirt as delegate of Archbishop Gröber of Freiburg in Breisgau, and a crowd filling the court room.[72]

In a document written on November 14, 1943, and later rescued from the prison, Father Metzger described many details of his trial. His counsel had warned him of the harsh tone of the People's Court and of the cleverness and capabilities of Freisler. Metzger nevertheless was quite collected and prepared to defend himself in a clear statement, specially explaining the motives of his action. He thought that if he were able to do this, and if there were still present among the magistrates "something of the humanity and integrity for which German Courts of Justice were formerly noted," he could at least hope to save his life. But after the introduction there was no doubt that here was only a mock trial; all hope was in vain. At the same time he felt bound

---

[70] *Ibid.*, 225-226.
[71] *Ibid.*, 233.
[72] *Ibid.*, 241.

to do all in his power to promote justice, "even if such a conception were unknown in the circle."[73]

Dr. Metzger wrote that he was not fearful of the great crowd of listeners and that after the sentence was pronounced he would have used the opportunity to speak strongly against the obvious injustices, had he not felt obliged to refrain himself for the sake of his Community. The decision, however, was arrived at before he could defend himself.[74] During the proceedings Freisler asked Metzger, "What is this Una Sancta?" Metzger calmly began to explain, "Christ has founded only one Church. . . ." But at this point Freisler shrieked "Una Sancta! Una Sancta! . . . Una! Una! That is us! And there is no other!" A little later, in his final speech, Freisler said, ". . . the accused must be eradicated. I have never until this moment in my career used the word 'eradicate,' but I use it here. Such a plague-boil must be eradicated. . . ."[75]

While waiting the few moments it took the judges to decide on the sentence, Metzger said he prayed and became resigned to whatever the verdict would be. When the death sentence came, a feeling of proud disdain came over him since he felt there was no shame, only honor, in being declared dishonorable by such a court. His greatest concern seemed to be for the two sisters at the trial, who Metzger thought must have been suffering as much as he. For just a few moments before being led away after the trial he was able to speak to Sister Gertrudis and Sister Judith and Dr. Hirt. He said, "Now it is over. I am at peace. I have offered my life to God for the peace of the world and the unity of the Church. If God accepts it I will be glad; if He grants me a longer life I shall also be thankful. As God wills."[76]

---

[73]*Ibid.*, 252.
[74]*Ibid.*, 252-253.
[75]*Ibid.*, 124-125.
[76]*Ibid.*, 241.

Several petitions had been filed by Archbishop Gröber and others, but to no avail. By this time with the eastern front deteriorating, the "SS" and Gestapo had locked Germany in their steel group. Decisions of the People's Court were almost never reversed.[77]

Metzger then waited many long months in hope and despair. On April 13, he learned that thirty executions were scheduled for April 17, but only twenty-nine names specifically listed. His name was not among the twenty-nine. Only on April 17, as the Judge read the official list of those to be executed, did the prison chaplain learn that Metzger was the thirtieth.[78] He rushed to inform Dr. Metzger; it was about noon. "Calmly and composed, like an ancient stoic, he received the news, laid his pen down and asked for Holy Viaticum. After the reception he sat on his cot and said, "Now, Lord Jesus, I come quickly."[79] The two farewell letters which Metzger was allowed to write were never recovered.[80] Shortly after three "he was led to the place of execution, upright as in his best days."[81] At 3:26 P.M. Max Josef Metzger, Bruder Paulus, was decapitated.[82] A prison employee said afterwards to a friend, "Never have I seen a man die like that."[83] About the same time the sisters at the mother house in Meitingen were saying the prayers for the dying, as they had been doing every Monday for years, for prison executions were usually on Mondays and the condemned often had no one to pray for them. When they received news of his execution they sang a *Te Deum*.[84]

---

[77]Cf. Stevenson, *Max Joseph Metzger*, 17.
[78]Metzger, *Gefangenschaftsbriefe* (1948), 302.
[79]Cf. *ibid.*; and Metzger, *Gefangenschaftsbriefe* (1947), 85; and Laros, *Metzger ein Blutzeuge*, 7.
[80]Metzger, *Gefangenschaftsbriefe* (1948), 302.
[81]Laros, *Metzger ein Blutzeuge*, 7.
[82]Metzger, *Gefangenschaftsbriefe* (1948), 303.
[83]Laros, *Metzger ein Blutzeuge*, 8.
[84]*Ibid.*

On September 14, 1946, the body of Father Metzger was translated to St. Hedwig's Cemetery in Berlin; a large number of mourners of various confessions were present. Father Buchholz delivered a moving memorial for the priest "who lived and died for the peace of nations and reunion in faith."[85]

[85]Michael Buchberger, *Aufbruch zur Einheit und Einigkeit im Glauben* (Freiburg, 1948), 17.

Chapter Nine

Postwar Expansion of the Una Sancta Movement

The War and Postwar as Contributing Factors

In May of 1945 Germany was in chaos. Its armies were smashed; its cities were largely rubble. Productive activity was almost at a standstill. In the months that followed, some 11.5 million German expellees driven from their homes, mainly in eastern Germany and the Czechoslovakian Sudetenland, poured into the western rump of the *Reich.* One of the results of this new "*Wanderung der Völker*" was that areas that had rarely seen a Catholic since the time of the Reformation were flooded with Catholic refugees, and sections which had contained no Protestants were now deluged with Protestant refugees. Every area of Western Germany was required to take its quota of eastern displaced Germans, and religion was not a controlling factor. Thus the number of Catholics living in the "diaspora" areas of northern and eastern Germany increased by over three and one-half million, from 4,303,000 to 7,934,000. In East Germany the almost two million Catholic refugees were scattered among fourteen million Protestants. Correspondingly the Protestant population in overwhelmingly Catholic areas swelled with the influx of refugees. In Upper Bavaria the Protestant population grew from ten per cent in 1938 to fourteen per cent in 1946. In the Regensburg diocese, bordering on the "Iron Curtain," the arrival of refugees meant that for every eight native Catholics there was one refugee Catholic; for every eight native Protestants there were sixty refugee Protestants. Even more important than the changes in ratio of Protestants to Catholics was the fact that formerly "pure" areas almost ceased to exist. The purely Catholic communities in Bavaria in 1910 numbered over 2300; after the second World War this number sank to nine. Where in 1910 there were 244 purely Protestant communities in Bavaria, today there are none. With this tremendous mixing of peoples and religions came the opportunity to observe the ideas and practices of the other religion and the melting away of century-long prejudices.

These refugees in Western Germany lacked almost every necessity, often including churches in which to hold their religious services. The only solution, one which under less disastrous conditions would have been considered sacrilegious, was for all the people to use those church buildings that were available, regardless of confessional differences. Thus, Protestants used Catholic Churches for certain hours for their religious services, and *vice versa*. Typical of the situation that existed all over Germany was that of the diocese of Rottenburg in Baden-Württemberg, where in 1949, 150 Protestant churches were being used by Catholics and fifteen Catholic ones were utilized by Protestants. The Catholic parish of Altenberg in Thüringen had thirty mission stations with 20,000 souls to care for; twenty-eight Protestant churches were put at the Catholics' disposal. Contrariwise in the area around Plattling where there previously had been only 500 Protestants with one church, in 1949 there were 15,000 Protestants; the bishop of Passau put 25 Catholic churches at their disposal.[1]

A public statement made at the *Katholikentag* in 1948 bears witness to the deep impression this cooperation made. "We are thinking particularly of the help given us in those areas of our Fatherland which earlier were almost entirely Protestant. The Protestant Christians there, clergy and laity, not only selflessly offered the use of their churches and in-

[1]Edgar Grüber, "Im Zeichen des 'schöpferischen Friedens,'" *Zeitwende*, XXI (1949), 293-295.

struction rooms, but also supported the Catholic priests in their burdensome office through many personal services.[2] These conditions persisted for almost a decade after the war ended; in 1954, seven hundred Protestant churches of the Kommissariat Magdeburg were also still being used by Catholics.[3] Even today, though the Catholics and Protestants are gradually building their own churches, many churches still stand double duty, particularly in East Germany.

Likewise the drive for a unified Protestant Church in Germany continued after the war. Although the *Bekennende Kirche* had its martyrs and its followers, its strength had fallen off considerably by the end of the war. At Eisenach in 1948 the *Evangelische Kirche in Deutschland* was founded on the basis of the experience of the *Bekennende Kirche.* The EKD, however, is not a unified church, for "the EKD lacks unity of faith and of teaching, and therefore it is not a church."[4] Rather the Evangelical Church in Germany is a federation of Lutheran, Reformed, and United Churches.

At the same place and in the same year, but shortly before the founding conference of the EKD the majority of Lutheran Churches in Germany gathered together to form the *Vereinigte evangelisch-lutherische Kirche Deutschlands.* The members recognize the VELKD as a "Church" because it is unified in the adherence of member Churches to the same confessional writings; the VELKD includes about twenty out of the twenty-two million Lutherans in Germany. The VELKD is itself ecumenical in outlook; Landesbischof Lilje in 1957 at the Hamburg General Synod of the VELKD declared that

---

[2]Quoted in Heinrich Hermelink, *Katholizismus und Protestantismus* (Stuttgart, 1949), 35.

[3]Juan C. Ruta and Johannes Straubinger, *Die katholische Kirche in Deutschland und ihre Probleme* (Stuttgart, 1954), 116.

[4]Ernst Zeeden, "Ueber die innere Entwicklungsgeschichte des Protestantismus seit der Reformation," *Theologie und Glaube,* XLI (1951), 232.

Lutheranism had "an ecumenical task."[5] The VELKD also belongs to the Lutheran World Federation, and it was this group which urged the plenary meeting in Minneapolis to found a large confessional studies institute of the Lutheran Federation to study Roman Catholic theology and practices. The initiation of this plan was put in the hands of Bishop Dietzfelbinger of Munich and Professor Kristen Skydsgaard of Copenhagen;[6] it was originally located in Copenhagen, but has since been transferred to Strassburg.

Even before the final catastrophe overtook Germany, the walls between the confessions had begun to crumble. Besides the seedling Una Sancta groups that had sprung up in the 1930's under Nazi Germany's persecution of the Christian Churches, numberless personal religious contacts between Catholics and Protestants were made during the long war years – in the trenches, foxholes and prisoner-of-war stockades, and above all in the concentration camps. Infamous Dachau was particularly fruitful in this regard;[7] of its 32,000 prisoners, 2000 were Protestant and Catholic clergymen, many of whom made life-long friendships with their confessional counterparts. Moving in the same direction of religious reconciliation, the Lutheran and Reformed Protestants, once almost as bitter antagonists of each other as of the Church of Rome, found themselves drawn closer to each other in the common persecution. In a conference for returning chaplains of both faiths in January of 1947, it was recommended to the proper ecclesiastical superiors that since they "were together at the front, in hospitals or prisons with brothers from different Protestant Churches in the hearing of the Word, in prayer and in common celebration of Holy Communion" and had discovered that they were no longer divided from each other as in the past, their newly discovered

[5]J. P. Michael, *Christen suchen eine Kirche* (Freiburg, 1958), 91.
[6]Interview with Kristen Skydsgaard, August 18, 1958.
[7]Wilfried Lempp, *Oekumenisch oder katholisch?* (Tübingen, 1948), 7.

closeness should be taken into consideration in the forming of the new Evangelical Church in Germany.[8] Carrying this conciliatory tendency even further, the delegates of the Prisoner-of-War Society of the YMCA, with the aid of the French Military Government, conducted a joint conference of all the chaplains of the prisoner-of-war camps of the French zone during the summer of 1947. The Protestant Landesbischof Wurm gave one talk, and the Catholic Archbishop Gröber of Freiburg was represented by his Domkapitular Eckert. All took part in morning and evening services which were alternately in Catholic and Protestant form, and in the common concluding liturgical celebration.[9]

It was these war and post-war experiences and conditions, plus the lifting of the weight of Nazi persecution, that stimulated the extraordinary growth of the Una Sancta Movement in Germany between 1945 and 1948. Just a little over a year after the collapse of Germany, Matthias Laros wrote that the Una Sancta Movement had reached a new level – not only because of the extreme material need of the times, but above all through the deaths of the common Christian martyrs. Whereas earlier there were only smaller, comparatively isolated circles working toward a reconciliation of the confessions, "there has arisen now in the broad masses of people – one can even say throughout the whole of the people – . . . an elemental will toward a final and at the same time positively fruitful elimination of the divisions of faith."[10] This will to unity, according to Laros, was not based on a desire to ignore or minimize the real differences and oppositions, as was the case with some romantics, for the modern Protestants too have become earnest dogmaticians, nor was

[8]Wilfrid Lempp, *Bekenntnis und Bekennen* (Schwäbisch Gmünd, n.d.), 2. See J.P. Michael, *Christen suchen,* for a description of the EKD.

[9]Kurt Hutten, "Das Gespräch zwischen den Konfessionen," *Für Arbeit und Besinnung,* I (1947), 227.

[10]Matthias Laros, *Una-Sancta-Einigung I. Rundbrief* (September, 1946), I.

it a type of secret propaganda or proselytizing of one confession at the expense of the other.

This will toward unity is primarily religiously directed; those active in the Una Sancta Movement are not directly interested in politics as such. The mixing of politics and religion in the past, to the detriment of both, has more than once been the cause of the widening of the rift between the confessions. But in no Una Sancta literature, in no reports of Una Sancta lectures and discussions, is there any treatment of politics beyond an occasional article pointing out that the mixing of politics and confessionalism has always had evil results.[11] Yet, although the Una Sancta Movement has no political overtones, some developments on the political scene can be viewed as contributing to the setting of the stage for the Una Sancta Movement. Before 1933 there had been a strong confessional Catholic political party, the Center Party, which arose out of the *Kulturkampf*. It naturally contributed to the polarity of Protestants and Catholics on the political level, and hence indirectly on other levels also. After the war the Center Party, for all practical purposes, disappeared from the political scene. There arose instead the Christian Democratic Union which was neither confessional, like the Center Party, nor non-confessional, like the Socialist Party (SPD), but rather inter-confessional; it is based specifically on Christian principles.[12] In the CDU Catholics and Protestants have worked together successfully, but at the same time disputes over religious issues have not been lacking, mainly because the Catholics as a group have had much political experience in the Center Party and have consequently become the predominating element in the party leadership.

---

[11]Cf. Franz Xaver Arnold, "Rivalität oder Zusammenarbeit der Konfessionen," *Hochland*, XLV (1952), 1-14; and "Konfessioneller Machtkampf oder Glaube?" *Universitas*, XI (1956), 385-388.

[12]Paul Weymar, *Adenauer His Authorized Biography* (New York, 1957), 168-173.

Wrangles, for example, over the number of Catholics and Protestants that should be appointed to various posts have often cropped up. In this respect the CDU has stressed the difference and opposition between Protestants and Catholics. But it is nevertheless true that 35 per cent of the party elite and 38 per cent of the CDU's *Bundestag* delegates are Protestant[13] and that 30 per cent of the voting support for the CDU has come from Protestants. Moreover 45 per cent of all Protestant and Catholic churchgoers indicated in 1952 their support for the CDU and only 22 per cent for the SPD.[14] This means that a large part of the former political polarity between Catholics and Protestants has been eliminated. Thus in some ways the post-war political situation has led to a lessening of religious tension, in some ways not.

UNA SANCTA CIRCLES DEVELOP

The number of cities and towns reporting the existence of one or more Una Sancta circles in the immediate post-was years was at least forty. It included most of the larger cities, several medium-sized ones, and a few smaller towns with particularly suitable circumstances, such as the presence of abbeys and seminaries. The heaviest concentration naturally occurred in those areas of greatly mixed religious groupings: the West and South, or what was later to become the West German Federal Republic. A comparison of this list to the smaller list of the pioneer inter-confessional groups of the 1930's shows considerable continuity, except for the Soviet zone, where apparently the emigrations and oppressive Communist rule eliminated many of the pre-war groups. Of the six cities with Una Sancta Circles in the Soviet zone, five were grouped within an area of a thirty mile radius. Leipzig was the most active of the group, for here there were not

[13] *Ibid.*, 63.

[14] Elisabeth Noelle Neumann and Erich Peter Neumann, *Jahrbuch der öffentlichen Meinung, 1957* (Allensbach, 1957), 29, 264.

only a relatively large number of Catholics in the midst of a heavily Protestant area, but also an important center of the Oratorian Fathers, who were both active in the liturgical movement and also strongly influenced by the ecumenical spirit of John Henry Cardinal Newman, himself an Oratorian.[15] Even the sixth city in the Soviet zone, Dresden, was only sixty miles from Leipzig. Berlin, outstanding as an island of freedom in the midst of the red sea, was probably the most active of all Una Sancta circles.[16]

The membership of the circles varied. Some were made up completely of theologians, such as the circle in Wuppertal, founded in 1938 by Arnold Rademacher; by 1957, the group was twenty-four strong, half Protestant and half Catholic. One Leipzig circle, because of the presence of members of the Protestant theological faculty and large numbers of Catholic priests, especially the Oratorians, was also composed mainly of theologians. However, this sort of a situation was comparatively rare. Most of the circles were a mixture of lay people and theologians, with the number of laymen usually outweighing that of the clergy; thus, Stuttgart reported that in each of its several circles there was always at least one Catholic and one Protestant clergyman.[17] Both Protestant Pastor Rehbach and the secretary

---

[15]Matthias Laros, *Una-Sancta-Einigung 3. Rundbrief* (January, 1947), 3.

[16]Letter from Kurt Krüger, secretary of the Una Sancta circles in Berlin, to Leonard Swidler, December 15, 1957. By 1946 Una Sancta circles were located in Aachen, Bamberg, Berlin, Bonn, Boppard, Darmstadt, Dresden, Düsseldorf, Eisleben, Erfurt, Essen, Frankfurt, Fulda, Giessen, Hagen, Hanover, Hamburg, Heidelberg, Jena, Kassel, Koblenz, Köln, Krefeld, Kreuzenach, Leipzig, Limburg, Marburg, München, Nürnberg, Paderborn, Passau, Ravensberg, Saarbrücken, Soest, Stuttgart Tübingen, Weingarten, Werl, Wiesbaden and Wuppertal. Laros, 1. *Rundbrief*, 3; Arnold Schulte, "Wuppertal," *Una Sancta,* XII (1957), 58; Hermann Hoffman, "Una Sancta Arbeit in der DDR," *Una Sancta,* XII (1957), 60; Hutten, "Das Gespräch," 230.

[17]Letter from Franz Kneer, leader in the Stuttgart Una Sancta circles since 1945, to Leonard Swidler, December 18, 1957.

of the Munich circle mentioned that their group was always largely composed of laymen.

Some circles, such as those in the state of Westphalia and the city of Leipzig, drew mostly gymnasium and university students. Some circles were mainly students, like some Stuttgart groups which drew on the student bodies of the Institute of Technology, the Art Academy, and the Pedagogical Institute, and on youth group leaders; or like the Tübingen circle where the university students have been meeting weekly in the Protestant student house since 1947. This Tübingen circle has the advantage of being located by a university with both Protestant and Catholic theological faculties which have had professors such as Karl Heim, Karl Adam, Heinrich Fries and Romano Guardini and now Hans Küng. In the Ruhr industrial area, where overall religious indifference was most widespread, the factory workers took a very active part. Many groups were of a very mixed sort, ranging from workers and secretaries to doctors. But by the very nature of discussion groups the appeal would be strongest to persons of at least a somewhat more advanced education.

All the circles included both Catholics and Lutherans, but often members of the Reformed Church also participated the secretary of the Una Sancta in Berlin was a Baptist, and one of the leaders of the movement in Krefeld was a Mennonite. Some of the larger cities like Munich and Berlin were able to gain Orthodox and even Old-Catholic participants.

It would be impossible to ascertain with any sort of accuracy the number of people who took an active part in the Una Sancta meetings. Edgar Grüber stated in 1949 that there were over ten thousand active participants.[18] Such a figure is possible. Nuremburg had over two hundred members; Stuttgart reported having several circles with from

---

[18]Grüber, "Im Zeichen," 215.

ten to fifty members each. Berlin not only had many separate circles, but when an Una Sancta evening with speeches by Baptist, Catholic, Lutheran and Orthodox speakers and with common singing and prayer was announced, the church with a capacity for 2500 persons was filled to over-flowing a half hour ahead of time. Dr. Laros said on New Year's of 1947 that the influence of the Una Sancta Movement in Swabia and Bavaria was spreading so rapidly from the cities to the country that in southern Germany one could speak of a "people's movement."[19] Even the Una Sancta circle of the small town of Weingarten near the Swiss border was able to fill the huge Abbey church "to the last place, and the ideas of the Una Sancta have carried over into the entire Swabian highlands."[20]

The frequency and type of Una Sancta meetings varied considerably. Most circles met at least monthly, but some met every two weeks and some even every week. Often the meeting would consist in whole or at least in part of the reading of Scriptures followed by a discussion. Berlin reported one group studying parts of the New Testament in the original Greek. However, quite often the meetings were conducted in the form Metzger had earlier suggested: a short talk by one or two speakers on some common religious theme, followed by discussions.

Una Sancta Activities Spread

At times an Una Sancta circle would sponsor a lecture on a more public basis; Friedrich Heiler was very often invited to give such lectures, as was also Josef Lortz. Sometimes a whole lecture series would be carried out on a monthly basis over the period of a year, as was the case in Munich, or as the Jena circle did; meetings were held every two weeks, with lectures and discussions of the material alter-

---

[19]Laros, *3. Rundbrief,* 6.
[20]Laros, *1. Rundbrief,* 3-4.

nating. In Eberswald a series of weekly lectures was sponsored by the Protestant, Catholic, and Free Churches; each time over a thousand listeners jammed the largest hall available. The lectures apparently met with equal success everywhere. Pastor Rehbach said hundreds attended the lectures in Munich;[21] Elizabeth Sorger, the Una Sancta secretary in Frankfurt, reported the same.[22] The Catholic theology professor Karl Adam delivered a series of three lectures on the Una Sancta in the huge Protestant Markuskirche in Stuttgart before overflowing crowds, and repeated the series in Karlsruhe. The Berlin Una Sancta complained that the requests for more lectures and discussions were constantly increasing and already the available speakers were unable to fulfill all the demands made on them.

In September of 1946 Dr. Laros wrote that several cities had sponsored "Ecumenical Weeks" in which four lectures on "The Ecumenical Problem Today," "Newman as an Ecumenical Figure," "Soederblom as an Ecumenical Figure," and "Creative Peace of the Confessions" were given by Catholic and Protestant university instructors; each time representatives from the two Churches led a discussion on the lecture the following day. A few months later Laros reported that these "Ecumenical Weeks" had become especially popular in the whole Rhineland with the immediate practical result that in many places the Protestant and Catholic pastors got together to present to each other brief courses of their own theologies, especially on points of crucial importance such as original sin, freedom of the will, justification, the sacrifice of the Mass, confession, indulgences, the veneration of Mary and the saints, the hierarchial structure of the Church, the primacy of the Pope, Papal infallibility, and the corresponding teachings of Luther and the Augsburg Confession.

---

[21]Interview with Pastor August Rehbach, October 15, 1959.
[22]Interview with Elizabeth Sorger, December 19, 1957.

The spirit of the Una Sancta sometimes manifested itself even more publicly. On December 11, 1946, in Krefeld, Christians of all faiths gathered at the Parkhof square; here the Catholic city dean and the Mennonite pastor gave addresses, the Lutheran pastor led the recitation of the Lord's Prayer, and all sang together both Protestant and Catholic chorales. The crowd then formed a silent procession through the city before separating and going to their own churches where all recited a commonly composed prayer, copies of which in Latin and English were even handed out to representatives of the occupation forces. In Karlsruhe the Una Sancta circle sponsored a joint adult education course, and Nuremberg did much the same thing; the problems of the two confessions, of course, were thoroughly treated. Bamberg and Frankfurt too had somewhat similar programs. Several circles, such as Krefeld and Soest, imitating St. Paul, took up collections for the needy Christians. Also in Soest, where the Una Sancta work was carried on under the energetic leadership of a retired Catholic Colonel Schunk, a sort of Una Sancta area center was set up to arrange for lectures and discussion material for all of Westphalla. Elizabeth Sorger of Frankfurt took on a similar task in her area.

In addition to these meetings for an evening or a day, various Una Sancta circles were able to conduct conferences of several days' length. Such conferences had been arranged already by Max Metzger in 1939 and 1940. There were several others during the early 1940's, but only on a local level. One such Una Sancta conference took place in Easter week, 1943, at Tübingen when members of the Stuttgart Una Sancta circle spent several days together. Pastor Rudolf Daur, the Protestant leader of the group, wrote of this conference, "Rich, unforgettable days! We decided then to repeat such a meeting within a year; but the times would not allow it."[23] The

---

[23]Rudolf Daur, *Um die Einheit der Gläubigen* (Stuttgart, 1946), 2.

Nazis, mainly through the Gestapo, put a stop to all such conferences during the last year and a half of the war.

As soon as the dust from the rubble settled, the desire for such conferences arose stronger than ever. In April, 1946, fifty members of the Stuttgart Una Sancta circle spent several days in Schönberg bei Ellwangen at a home run by Catholic sisters. The participants were about equally divided between Protestants and Catholics, including both theologians and laymen from all stations in life and age groups. Each day was begun with a liturgical celebration held in common. On the first evening the Mass was explained with great care so that the Protestant members could attend with more understanding. One Protestant said, "We Protestant guests did not communicate. But we were nevertheless not left standing outside like strangers and onlookers; rather we felt ourselves, despite the external barriers separating us, within the *Communio Sanctorum*."[24] The second morning the Lutheran "German Mass" was celebrated. In one of the discussion periods an attending Catholic priest said that he was moved to tears by this liturgy, that he had never felt so deeply the unity nor so painfully the division of Christians as by the service which the Lutherans had celebrated with such earnestness and in such a noble and worthy manner. The rest of the days were filled out with two lectures from Catholics and two from Protestants, discussion periods, organ music and "still walks through the spring-green forest."[25]

About the same time a Protestant friend of the prior of the Benedictine Abbey of Niederaltaich expressed the desire to participate sometime in a Catholic retreat. Prior Emmanuel Heufelder invited him to come to the retreat in August, 1946, which he was preparing for a group of Catholic priests on "The spiritual life according to the rule of St. Benedict." The pastor came and brought with him a number of fellow

[24] *Ibid.*, 3.
[25] *Ibid.*, 4.

Protestants—pastors, theologians, and laymen. The joint retreat was found so successful that a second one was arranged for the following Easter week. Still more Protestants took part in this Easter retreat, one which was especially significant because of the concrete formulation of the paths leading to the *Una Sancta.* Three steps were distinguished. 1. In the effort toward mutual understanding, there must be a preparedness to learn from one another, to practice true Christian love. 2. In the striving toward Christian truth it is necessary that the divisive points be clearly seen. A union must not result at the expense of the truth. 3. The actual union is the work of God. God however works in history. Great historical events, great common needs can become in the hands of God decisive means of his grace when the hour has become ripe. "We can and must already now prepare ourselves for such a working of God's grace by taking the first two steps and by sincere prayer for unity."[26] The following August 18-23, another Una Sancta retreat was held with great success. This time there were thirty-five participants, two-thirds of whom were Protestant.

The Stuttgart Una Sancta circle, about a year after its conference at Schönberg bei Ellwangen, sponsored another Una Sancta conference at the Benedictine Abbey of Neresheim between Ulm and Ellwangen in eastern Würtemberg from April 14-18. Many important leaders were among the 120 participants. The main lectures were delivered by Abbot Bernhard Durst of Neresheim, Hans Asmussen, then the President of the Chancery of the Evangelical Church in Germany, the Protestant Prelate Wilfrid Lempp of the Stuttgart State Church Directory, the Catholic Dean Lämmle, Catholic theology Professor Franz Arnold from Tübingen, Prior Heufelder from Niederaltaich Abbey, and the Protestant City Pastor Daur of Stuttgart. Although the main theme of the

[26]Benedikt Ewaldt, "In Christo Unum," *Die beiden Türme,* Sonderheft (1958), 44-45.

conference was the meaning of ecclesiastical jurisdiction in Protestant and Catholic theology, two lectures, one by a Catholic and one by a Protestant, were delivered in memory of Dr. Max Josef Metzger as "founder and blood martyr of the Una Sancta Movement." The earlier practice of beginning each day with alternate forms of the liturgy was retained and extended. On the first day a Catholic Solemn High Mass was celebrated; the second day the Lutheran "German Mass" was done in the Berneuchner manner; on the third day a Pontifical High Mass in the Russian Rite was celebrated by the Russian Paul Meltijew, formerly Orthodox Bishop of Briansk and Smolensk under the Czar, but shortly before 1947 newly named Bishop of Herokleopolis in union with Rome. The whole conference received official approval in the form of greetings sent by both the Protestant Landesbischof Wurm and the Catholic Bishop Sproll.[27]

The practice of Una Sancta conferences spread and their frequency continued to increase rapidly in the next year. Later that same year, 1947, the famous Benedictine Abbey in the Rhineland, Maria Laach, played host for two weeks to fourteen Protestant theology students. Early the following year Niederaltaich Abbey conducted a "Singweek" for members of all confessions, during which there was considerable discussion about the meeting of the faiths. That May there was another Una Sancta conference at the Evangelical Academy at Bad Boll from the tenth to the fourteenth, and in early June still another Una Sancta conference was held at Berg Gemen in Münsterland. The liturgical procedure here was a little different: the day began with a common recitation of Prime, but then the Catholics and Protestants separated to celebrate the Catholic Mass and the "German Mass."

---

[27]Anton Frey, *Um die Wiedervereinigung im Glauben* (Stuttgart, 1947), 7; Michael Buchberger, *Aufbruch zur Einhalt und Einigkeit im Glauben* (Freiburg, 1948), 41; Hutten, "Das Gespräch," 205.

INTERNATIONAL UNA SANCTA CONFERENCE

But much larger than any of these conferences was to be the Una Sancta conference to take place at the end of September, 1947, in Constance, on the border between Germany and Switzerland. Plans were laid for the conference by the neighboring Una Sancta circles of Constance and Meersburg in conjunction with the Munich circle. There were applications from hundreds of people in all parts of Germany, and from leading personalities in France, Holland and Switzerland. At the last minute, however, the conference had to be cancelled because of a ban by the French Military Government made at the request of the German Catholic Archbishop Gröber of Freiburg. Although approached both by letter and in person, the archbishop refused to change his decision and declined to give a reason for his disapproval.[28] It is not surprising to discover that Archbishop Gröber also had for years opposed energetically the liturgical movement and had refused Father Metzger permission to lecture on Christian reunion.[29]

This reversal did not put a stop to plans for a large scale Una Sancta conference in southern Germany. The following year a location was chosen in the American zone, at Seeshaupt on Starnbergersee near Munich. In the meanwhile the framework of the conference had grown considerably: members of the Old Catholic Church began to take an active part in the Una Sancta activities in Munich, and the relations with the Orthodox grew even better, with the result that the cover of the conference brochure read, "Catholic, Orthodox, Evangelical, Old Catholic Christians meet each other in

---

[28]"Una Sancta-Gespräch in Konstanz musste abgesagt werden," *Der Ueberblick,* II (October 22, 1947), 10.

[29]Cf. Ernest Koenker, *The Liturgical Renaissance in the Roman Catholic Church* (Chicago, 1954), *passim,* and Gordon Zahn, *German Catholics and Hitler's Wars* (New York, 1962), 135.

prayer and discussion." On the first evening Catholic Compline was to be recited by all in German; the next day was to be opened by the Protestant form of Matins and closed with an Old Catholic service. On the second day there would be the Lutheran "German Mass," the third day the Orthodox Liturgy, and on the last day a Catholic High Mass. The lectures were to be delivered by Catholic, Protestant and Orthodox theologians. Sister Gertrudis of the Society of Christ the King was to give a description of the Una Sancta work of Dr. Metzger. Although the proposed lodgings could handle only a hundred, within a very short time of the announcement there were 350 applicants from all parts of Germany and from other countries, cutting across all confessions, social levels and age groups. To meet the crisis, the Munich Una Sancta procured tents and cots, warned people ahead of time to bring bedding and dishes, and arranged for a bus to take people to lodgings in nearby areas.

The conference was to take place from June 25 to 29, 1948. On June 8 the press published the *Monitum,* dated June 5, from the Holy Office in Rome which pointed anew to the provisions of Canons 1325, Par. 3 and 721, Par. 2, which forbade Catholics to participate in inter-confessional meetings without first obtaining permission from Rome and forbade Catholic participation in non-Catholic services. The Catholic members of the Munich Una Sancta circle had already laid their plans for the conference before Archbishop Jäger of Paderborn, who had been designated the representative for Una Sancta questions in the Fulda Bishops Conference of the German bishops. Their plans had received his warmest best wishes and blessings, and he had written on May 29, that on his trip to Rome he had had the opportunity to speak to the Holy Father about the Una Sancta Movement and that it was a joy to see with what eagerness the Pope followed all ecumenical efforts. It was then only as a result of the quick intervention of Archbishop Jäger that "the conference permission was granted by telegraph from the highest office," on the condition that no liturgical services be celebrated in common.[30]

With the reception of this permission the Munich Una Sancta circle's difficulties were not yet at an end. On June 20 the West German government imposed a currency reform: every German was to hand in all his old currency and receive 40 Marks, no more. This of course meant that most of the Germans were unable to travel, especially any great distance; only fifty were able to attend the conference. The smaller number, however, had its own advantages. A member from one of the Swiss Una Sancta circles commented that there developed between Catholics, Orthodox, Evangelical and Old Catholic Christians, theologians and laity, an intensity of discussion and probably also of prayer that would have been impossible in a larger group.[31]

THE UNA SANCTA AND OTHER ORGANIZATIONS

Una Sancta work gained popularity also among the youth in the immediate post-war years. Shortly after the end of the war Franz Ranft covered seven dioceses in central and eastern Germany, speaking to Catholic theology students. He said, "Naturally the interest in the Protestant-Catholic problem is especially strong among the theology students, who, at least in the upper division, are all war veterans." They put to him the following questions: "What is the situation in the Protestant Church today? What does present day Protestantism believe? What are the liturgical forms used by the different Protestant groups? What success have the Protestant-Catholic conferences had? What exactly are the activities and aims of Meitingen?"[32] Already in 1946 the

---

[30]Der Münchner Arbeitkreis der Una Sancta, *Liebe Freunde der Una Sancta München und liebe neue Freunde in der Schweiz.* (Munich, 1948), 2.

[31]Alfons Rosenberg, *Una Sancta Tagung Seehaupt-München,* mimeographed report (1948), 1.

[32]Franz Ranft, *Zur Begegnung von Katholiken und Protestanten* (Fulda, 1947), 7.

instructors and students of the Protestant Pedagogical Academy and Catholic theological seminary at Aachen met together for an Una Sancta discussion.

Early in January of 1947 a number of Protestant and Catholic student chaplains of the British zone held a conference in Hardeshaufen to discuss the possibilities of cooperation between the student congregations. It was decided that a general process of getting to know each other better through mutual invitations, common lectures, and programs should be inaugurated. They even expressed a desire to publish a common hymn book and a common collection of prayers so that they could at least pray together. Some of these suggestions had already been incorporated in the work of such student groups as the one at the University of Berlin. Here the Catholic and Protestant student congregations had arranged within their winter programs of 1946-1947 two common evenings; one time a Catholic theologian addressed them in the Protestant cathedral and the other time a Protestant pastor spoke.

Arrangements for joint projects were agreed upon by Manfred Müller, chairman of the Youth Division of the Evangelical Church in Germany, and Josef Rommerskirchen, director of the Catholic youth groups of Germany. In many areas the Protestant and Catholic youth groups set up cooperation committees. At Paderborn, for example, the Catholic St. Georg Society and the Evangelical Youth Society set up such a committee which issued the following statement: "Our salvation lies not in a blurring of doctrine, but rather in cooperating with each other in our common task: Christianization and pacification of our people and the world."[33] By September of 1949 good relations had developed so far that the Protestant youth leaders were able to invite the Catholic youth leaders to Marburg for a discussion of mutual problems. In 1950 the Catholics returned the gesture by

[33]Grüber, *Im Zeichen*, 295.

inviting the Protestant youth leaders to Fulda for a conference; seventy people participated. On October 27, 1946, between three and four thousand members of Protestant and Catholic youth groups gathered under the open sky at Olympia stadium, Berlin, in a public demonstration for all baptized youth. About the same time a similar demonstration was put on by several thousand youths at the Cologne university.

There were many other kinds of organizations that took up Una Sancta work at this time. One was the Society for Metaphysics, founded after the war by Protestants and Catholics to promote mutual understanding and religious tolerance through the science of comparative religion. Alike in goal but issuing mainly from the Protestant side was the "Reconciliation Society," centered in Petzen bei Bückburg, which aimed at peace and cooperation of all nations and creeds. Also Protestant was the *Humiliaten* Order which in 1946 was twenty-five years old; under the direction of Abbot Richard Walter the Order was "placed completely in the services of the Una Sancta idea."[34] On the Catholic side was the Catholic Academic Union of Hanover, which worked in three groups, one social, one liturgical and one Una Sancta; the last was concerned with the theme "The Christian conscience in the Protestant and Catholic view."[35] Similarly the Protestant and Catholic Senior Academic Unions conducted a joint Advent celebration in 1946. And under the direction of the Franciscan Saturnin Pauleser the Christ the King Confraternity was founded in Miltenberg to promote inter-faith understanding which would eventually lead to a reunion in faith; it was mainly an information and prayer movement.

Inter-confessional cooperation in organized historical research developed soon after the war. The Institute for

---

[34]Laros, *3. Rundbrief*, 8.
[35]Hutten, "Das Gespräch," 228.

Reformation Research in Munich received its license from the American Military Government on December 9, 1946, and although the formalities were not completed until June of 1948, the initial meeting was held on January 12, 1947, when Karl August Meissinger, a Lutheran, was elected president and Hugo Lang, O.S.B., vice-president. Meissinger was a highly respected Reformation scholar, who, besides having done a great deal of work on the Weimar edition of Luther's writings, had published a number of scholarly books on the Reformation, including "A Luther Breviary," designed especially to inform Catholics of the lights and shadows of Luther's personality and history; he had for quite some time been active in the Una Sancta Movement.[36] Professor Hugo Lang, who later became the Abbot of St. Boniface's Abbey in Munich, was one of the original members of the Una Sancta circle started in Munich in 1938 and was appointed by Cardinal Faulhaber of Munich to be his representative in Una Sancta affairs.[37]

The aims of the institute and the principles upon which it was based were similar to those of the Una Sancta Movement. There should be: "1. scholarly cooperation between Protestants and Catholics. 2. No watering down, but rather a clear delineation of the doctrinal differences of both sides, not however for the selfish purpose of controversy, but rather in a believing, common seeking for the one truth."[38] The institute was not only to serve research scholars but also younger students of both faiths; there was to be a "cooperative working together of teachers and learners in a continuing work team, under one roof and under the direction of the president."[39] But in addition to the purely scholarly projects, which were the main purpose of the institute, and the closely associated

---

[36]Karl Meissinger, *Institut für Reformations-forschung* (Munich, n.d.), 3.
[37]Interview with Abbot Hugo Lang, October 28, 1959.
[38]Meissinger, *Institut,* 3.
[39]*Ibid.,* 4.

training of young intelligent future leaders in Una Sancta work, a third task became increasingly important to the institute, "to work in an immediate way on the laity of the *Una Sancta* and the broadest public in general."[40] Unfortunately, in 1950, before the institute could really get on its feet and become self-sustaining, its guiding spirit, Karl Meissinger, died, and the institute with him.

UNA SANCTA PUBLISHING

The cooperation of the confessions on a religious basis spread over into the field of publishing. In the French zone a joint committee called "Christian Germany" was set up which worked together to publish documents and reports mainly of Christian resistance to the Nazis. The Herder Publishing Company in Freiburg published the Catholic books and the Furche Publishing Company in Tübingen the Protestant. But even more in the spirit of *Una Sancta* was the work of the Schwaben Publishing Company in Stuttgart. This group set up the "Peter and Paul Book Series," "an organ, in which Catholic and Protestant authors of the present and the past are found together in order to serve unity in faith."[41] The amount of periodical literature was voluminous after the war; the traditionally intellectual periodicals like *Stimmen der Zeit, Glaube und Wahrheit, Christliche Welt* and *Hochland* often contained articles on Catholic-Protestant cooperation and relations. Such periodicals as the *Herder-Korrespondenz, Begegnung, Die Besinnung, Die Seele, Frankfurter Hefte, Die Lücke* and *Ueberblick* took up the cause of Catholic-Protestant ecumenism with even greater energy; almost every issue of these periodicals contained something on this subject.

After the war Sister Gertrudis, the Mother General of the Society of Christ the King, began to search for someone to

---

[40] *Ibid.*, 6.

[41] On jacket of Ulrich Valeske, *Die Stunde ist Da* (Stuttgart, 1948).

take Dr. Metzger's place as leader of the Una Sancta Movement. She soon found Dr. Matthias Laros, a Catholic pastor at Kapellen-Stolzenfels in the Rhineland. Dr. Laros had long been interested in the Lay Apostolate and in confessional peace and had written on these and other subjects in theological and cultural periodicals; he had also been a personal friend of Max Metzger. Dr. Laros agreed to take over the work. He visited the center at Meitingen once for five weeks and at other times for shorter periods, besides keeping in contact through correspondence. He published a number of articles in different periodicals and spoke over the radio a number of times about the Una Sancta Movement. Of Laros' various publications, probably the most important was the *Una Sancta Einigung Rundbriefe,* which came out about four times a year. Early in 1946 Sister Gertrudis circulated a mimeographed page telling of the death of Dr. Metzger and asking for people's addresses; all correspondence, documents and equipment had been confiscated by the Nazis so that it was necessary to start anew. That September the first *Rundbriefe* (circular letter), written by Dr. Laros and mainly describing the situation of the various Una Sancta circles in Germany, appeared. These *Rundbriefe* were eight pages in length, and, regardless of what numbers they were printed in, always found readers. Sometimes five, eight, ten, fifteen, twenty, and once even forty-five thousand copies were printed and distributed. Sister Gertrudis thought that each time over fifty thousand copies could easily have been used, so great was the demand before 1948.

Dr. Laros edited the prison letters of Dr. Metzger in 1947 as the first of the "Una Sancta Book Series" which the Kyrios Publishing Company of the Society of Christ the King started to publish. In 1948 they printed a second edition of the prison letters, this time with an introduction by Hannes Baecker; their plans were then completely disrupted by the currency reform of June, 1948. Laros, who had been a student of Arnold Rademacher and a member of the circle about him, was also early interested in the important ecumenical figure Cardinal Newman. As early as 1922 he helped to edit some of Newman's writings in German.[42] In 1950 Laros published his largest piece of work on the Una Sancta. He called it *Schöpferische Friede der Konfessionen* (Creative Peace of of the Confessions),[43] a term he has been using at least since 1935 when he wrote an article called "Concerning the Creative Peace of the Confessions."[44] The term had become a motto for Laros. To him it meant that while men obviously could not create unity in the Church—only God could do that—it was possible for man to perform the essential work of preparation, so

> that the Christians of the different confessions relinquish their oppositional attitude held until now and help one another as brothers and sisters in Christ—to overcome the mutual prejudices and misunderstandings and transmit everything of positive religious value to each other; also through a positive critique to probe, with all possible objectivity, to the very foundations of the mutual misunderstandings and finally the real oppositions of faith and church discipline; so that the minds and souls will be prepared for the actual union in the sense of the Lord.[45]

THE UNA SANCTA VIS-A-VIS THE HIERARCHY AND THEOLOGIANS

Did this Una Sancta Movement exist in a "no-man's land" between the confessions with the pope and hierarchy standing negatively apart, as some apparently thought? The evidence points in the other direction. Already in 1946 Laros was able to write that the considerable misgivings which the Protestant and Catholic church authorities had previously

---

[42]Cf. Hermelink, *Katholizismus und Protestantismus,* 23.

[43]Matthias Laros, *Schöpferischer Friede der Konfessionen* (Rechlingshausen, 1950).

[44]Matthias Laros, "Um den Schöpferischen Frieden der Konfessionen," *Schönere Zukunft,* X (1935), 1073-75.

[45]Laros, *Schöpferischer Friede,* 199.

held toward the Una Sancta Movement were disappearing; this was true mainly because three things became clear: the danger of an unclear "Mischmasch" which would end in a watered-down "Super-church" did not exist in the movement; the Una Sancta did *not* look upon the mixed marriage as an ideal; the Movement did not belittle the importance of the confessional school.

The Protestant church historian Heinrich Hermelink wrote that Pius XII never missed an opportunity to send a greeting out over the borders of the Roman Catholic Church to all Christians of other denominations;[46] Archbishop Jäger's report of his visit with the Holy Father and his interest in ecumenical matters bore this impression out. More specifically, Hermelink added that the Catholic bishops of north and south Germany have not omitted sending a friendly word now and again to the "circles of agreement" which have opened the friendly conversations between Catholics and Protestants in their dioceses. But three German bishops were outstanding in their leadership in support of the Una Sancta Movement in this early period: Archbishop Buchberger, Cardinal Faulhaber and Archbishop Jäger.

Archbishop Buchberger of Regensburg, the first editor of the multi-volume *Lexikon für Theologie und Kirche* (1931), was also a frequent contributor to the irenic periodical *Schönere Zukunft* in the middle 1930's when Lortzing was also publishing there his Una Sancta type of articles. He took a very favorable attitude toward the Una Sancta Movement In 1948 he delivered a sermon which was the result of long and painstaking collecting of information on Catholic-Protestant ecumenical activities in Germany since the 1930's; the sermon was published a short time later under the title "Breakthrough Toward Unity."

---

[46]Heinrich Hermelink, *Die katholische Kirche unter den Pius-Päpsten des 20. Jahrhunderts* (Zurich, 1949), 130.

The relationship of the rise of the Lay Apostolate in the Catholic Church to the Una Sancta Movement can be seen in the person of Cardinal Faulhaber of Munich. Faulhaber considered Pius XI's encyclical of 1925, *Quas Primas,* which outlined the program for Catholic Action, "the solution for a century."[47] The Cardinal delivered his well-known outline for the Lay Apostolate in a semon three years later, on December 12, 1928; it was still being quoted by non-Catholics after almost thirty years. Cardinal Faulhaber also directly involved himself in Una Sancta work when he appointed Hugo Lang to be his representative in all Una Sancta work in the diocese. And on March 3, 1940, the Cardinal showed himself completely one with the ideas of the Una Sancta Movement when he said in a sermon that the ecumenical discussions do not aim at making converts; rather they wish

> to build bridges of understanding, reconciliation and Christian love. . . . They do not further any proselytization in the pejorative sense of the word because at these discussions it is not teacher and pupil that face each other, but rather one as well as the other declare themselves pupils of Him who in the gospel is called the *Unus Magister,* the one teacher.[48]

At the 1946 annual conference of all the German bishops at Fulda, Archbishop Jäger of Paderborn was chosen to take responsibility for all Una Sancta work in Germany and was encouraged to set up a center for such work. He received plans for Una Sancta conferences at Seeshaupt and formed what amounted to his own high-level Una Sancta circle; he then in turn kept the German bishops and the Holy Father informed of the development of Una Sancta matters. The Movement, therefore, existed with the knowledge and approval of the German bishops and apparently the Pope;

---

[47]Walther von Loewenich, *Der moderne Katholizismus* (Witten, 1956), 129.
[48]Max Pribilla, "Zum Gespräch zwischen den Konfessionen," *Stimmen der Zeit,* LXXI (1941), 213.

however, difficulties with the Holy Office in Rome were to develop later.

Max Pribilla, already active in ecumenical affairs in the 1920's and 1930's, continued to make his influence and leadership felt in the 1940's, especially as the editor of the influential *Stimmen der Zeit;* in 1948 he even wrote a pamphlet describing the Una Sancta Movement.[49] Pribilla encouraged the timid by showing how pioneers are needed to break the paths and put up bridges; the work already done must be continued in patience, and one must not become discouraged through reverses, hostilities, misinterpretations or personal inadequacies. "If the Christians cannot eliminate the division in faith itself, they nevertheless have the possibility, and therefore the duty, to lessen the consequences of this great evil. Therein lies the encompassing and very promising task of the Una Sancta Movement."[50]

When on three successive evenings, from April 27 to 29, 1947, the Catholic theologian Karl Adam delivered three sermons in the Protestant St. Mark's Church of Stuttgart, his theme was "Una Sancta from the Catholic Viewpoint." The same sermons, thereafter repeated in Karlsruhe, were published in German[51] and later in English.[52] The main life-long theme of Adam's theological writing, Christ as the center of the Christian faith, can be seen by a glance at the titles of some of his books: *Son of God, Christ Our Brother, The Christ of Faith.* It was the first two of these books which J. Lortzing referred to as symptomatic of a tendency in contemporary Catholic theology which was drawing the Catholic Church closer to Protestantism: "Christocentrism."[53] This tendency was reinforced by Pius XII's encyclical on the

[49]Max Pribilla, *Die Una Sancta-Bewegung* (Meitingen, 1948).
[50]*Ibid.,* 8.
[51]Karl Adam, *Una Sancta in katholischer Sicht* (Düsseldorf, 1947).
[52]Karl Adam, *One and Holy* (New York, 1951).
[53]J. Lortzing, "Wir wandern uns entgegen!" *Schönere Zukunft,* IX (1934), 518.

Mystical Body and by both the liturgical and Bible movements, which pointed to Christ in "*Wort und Sakrament*." It was only as a logical outgrowth of his theology that Karl Adam's sympathy with the aims of the Una Sancta Movement developed.

The first of Adam's three sermons concerned the roots of the Reformation, the second Luther's leaving the Church and the possibility of reunion, the third the methods of achieving reunion. For the first two Adam named as his sources Karl Bihlmeyer's church history and "Josef Lortz's brilliant and psychologically penetrating *Reformation in Deutschland*." Following Lortz, Adam painted the many shadows as well as the lights in the pre-Reformation Church. He did not hesitate to discuss frankly the corruption, superstition, immorality, the great need of reform that existed in the clergy high and low and in the laity at the beginning of the sixteenth century. Still finding his support in Lortz, Adam described Luther not in the old manner as an evil runaway monk or a psychotic, but rather as a man with marvelous gifts of heart and mind, a warm penetration of the essence of Christianity, a passionate defiance of all unholiness, and a soul-shattering power of speech. Had he brought these gifts to the reform of the Church and remained a faithful member, then "he would be forever our great Reformer, our true man of God, our teacher and leader, comparable to Thomas Aquinas and Francis of Assisi. He would have been the greatest saint of our people, the refounder of the Church in Germany, a second Boniface."[54]

In discussing the possibilities of whole communities entering into a reunion with Rome, Adam offered suggestions that were reminiscent of the plans recommended by J. Lortzing, Karl Thieme and Friedrich Heiler in the early 1930's. Adam pointed out that Rome might allow a married clergy

[54]Adam, *One and Holy*, 26.

at least for those new communities, just as she did for the Uniate Orthodox; since Rome in the past permitted other reunited groups to keep their traditional liturgical language, she could certainly do it again. Part of this was carried out in the 1950's, at least on an individual basis, when the former Protestant Pastor Goethe from the Rhineland was ordained a Catholic priest and allowed to remain in the married state. By 1957 two other Protestant converts enjoyed the same privilege and another five were preparing for ordination.[55] To Adam a reunion of the Church would not merely undo the harm of the split but would mean "the building up of a new, more embracing, richer unity than was there in the first place, a unity which will really have taken into itself new human values. It will be an *advance* upon the situation that preceded the schism. . . . If reunion comes it will come at a *maximum* level, not a minimum, in abundance, not in poverty."[56] In a reunion the Protestant groups would bring with them the valuable services their theology has rendered in the fields of religious history, religious psychology, history of dogma, and Scripture studies; they would bring a real interest in and deep familiarity with the Bible, and the evangelical form of church music, the chorale.

But because, says Adam, union could only come under the Holy Father, and because churches like other collective entities obey not only religious laws but also sociological laws, which lead every corporate body to maintain its own existence as long as possible, there can be no expectation of corporate union in the near future. Nevertheless, every Christian must do everything possible to prepare for a unity in love which will lead to a unity in faith.

---

[55]Eva-Maria Jung, "L 'attività dell' *'Una Sancta.'*" *Communita,* XI (1957), 46. Cf. Rudolf Goethe et al., *We Are Now Catholics* (Westminster, 1959).

[56]Adam, *One and Holy,* 122.

THE UNA SANCTA AND PROTESTANTS

The first World War had broken the close alliance between the Protestant Churches in Germany and the German "Lands"; the structure of the Churches was almost completely shattered by the pressure of the Nazis and the resistance of the *Bekennende Kirche.* At the same time the influence of the concepts of the Church's importance, of the teaching office of the Church, and of the bishop began to make themselves felt. Consequently the Protestant Church of Germany in 1945 had to work mightly to lift itself out of its own tangled disorder, to say nothing of the physical disorder of Germany. This, of course, engaged much of the energy of the Protestant Church leaders. Nevertheless a number of them did express themselves on ecumenical and Una Sancta work.

The Protestant Landesbischof Dr. Lilje of Hanover declared in 1949 that the Protestant and Catholic Churches had been cooperating very closely ever since the collapse of Germany in 1945 to overcome the postwar chaos. He added that never since the Reformation had the willingness of the two Churches to cooperate been so manifest as then. Hans Asmussen, a leader of the *Bekennende Kirche* in the resistance against the Nazis and after the war the President of the Chancery of the Evangelical Church in Germany became one of the chief interlocutors in the Una Sancta discussions, both through his writings and his appearances on the speakers' platform.[57] The ecumenical-minded Otto Dibelius, who already in the 1920's said that this was to be the "century of the Church," was the Protestant bishop in Berlin, where one of the oldest and most active groups of the Una Sancta circles existed; late in the 1950's he, in conjunction with Cardinal Döpfner, set up an official committee to regulate Una Sancta affairs. The belligerently anti-Catholic *Evangelischer Bund* began to lose some of its force by the late 1930's and by the end of

[57]Grüber, *Im Zeichen,* 209, 211.

the war had undergone quite a metamorphosis. The *Bund's* president for Hamburg, Pastor Staack, declared his genuine joy over the relaxation of tension between the two Churches.

Another Protestant leader who became deeply involved in Una Sancta affairs was Professor Wilhelm Stählin, who was made bishop of the Evangelical Lutheran Church in Oldenburg in 1945. Already in the 1920's he had been one of the leaders of the Protestant liturgical movement and one of the founders of the Berneuchner Circle; this concern for the liturgy naturally brought him into close contact with the Catholic Church on many levels. It was likewise this association with the liturgical movement and its parallels with many Catholic concepts that brought him to deliver a sermon on July 5, 1946, in Oldenburg on "Catholicizing Tendencies in the Evangelical Church"; the sermon was later published in the "Peter and Paul Series" as "a contribution to the discussion between the confessions." Bishop Stählin insisted in this sermon that Protestantism did not mean a "subtraction" of things found in the Catholic Church from the body of Christian truths and practices; the Reformation was specifically a protest against the late medieval Church that in many aspects contradicted the *fullness* of the gospel. Consequently, since truth and goodness are one, many things in a vital Protestantism and a vital Catholic Church are bound to be similar. As for the specifically liturgical matters, Bishop Stählin pointed out that Luther himself had been much closer to the Catholic Church in his liturgical ideas and practices than was the Lutheran Church before the first World War; what was being added through the liturgical movement was a regaining of Lutheranism, of true Catholicism.[58]

The Protestant theologian von Loewenich, commenting in 1948 on the relations between Catholicism and Protestantism,

---

[58]Wilheim Stählin, *Katholisierende Neigungen in der evangelischen Kirche* (Stuttgart, 1947).

wrote that the time of polemic is finally past; the last twelve years had shown that Catholicism and Protestantism stood in a common front against the anti-Christian spirit of the times. Protestants can no longer say that Bismarck was right and the Catholic Church wrong in the *Kulturkampf*, nor can they continue to accuse the Catholic Church of internationalism: they have learned in the past generation to appreciate that there is one Church and that it is not bound by narrow national boundaries and the hate-psychoses of nationalism that too often go with them in our own time: rather, the Church is ecumenical and catholic, and by thus recognizing her, people best serve their fatherlands.[59]

After compiling a bookful of quotations from Protestant and Catholic leaders and thinkers, the Protestant Ulrich Valeske came to the conclusion that "the hour is here" for the two Churches to cooperate energetically in preparing the way for unity.[60]

Anyone who was *au fait* of religious activities in postwar Germany was at least aware of the existence of the Una Sancta Movement, although not all were enthusiastic supporters. The reaction of the clergy in the Stuttgart area was typical: the majority were uninterested or even antagonistic in their attitude. Laros spoke of Protestant critics of the Una Sancta who referred to it as a "sapping operation," or who were skeptically awaiting a disavowal "as *Mortalium Animos* was to the ecumenical efforts twenty years ago"; catholic critics feared a "heretical infection," the fostering of mixed marriages, joint schools, and a blurring of doctrines.[61] Thomas Sartory, O.S.B., the successor to Laros, while admitting that criticism, skepticism, and even opposition to

---

[59]Walther von Loewenich, "Der Katholizismus und Wir," *Zeitwende*, XX (1948), 718, 720.

[60]Valeske, *Stunde*.

[61]Matthias Laros, "Die 'Una-Sancta'-Bewegung," *Deutsche Rundschau*, LXXI (1948), 179.

Una Sancta work equals the friendship and support shown it, maintained that if one examined the arguments of the opponents of the Una Sancta Movement, "one would sense a misunderstanding or even often a complete ignorance of the actual motives of this work."[62] Obviously no new movement finds unanimous support. But the Una Sancta Movement found not only many followers in the masses, but also had its supporters in high places.

High-Level Support

The most striking example of support for the Una Sancta type of work comes from the highest theological and hierarchical levels in Germany. Since 1946 over a dozen of the leading Protestant and Catholic theologians have been meeting twice annually under the leadership of the Protestant Bishop Wilhelm Stählin of Oldenburg and the Catholic Archbishop Lorenz Jäger of Paderborn. The Catholic Dompropst of Paderborn, Paul Simon, who had been the leader of the Catholic-Protestant theologians' meeting in Berlin in 1934, was also the leading spirit in this post-war theologians' conference, and although he died shortly after the initial meeting, the work has continued to flourish. Archbishop Jäger, who is always present at the meetings, serves as an official link between the Protestant theologians and the Catholic bishops, since he was appointed by the German bishops to be responsible for Una Sancta work; and in addition he has kept Rome informed of the inter-confessional developments, particularly since 1948. Bishop Stählin, who had been theology professor for many years at the University at Münster, where there is also a Catholic theology faculty, served on his side as the official connection with Protestant church leaders.

Once each year the Catholics invited the Protestants to Paderborn for a conference; for the second semi-annual con-

[62]Thomas Sartory, "Gespräch um die Una Sancta," *Benedictinische Monatsschrift,* XXIX (1953), 406.

ference the Protestants were the hosts. The conferences always began on a Monday and ran to Friday; the participants lived, ate and worked together. Usually about four lectures were delivered on previously selected themes, and much time was given over to open, often very energetic, discussion. The personnel of the conferences has remained almost constant, about twelve theologians and one or two non-theologians from each side; no one new may be invited without the approval of both sides.[63] The subjects of the conferences have been of the most profound and often controversial sort, such as death, immortality, faith and works, and Mary. When differences of opinion arise the spirit is not always Catholic versus Protestant; it sometimes cuts across both sides. The meetings have taken place regularly without fail, even during the troubled years between 1948 and 1951, although since about 1957 they have been cut down to one a year at the request of the Protestant members, who felt themselves pressed with so much other demanding work. When asked in 1959 what results he thought he could see in the thirteen years of meeting, Bishop Stählin said that the opinion and understanding both sides have of each other have vastly improved; today's situation would have been considered absolutely impossible a few years ago.[64]

---

[63]Among the Protestants who took part in the meetings were Wilhelm Stählin, Hans Asmussen, Otto Dibelius, Gerhard Krueger, Edmund Schlink, Peter Brunner, Hans von Campenhausen, Ernst Kinder, Heinz Wendland, Georg Friedrich, Wilfried Joest, Wilhelm Panenberg, Kristen Skydsgaard, and Wilhelm Mumm; among the Catholics, Lorenz Jäger, Robert Grosche, Josef Lortz, Hermann Volk, Karl Rahner, Josef Pascher, Gottlieb Söhngen, Michael Schmaus, Friedrich Buuch, Otto Kuss, Josef Höfer, Victor Warnach and Josef Pieper.

[64]Interview with Wilhelm Stählin, November 10, 1959.

Chapter Ten

The Crisis Years

BY the first part of 1948 the future of Catholic-Protestant understanding looked very promising. In addition to the growing cooperation in Germany, the ecumenical movement in most of Christendom was rapidly gathering momentum again after the war; the ecumenical conference which was to unite the Faith and Order Movement and the Life and Work Movement was scheduled for the summer of 1948 at Amsterdam. But the years 1948 to 1951 brought a long series of crises for the Una Sancta Movement: a *Monitum*, or warning concerning inter-confessional religious meetings was published by the Vatican in 1948; Catholics were forbidden to attend the Amsterdam Ecumenical Conference; a further *Instructio* on inter-confessional meetings was issued by Rome in 1949; in 1949 Dr. Laros resigned from the Catholic leadership of the Una Sancta Movement; the encyclical *Humani generis* condemning "false irenicism" came out in 1950; and finally the Assumption of Mary was defined as dogma by the pope in 1950. Each of these events, with varying impact, affected the Una Sancta Movement and left it considerably changed.

PAPAL ATTITUDE TOWARD UNA SANCTA MOVEMENT

The attitude of the papacy toward ecumenical activity and Catholic participation in it had undergone a slow evolution from the time of the first World War. On the whole it grew gradually more favorable, but in outward appearances it was not an even, constant development. At times the papacy was not as favorably inclined as many thought, whereas at other times observers took a too pessimistic view of papal attitudes.

The attitude of Pius XI toward ecumenical activity at the beginning of his pontificate seemed to be quite encouraging, at least as far as the Malines Conversations were concerned. Though they had already started before he ascended the papal throne, he followed them with interest and gave them his blessing. However, when the large ecumenical organizations were being formed and invited him to participate in the initial meetings, he politely refused. It was one thing for six or ten theologians of known probity to carry on interconfessional discussions, and entirely another for hundreds of delegates of often unknown background to try to do the same thing.

After the first conference at Stockholm and Lausanne, the papal attitude grew even less sympathetic; its expression was *Mortalium animos.* Pius XI saw in the undertones and assumptions of the new organizations a new form of the "modernism" Rome had so recently condemned. Although this danger of "modernism" with its characteristic religious indifferentism was avoided in the ensuing history of the ecumenical movement, the Holy See, not having the advantage of hindsight, chose a more cautious course. But since conditions within the ecumenical movement changed considerably, the encyclical *Mortalium animos* eventually was no longer considered representative of the attitude of the Holy See. Father George Tavard remarked that its interest "is now mainly historical."[1] Robert McAfee Brown wrote: "A Protestant may offer the less cautious opinion that the document is dated, and remind Protestants that it is irrelevant to offer it as evidence that Rome has no interest in Protestant ecumenism."[2] Before the end of his pontificate Pius XI was making statements which reflected his growing estimation of the ecumenical movement:

[1]George Tavard, *The Catholic Approach to Protestantism* (New York, 1955), 107.

[2]Robert McAfee Brown and Gustave Weigel, *An American Dialogue* (New York, 1960), 97.

> For a reunion it is above all necessary to know and to love one another. To know one another, because if the efforts of reunion have failed so many times, this is in large measure due to mutual ignorance. If there are prejudices on both sides, these prejudices must fall. Incredible are the errors and equivocations which persist and are handed down among the separated brethren against the Catholic Church; on the other hand, Catholics also have sometimes failed in justly evaluating the truth or, on account of insufficient knowledge, in showing a fraternal spirit. Do we know all that is valuable, good, and Christian in the fragments of ancient Catholic truth? Detached fragments of a gold-bearing rock also contain precious ore.[3]

Pius XI felt that "from the full and perfect unity of all Christians the Mystical Body of Christ and all its members, one by one, are bound to obtain a great increment."[4]

At the very beginning of his pontificate Pius XII indicated a very friendly attitude toward non-Catholic Christians. He said:

> Our thought also goes to all who are outside the fold of the Catholic Church. We trust that they also will gladly know that in this solemn moment we beseech the all-bounteous and almighty God to grant them His divine assistance. . . . We truly entertain the firm hope that you, our sons, and you, our brothers, will not bring to nought our most burning wish to ensure peace.[5]

Every Christmas Pius XII expressed his plan for world peace, a plan whose basic principles had been outlined in conjunction with the Anglican Archbishop Temple through Temple's friend Cardinal Hinsley.[6] The Pope addressed himself to "all who are united to us through the bonds of faith" (Christmas, 1939) and "all who, without belonging to the visible body of the Catholic Church, are near to us through

---

[3]Quoted in *ibid.*
[4]Quoted in *ibid.*, 98.
[5]Quoted in Tavard, *Catholic Approach*, 108.
[6]J. P. Michael, *Christen suchen eine Kirche*, (Freiburg, 1958), 48.

faith in God and Jesus Christ" (Christmas, 1941).[7] Moreover, on July 12, 1939, Archbishop Temple received a letter from the Apostolic Delegate in Great Britain written in the name of the Cardinal Secretary of State: "There is no obstacle in the way of consultation with the Bishops and the Apostolic Delegate. Likewise there is nothing in the way of exchange of confidential information with Catholic theologians, who will, naturally, make reply in their own name."[8] Unfortunately Archbishop Temple died in 1944.

Thus there was great optimism concerning the papal attitude toward ecumenical activity; it was hoped by many, for example, that Rome would participate in the founding conference of the World Council of Churches in August, 1948, at Amsterdam. This hope was disappointed.

"MONITUM" FROM HOLY OFFICE

On June 5, 1948, the Holy Office in Rome, which has charge of all matters concerning doctrine, issued a *Monitum,* beginning with the words *Cum compertum,* dealing with the meeting of Catholics and non-Catholics to discuss matters of faith.[9] Actually the *Monitum* stated no new policy but rather called attention to the existing canons which covered the matter. It stated that it had come to the knowledge of the Holy Office that Catholics were taking part in inter-confessional meetings, an action forbidden by canon 1325, section 3, except by special permission; *a fortiori* Catholics were not allowed to organize and publicize such meetings. This proscription was also applied to "ecumenical" meetings. It had also been learned that groups had been celebrating common religious services, which, it was pointed out, was forbidden by canons 1278 and 731, section 2.

---

[7]Quoted in Tavard, *Catholic Approach,* 109.
[8]Quoted in *ibid.,* 112.
[9]*Acta apostolica sedis* 40 (1948), 257. See appendix for text.

Canon 1325, section 3, forbids Catholics to participate in public disputations or discussions with non-Catholics without first obtaining the approval of the Holy See or, in urgent cases, of the Bishop Ordinary. Canon 1258 forbids Catholics from ever taking an active part in non-Catholic religious services although a passive presence at funerals, weddings, and other solemnities could be tolerated if there is no danger of scandal. Canon 731, section 2, prohibits the administering of the sacraments to heretics and schismatics.[10]

The immediate reaction of most Protestants was, as the Catholic theologian Michael Schmaus pointed out, "extremely negative."[11] The Protestant theologian von Loewenich wrote that the *Monitum* appeared to many to be a death sentence for the Una Sancta Movement; Edgar Grüber noted that the *Monitum* with its "commentary-less hardness and sternness" was extremely disillusioning not only in Una Sancta Circles but also in the Protestant Church itself.[12] Landesbischof Wurm, then the chairman of the Council of the Evangelical Church in Germany (EKD), took a strong position on the *Monitum* at the huge Protestant "*Kirchentag*" which was held at Eisenach in June of 1948. "The cause of Christ has not been served by the action. How terrible must be the centuries-long pressure of tradition when even so far-seeing and magnanimous a man as the present occupant of the Papal See ordered or sanctioned such a trenchant measure. . . ."[13]

Within the Catholic Church the *Monitum* caused a "considerable sensation" and, in the affected circles, "depending on their standpoint, applause, wonderment, disarmament, gloating or confusion. Many went so far as to see in the

---

[10]See appendix for text.

[11]Michael Schmaus, *Der Vatikan und die ökumenische Bewegung* (Meitingen, 1950), 2. This is a four-page pamphlet.

[12]Edgar Grüber, "Im Zeichen des 'Schoepferischen Friedens," *Zeitwende,* XX (1949), 211.

[13]*Ibid.,* 211-212.

Monitum a complete rejection of all efforts toward Christian unity and inter-confessional discussions; the Catholic Church withdraws itself thereby back into the fortress and turns to all non-believers a cold shoulder."[14] Friedrich Heiler corroborated this statement; the reaction of Catholics he observed ran the whole scale from the bitter remark of a pioneer of the Una Sancta, "*Difficile est satiram non scribere*" and the painful cry of a Catholic newspaper, "A frost fell on a spring night," to the calming declaration of a religious, "The decree has nothing to do with us."[15]

CLARIFICATIONS AND QUALIFICATIONS

After the first shock and confusion, a number of clarifying and moderating commentaries began to appear from various sources, including authoritative persons in Rome. It was pointed out that the *Monitum* was not an infallible dogmatic decision, but rather only a disciplinary action growing out of the time as the Roman authorities saw them. Consequently Catholics had the right to maintain a questioning attitude or even critical opinion and submit to the papal authorities contrary arguments or further information which would perhaps supply a more complete picture. At the same time it was added that the highest ecclesiastical authorities did not issue any lightly made decisions or warnings. The German leaders had apparently failed to inform Rome adequately of Una Sancta activities, and at the same time it was a notorious fact that on many occasions the prescriptions on inter-confessional disputations and on active participation in non-Catholic religious services were not sufficiently well observed.[16] The *Salzburger Klerusblatt* quoted a Vatican source

[14]Max Pribilla, "Rom und die ökumenische Bewegung," *Stimmen der Zeit*, CXLVI (1950), 37.

[15]Friedrich Heiler, "Die Krise der Una-Sancta-Bewegung," *Oekumenische Einheit*, I (1948), 117-118.

[16]Laros, *II. Rundbrief*, 3.

as saying that there was a conference at which, in a Catholic Church, a Catholic Mass, a Protestant service and an Orthodox Liturgy were celebrated on successive days for the religiously mixed participants, and another case where the Catholic Mass, Protestant Liturgy and Orthodox liturgy were celebrated simultaneously at three different altars in a Catholic Church. Although these were admittedly extreme cases, it was indicated that participation in some form or other of joint religious service or prayer was not infrequent.[17] Archbishop Jäger himself substantiated these statements in a letter to Dr. Laros on June 28, 1948.

"It cannot be denied that at many of the Una Sancta conferences called by untrained laymen uncautious and unwise acts have been committed, and that through the accompanying discussions considerable confusion was spread among some participants; the notion was aroused that the two confessions were in fundamentals really the same and therefore in the end it did not matter which confession one belonged to. Likewise various *'Communicatio in sacris'* have taken place. These things have become known in Rome and the Holy Office had to act upon such evidence."[18]

Cardinal Ottaviani of the Holy Office remarked to journalists that the Vatican condemned particularly the common religious services held by non-Catholics and Catholics in Germany, Switzerland and the United States.[19] A speaker on the Vatican radio pointed the *Monitum* even more directly toward the Una Sancta Movement when he declared that the admonition "was obviously directed in a particular manner toward German Catholics."[20] "We wished particularly to point out the wild growth which has become visible on the edges of the Una Sancta Movement and which has mean-

---

[17]B.A., "Christliche Kultur," 100.
[18]Laros, *II. Rundbrief*, 5.
[19]*Oekumenischer Pressedienst* (Geneva), June 18/25, 1948.
[20]*Ibid.*

while worked its way into the center."[21] The radio speaker went on expressly to find fault with those Catholics active in the Una Sancta Movement who overstressed and idealized the personality of Martin Luther and who maintained that the non-Catholic Churches were in a position to contribute "something valuable and important to life which the Roman Church lacks or has lost."[22] Although the *Salzburger Klerusblatt's* comment on this attitude was, "We need not bother saying that this position is erroneous,"[23] Karl Rahner, S.J., one of the foremost Catholic theologians in German-speaking lands, treated the problem somewhat differently. He said that although it was true that the Catholic Church possessed the entire truth in the sense of the metaphysical essence of the truth which of course was unchangeable and indivisible, it can be questioned whether the Catholic Church also apprehends and lives this unchangeable and indivisible truth in the most profound manner, or whether it is formulated in the clearest possible manner; in this question of making the faith really effective in the everyday life of individual Christians and in history, Catholics can always learn from Protestants, as can Protestants from Catholics.[24]

It also became clear that the *Monitum* was by no means an absolute prohibition of meetings between Protestants and Catholics, as apparently had been thought by some. A consultor of the Holy Office in a publication of the Gregorian University in Rome commented that "confessional meetings which are devoted to scholarly, social, economic and other questions are in no way affected, but only those which concern questions of faith."[25] Nor were religious meetings completely forbidden. The same consultor of the Holy Office remarked that "it must be further recognized that it is not

---

[21] *Ibid.*
[22] *Ibid.*
[23] B.A., "Christliche Kultur," 100.
[24] Schmaus, *Der Vatikan,* 3.
[25] *Oekumenischer Pressedienst* (Geneva), July 30, 1948.

the fact of inter-confessional cooperation toward the discussion of questions of faith as such that is condemned, but rather simply the participation in such conferences without the previous agreement of the Holy See or in urgent cases of the responsible diocesan bishop.[26] The almost immediate action which backed up these words was the permission from Rome by telegraph allowing the large international Una Sancta meeting on Starnbergersee July, 1948.[27] Moreover, even this permission was not necessary for non-public, private religious discussions. This point was made quite clear by the radio commentator when he said, "Religious discussions in small private circles in which the differences between the denominations is clearly explained are not affected by the *Monitum*. This indeed is also what happens in the instruction of those persons who are preparing for conversion."[28]

The June 5 *Monitum* was not only not a new dogmatic statement; it was not even a new statement of law. It merely called attention to already existing canons, most particularly canon 1325, section 3, forbidding Catholics to participate in public religious discussions without previous consent. According to the pertinent footnotes of the *Codex Juris Canonici*, canon 1325, section 3, stemmed from the decisions of the Roman authorities in March 9, 1625, and December 18, 1862, man who directed the codification of the *CJC*, Cardinal Gasparri, also began a source book on the 1917 Code, *Codicis Juris Canonici Fontes*. The decree of 1625 specifically declared that public disputations with non-Catholics were forbidden because often either through the garrulousness or arrogance of the speaker or through the acclamation of the

[26] *Ibid.*
[27] See chapter IX.
[28] *Oekumenischer Pressedienst* (Geneva), June 18/25, 1948.

and must be explained in the light of those decisions.[29] The

[29] Pietro Gasparri, *Codex Juris Canonici* (Typis Polyglottis Vaticanis, 1948), footnote to Canon 1325 # 3.

crowd the Catholic truth was suppressed.[30] The 1625 decision stated that discussions and public disputations with heretics could in certain circumstances be allowed, but that experience has shown that for the most part bad results rather than good can be expected from them.[31] In 1662 the decision declared that the Holy See, having been taught through long experience, must forbid public conferences and disputations with non-Catholics so long as the desired assurances are not forthcoming; the previous approval of Rome, therefore, must always be obtained.[32]

AFTERMATH OF THE "MONITUM"

Three months after the *Monitum*, on September 5, Pope Pius XII, speaking over the Vatican radio to the "*Katholikentag*" at Mainz, Germany, said of the efforts toward Christian unity: "We know how intense is the yearning on the part of many of your nation, Catholic and non-Catholic, toward unity in faith. Who could feel more vitally this yearning than the representative of Christ himself?"[33] Archbishop Jäger re-emphasized the pope's appreciation of the Una Sancta. When addressing the German nation over the Vatican radio, Archbishop Jäger declared: "Nor may I leave unmentioned the fatherly love which the Holy Father has for the fellow Christians who are separated from the Church and his watchful interest for all questions of the Una Sancta in our Fatherland. He knows from his residence of many years in Germany the manifold opposing difficulties. He knows better than any other that the reunion of Christendom is not made by men, but only can be given by God in grace. We men can and must pray for this grace: we must above all do everything possible to remove the hindrances which stand

[30]See appendix for full text.
[31]See appendix for full text.
[32]See appendix for full text.
[33]*Acta apostolica sedis* 40 (1948), 419.

in the way of God's grace. That is the dearest wish of the Holy Father."[34]

Many Protestant writers, however, did not see the address of Pius XII as an attempt at conciliation but rather as a reiteration, though without harshness nevertheless with firmness, of the exclusive claims of Rome.[35] Von Loewenich[36] and especially Heiler spoke of many Christians being disillusioned in Pius XII, who had given promise of fulfilling the alleged prophecy of Malachias about the coming of a *"Pastor Angelicus"* and realizing somewhat the ideal of the *"Papa Angelico"* which many pious Catholics of medieval and modern times had envisioned; to the latter belonged the work of restoring the unity of Christendom. The loving turning toward non-Catholic Christians by Pius XII in his inaugural encyclical, his announcement of his election to the Orthodox Patriarch of Constantinople and his letter of congratulations to the new Orthodox Patriarch of Alexandria seemed to indicate to Heiler and others that Pius XII would "overcome the exclusiveness of his predecessors."[37] But Heiler though the encyclical *Mystici Corporis* and the *Monitum*

---

[34]Laros, 11. *Rundbrief*, 2.

[35]*Acta apostolica sedis* 40 (1948), 419. The text of the pertinent part is as follows: "We know how intense the yearning is on the part of many of your nation, Catholic and non-Catholic, toward unity in faith. Who could feel more vitally this yearning than the represensative of Christ himself? The Church embraces the brethren separated in faith with an 'unfeigned love' and with the ardor of prayer for their return to the mother from whom God knows how many of them without personal guilt remain distant. When the Church remains unyielding before everything that awakens even only the appearance of a compromise, of the placing of the Catholic faith on the same level with other confessions or of mixing with them, she does so because she knows that there has always been and will always be only one infallible, certain source of the whole truth and the fullness of grace, which has come to us through Christ, and that this institution according to the express wish of its divine founder is obviously the Church itself."

[36]Cf. von Loewenich, *Moderne Katholizismus*, 359.

[37]Heiler, "Die Krise," 214.

showed that Pius XII, all his personal conciliatoriness notwithstanding, was willing to continue the old totalitarian-exclusive line of the Roman papacy, "or—perhaps more correctly stated—that despite his personally broad view he was not able to loose himself from the inflexible demands of absolutism, of Roman 'Curialism.'"[38]

The Una Sancta Movement nevertheless apparently continued to have the wholehearted support of Archbishop Jäger and others of the German hierarchy. On July 28, 1948, Jäger wrote to Laros "that on the part of the German Episcopacy ways are being sought to be able to continue the Una Sancta work without disobeying the existing ecclesiastical prescriptions. . . . It is of great importance to me that the sincere efforts continue and that this work be carried on in the atmosphere of mutual trust."[39] Dr. Laros waited until six months after the *Monitum* before he wrote another *Una Sancta-Einigung Rundbrief*. When he did, it was quite optimistic. He gave a detailed explanation of the *Monitum* and commented that it was intended to prune away the "wild growths in single Una Sancta circles," but that in no way should the solid work done in the majority of the circles be hindered.[40] Along with a number of practical recommendations he suggested that by conducting Una Sancta work in such a way as to avoid the dangers warned against in the *Monitum*, there could be expected not only no hindrances but the greatest encouragement from ecclesiastical authorities on both sides.[41]

A significant exchange of statements took place between the annual *Katholikentag* and the *Evangelische Kirchentag*. The September, 1948, *Katholikentag* at Mainz, the same

---

[38]*Ibid.*
[39]Matthias Laros, "Das römische Monitum und die 'Una-Sancta,'" *Die neue Ordnung*, III (1949), 79.
[40]Laros, 11. *Rundbrief*, 5.
[41]*Ibid.*, 5-8.

which Pius XII addressed over the Vatican radio, sent a "Message to the Separated Brethren":

> The theological conversations between Catholics and non-Catholics have reached a stage where they no longer involve a polemic exchange or irenic attempts at bridgebuilding but rather are strictly concerned with the question of truth. The matter therefore is a concern of the pastoral office and the responsible persons appointed by the Churches. A Roman decree has just recently re-expressed this notion. We declare with satisfaction that this position in the matter was also acknowledged and affirmed by the leaders of the ecumenical movement.

The message then went on to describe the help rendered displaced Catholics by the Protestants and added, "For this we wish to thank you today with our whole heart and at the same time ask you not to discontinue this brotherly service."[42] At the August, 1949, *Evangelische Kirchentag* in Hanover, a "Message to the Catholic Christians" was formulated: "The participants of the 1949 German Evangelical *Kirchentag* in Hanover have heard the message of the German *Katholikentag* in Mainz 'to the separated brethren' and express their gratitude for it."[43]

After the first period of confusion passed, Protestant church authorities began to accept the stipulation of the *Monitum* that the Una Sancta work be carried on under the direction of the church authority.[44] During the Una Sancta discussion of 1948 held over the Frankfurt radio station on the Protestant "Penance and Prayer Day," the Protestants expressly emphasized that they felt that ecumenical work must under all circumstances be placed under ecclesiastical authority in order to avoid erroneous developments and to lead to a

---

[42]Heinrich Hermelink, *Die katholische Kirche unter den Pius-Päpsten des 20. Jahrhunderts* (Zurich, 1949), 35-36.

[43]Grüber, "Im Zeichen," 211.

[44]Matthias Laros, *Una Sancta-Einigung 14. Rundbrief*, August 1949, 1.

fruitful cooperation.[45] Not only did the theologians' discussions under the leadership of Stählin and Jäger not break off,[46] but in April of 1949 they were approved by the Berlin Synod of the EKD as official.[47] Many Protestant theologians pointed out that the *Monitum* was nothing new on the part of the Catholic Church. Writers like Heiler[48] and von Loewenich[49] nevertheless indicated their disappointment at the same time; Stammler, writing for Bishop Lilje's *Sonntagsblatt*, said it was a good thing that the Vatican has re-stated its position so clearly and eliminated those enthusiastic hopes which had cropped up in some Una Sancta circles. Stammler insisted, however, that even though an early reunion was not to be expected, the discussions were of value in eliminating misunderstandings and prejudices and should therefore continue.[50]

The core members of some of the Una Sancta circles apparently were not long disturbed by the *Monitum*;[51] nevertheless, most activity came to a halt for many months and revived as it did probably mainly because of the personal friendships that had grown up within the circles.[52] A discussion between Protestants and Catholics took place in January of 1949 on exactly this subject, "the taking up again of the ecumenical discussions between the confessions, which for several months after the papal *Monitum* have been discontinued."[53] Some circles, however, never recovered from the *Monitum* and the other difficulties that followed it: the Nuremberg circle which had contained 200 members before

---

45Laros, 11. *Rundbrief*, 4.
46Interview with Landesbischof Wilhelm Stählin, November 10, 1959.
47J. P. Michael, "Maria und die Protestanten," *Begegnung*, VI (1951), 60.
48Heiler, "Die Krise," 122 ff.
49Von Loewenich, *Moderne Katholizismus*, 356 ff.
50*Sonntagsblatt* (Hamburg), I, 31 (1948), 13.
51Interview with Pastor August Rehbach, October 15, 1959.
52Interview with Sister Gertrudis, November 9, 1959.
53Grueber, "Im Zeichen," 212-213.

the *Monitum* has since melted to between 30 and 50 members.[54]

The *Monitum* came when it did most probably because of the approaching Amsterdam Conference in August of 1948; in June it was still unknown whether Catholics would attend or not. Conservatism and caution still prevailed in the Vatican. To many it seemed like a reversal of Pius XII's earlier attitude. But it must be remembered that he had never before had the occasion to accept or refuse participation in an ecumenical conference; the last one had been in 1937, two years before he became pope. After he was more sure of the situation, he changed the policy somewhat; observers were sent to ecumenical meetings in 1952 (Lund) and 1957 (Oberlin), both during his pontificate.

As far as the Una Sancta Movement in Germany was concerned, the *Monitum* was not so much a reversal of a previous position as it was a tightening of a discipline based on, not false evidence, for there were abuses, but on incomplete evidence. That this was the case is borne out by the appearance of a much milder document after personal inspection of the situation in Germany by a cleric from the Vatican. Thus the issuance of the strict *Mortalium animos* by Pius XI and the subsequent moderation of its position were analogously repeated with the *Monitum* and its consequences.

"INSTRUCTIO" BY HOLY OFFICE

On March 1, 1950, the *Osservatore Romano* published a four thousand word *"Instructio"* by the Holy Office on the "Ecumenical Movement"; the *"Instructio,"* beginning with the words *"Ecclesia Catholica,"* was addressed to all diocesan bishops, and was signed by the secretary of the Holy

---

[54]Letter from Anton Kreiner of the Nuremberg Una Sancta Circle to Leonard Swidler, December 11, 1957.

Office, Cardinal Marchetti-Salvaggiani; it was dated December 20, 1949.[55]

The opening and closing paragraphs, as Max Pribilla pointed out, set the tone in which the individual parts of the instruction were to be interpreted.[56] The Holy Office wrote that although the Catholic Church had not taken part in the Ecumenical Conferences it nevertheless was and always would be vitally interested in efforts toward Christian unity and would continually offer prayers for their success. Reunion work was referred to as a "most significant work" which more and more must become one of the primary tasks of all pastoral work. It was stated that the faithful, priests and religious should be kept informed by pastoral letters and other means of developments in ecumenical matters so that they might foster success in them through prayer and sacrifice. Michael Schmaus pointed out that the language of the *Instructio* would have been other than it was had it been addressed to Germany alone, but since it was sent to all bishops and through them to all the faithful it had to take into consideration all the various circumstances and mentalities of the different peoples and so express itself as to create no misunderstandings; this should be kept in mind when reading the *Instructio*.[57]

In several places the *Instructio* was basically a recapitulation of previous statements from Rome. Care should be taken not to overstress the faults of Catholics and underplay the responsibility of the Reformers in the Reformation. Catholic doctrine must be clearly presented, including the teaching that unity will come only by a return to the Church of Rome: not that Protestants must reject everything in their religious tradition, rather they may keep what is good and they will find this completed and perfected in the Catholic Church;

[55]*Acta apostolica sedis* 42 (1950), 142-147.
[56]Pribilla, "Rom," 38.
[57]Schmaus, *Der Vatikan,* 4.

the impression however should not be given that the converts bring the Church something essential which she had been lacking until now. Also the faithful ought not to attend inter-confessional meetings unless they have first obtained permission; only those priests should be sent to such meetings who are well grounded in theology and are staunch in their faith, for the Holy See knows by much experience that the results to be expected from inter-confessional meetings are small and the danger of indifferentism is great. However, these restrictions do not apply to catechetical or convert instructions or to mixed meetings where no questions of faith or morals are discussed but which meet for the joint defense of the Christian religions against the enemies of God, or concern questions of the social order and like problems.

One section of the *Instructio* in effect anticipated part of the encyclical *Humani generis* which was published later in 1950. A "false irenicism" which overemphasized unifying doctrines in comparison to the divisive ones, thereby leading to indifferentism, was not to be embraced. The bishops were also to see that such statements as "the teachings of the encyclicals need not be taken too seriously because everything in them is not an object of faith," were avoided.[58]

But there were also some new aspects to the *Instructio*. The *Monitum* had called attention to the already existing canons concerning inter-confessional meetings, which canons reserved to the Holy See the power to grant permission to attend such meetings, except in urgent cases when the diocesan bishop might give the permission. With the *Instructio* a large share of the burden of making decisions in ecumenical matters was passed on to the bishops. As the efforts toward reunion were a primary concern of the Church, it was imperative that the bishops give this work their very special attention, not just by overseeing it but also by fostering and

[58]*Acta apostolica sedis* 42 (1950), 143.

directing it. For this reason every bishop should appoint a priest to be responsible for this work in his diocese and to keep the bishop informed on all developments.

In regard to inter-confessional meetings two new developments appeared in the *Instructio.* Catholics needed previous ecclesiastical permission for those inter-confessional meetings which consisted of "speeches and counter-speeches about questions on doctrines of faith and morals whereby each presents the teaching of his own faith as his own view;[59] Catholic and non-Catholic participants were spoken of as acting as equals, "*par cum pari agens,*"[60] a redeeming statement for the German Una Sancta Movement.[61] In addition the bishops were granted for three years the power to give permissions to attend those inter-confessional meetings described by the *Monitum* as requiring papal permission, and which were not inter-diocesan, national or international in scope; this was of particularly great assistance to the German dioceses with manifold Una Sancta activities. The bishops, however, were required to give an annual report to the Holy Office on the occurrence and results of these activities. The same prescriptions held for meetings between theologians alone, except that additional information for the annual report was required: what questions were discussed, who the participants were, and who read papers. This section apparently was intended specifically for Germany, for the *Instructio* spoke of the report being made by the bishop in whose diocese the theologians' meeting took place or "by the bishop who has been delegated to direct this entire work by the other bishops in a joint decision,"[62] an obvious reference to Archbishop Jäger's appointment by the German bishops and his semi-annual theologians' meetings under the joint leader-

---

[59]*Ibid.,* 145.
[60]*Ibid.*
[61]Interview with Sister Gertrudis.
[62]*Acta apostolica sedis* 42 (1950), 146.

ship of Landesbischof Stählin. Later on, in paragraph 7, the *Instructio* even recommended an arrangement similar to that of the German bishops'. It stated that although it was the duty of each bishop to carry out the ecumenical work in his own diocese, it may be found helpful, indeed necessary, for a number of bishops to set up joint organizations to conduct the work more effectively.

Although Catholics taking part in inter-confessional meetings still had to avoid all "*communicatio in Sacris,*" the *Instructio* said that it was not forbidden at the beginning and close of the activities to say in common the Our Father or some other prayer approved by the Catholic Church.

REACTION TO THE "INSTRUCTIO"

The reaction to the *Instructio,* like the *Monitum,* was extremely varied. On the Protestant side the church historian Heinrich Hermelink rebelled strongly against the notion of the Catholic hierarchy's official involvement in Una Sancta activities; he saw the *instructio* as an attempt to centralize the previously spontaneous discussions, "that is to subordinate them to the bishops and through them to the Holy Office (even the names of the Protestant speakers and participating theologians must be reported to Rome!)" and this meant "an essential changing of the whole character of these discussions."[63]

Landesbishof Wurm found the *Instructio* "a clear nuance friendlier" than the *Monitum;* whereas with the former Catholics had to listen to an admonishment, with the latter they were given encouragement. "This decree however does not indicate a change of attitude of the Roman Church toward the ecumenical movement."[64] The *Instructio* nevertheless

[63]Heinrich Hermelink, "Catholica und Una Sancta," *Theologische Literaturzeitung,* LXXV (1950), 534.

[64]"Unser Verhältnis zur römisch-katholischen Kirche heute," *Junge Kirche,* XI (1950), 194.

made it difficult for Protestants to participate in Una Sancta work, for they started out from different premises than those maintained by the Roman Church; Rome assumed reunion would have to come through Roman direction, whereas the Protestants believed all Churches needed to learn from each other and be corrected by a constant investigation of the Scriptures under the direction of the Holy Ghost.[65]

The *Sonntagsblatt* edited by Landesbischof Lilje took a mildly favorable, wait-and-see attitude. It noted that this was the first time the pope had allowed Catholic participation in inter-confessional meetings and common prayer, but before judging the new decree a step forward the writer would wait to see how it worked in practice. Bishop Dibelius, President of the Council of the Evangelical Church in Germany (EKD), told a press conference after a meeting of the Council that the Evangelical Church is "always ready for a discussion with the Catholic Church; it only regrets the fact that the Catholic Church does not participate in the ecumenical efforts."[66] The general secretary of the World Council of Churches, Visser 't Hooft, also answered the *Instructio* with cautious optimism. He said that the very fact that such a document could even be issued was a sign that the ecumenical movement was finally making its influence felt among Catholic laity and clergy; he thought this was the first time Catholics were allowed to pray in common with others. "This is a step forward."[67]

One of the most optimistic articles written on the *Instructio* appeared as a full page review in the *Westfalen Zeitung* with the banner headline *"Das 'Ja' des Heiligen Officiums,"* signed with the pseudonym *"Oekumenikus alienus."* The author thought that in the *Instructio* Pope Pius XII, himself the

---

[65]*Ibid.*

[66]"Vatikan und Oekumene," *Evangelische Welt,* IV (1950), 163-164.

[67]"Die neue Anweisung des Vatikans über das Verhältnis der katholischen Kirche zur ökumenischen Bewegung," *Junge Kirche,* XI (1950), 103.

head of the Holy Office, took a step closer to the separated brethren by making the bishops responsible not for isolated private ecumenical efforts but for the leadership of the whole Church in this task, and by requesting that the bishops set up long-range organizations and send out their best priests to this work not only to explain Catholic doctrine but also to learn "why the separated brethren hold to certain truths with earnestness and believe they must maintain themselves outside of the Church."[68]

The reaction on the Catholic side was also varied. Michael Schmaus, theology professor from the University of Munich, in an explanation of the *Instructio* for the *Süddeutsche Zeitung* (Munich) pointed out that the Holy Office, writing in the Roman tradition, was using a metaphysical style, whereas most Protestants were probably more used to the historical style; this was a cause of a good deal of misunderstanding on the part of the Protestant readers. Many thought the Catholic claim of possessing the fullness of truth the height of overweening pride, but the Church had in mind the unchangeable metaphysical essence of truth and not its historical incarnation and completion, as Professor Karl Rahner of Innsbruck had explained earlier. Schmaus ended his article, which was later published in pamphlet form by the Kyrios Publishing Company, with the statement that Protestants and Catholics need not despair just because of the difficulties in Una Sancta work, but "that there remains not much else to us except to strive toward unity simply because this is the mission of Christ."[69]

Some Catholic writers described the effect of the *Instructio* in more negative terms. The convert J. P. Michael, spoke of the *Instructio* as well as the *Monitum* as having a dampening effect on Una Sancta efforts, although its tone was an

---

[68]Oekumenicus alienus, "Das 'Ja' des Heiligen Officiums," *Westfalen Zeitung,* March 18, 1950.
[69]Schmaus, *Der Vatikan,* 4.

improvement.[70] Matthias Laros spoke of the *Instructio* working negatively still deeper than the *Monitum;* with so much power of initiative placed officially in the hands of the Catholic bishops, the Protestant Christians withdrew even further and in general waited to see what would be forthcoming from official sources and what the *Instructio* would accomplish. "Things become ever more still about the Una Sancta."[71]

It was doubtless because of the continual stream of information that poured into the Holy Office as a result of the *Instructio* and the necessarily concomitant elimination of abuses under episcopal supervision, that Cardinal Ottaviani, next to Pius XII in charge of the Holy Office, expressed himself so favorably toward the Una Sancta Movement near the end of the 1950's.

"Humani Generis" Condemns False Irenicism

A few short months after the *Instructio* was published, Pope Pius XII issued an encyclical, *Humani generis,* on August 12, 1950, which again threw consternation into the ranks of the Una Sancta Movement. The encyclical was directed against a number of prominent "errors of the times," and included a few paragraphs on the dangers of a false "irenicism," obviously aimed at certain ecumenical efforts.

> There appears also another danger which is so much the greater as it is covered up more with the appearance of virtue. Many who lament the division and going astray of souls let themselves be driven by an unwise zeal and burn in a long nourished yearning to do away with the walls by which good and upright men are divided from each other; they give themselves over to such "irenicism" that in the setting aside of the dividing questions they concern themselves not

---

[70]Michael, *Christen suchen,* 60-61.

[71]Matthias Laros, "Die Auswirkung des 'neuen Mariendogmas' auf die Begegung der Konfessionen," *Begegnung,* VI (1951), 305.

only with atheism, which they combat with united forces, but also with the removal of the controversial points in the teachings of faith. . . .

If these people had only the intention of adapting the Church's teaching and her method to modern conditions and demands by the introduction of some sort of innovation, there would hardly be any ground for concern; but in the imprudent overzealousness of their "irenicism" apparently some also consider as hindrances to brotherly understanding those things which rest on the laws and principles of Christ and those of the institutions founded by Him; when these fall then indeed all is united, but only in universal ruin.[72]

Friedrich Heiler referred to "irenicism" as a "hateful neologism" which should have been prevented by Christ's using of the term "*Eirenopoioi*," peacemakers, in the Sermon on the Mount, and concluded that the papal condemnation of this irenicism must have been discouraging to the pioneers of Christian unity[73]—he apparently spoke from his own experience. The reaction of other Protestant theologians and writers was similar.[74]

ASSUMPTION UNDERMINES UNA SANCTA MOVEMENT

But the encyclical *Humani generis* and the reaction to it in ecumenical circles were quickly lost in the crescendo of storm over the definition of the bodily assumption of the Blessed Virgin Mary into heaven. The *ex cathedra* definition was proclaimed on November 1, 1950, in the apostolic

---

[72]"Humani generis," *Herder-Korrespondenz*, V (1950), 26.

[73]Friedrich Heiler, "Das neue Mariendogma im Lichte der Geschichte und im Urteil der Oekumene," *Oekumenische Einheit*, II (1951), 41.

[74]Cf. Josef Loosen, "Gestörtes Una-Sancta Gespräch?" in *Das neue Dogma in Widerstreit* ed. by Otto Semmelroth (Würzburg, 1951), 13; and Werner Meyer, "Oekumenische Kreise Zürich I und II Brief der evangelischen Gesprächsteilnehmer an die katholischen Brüder, eine Zusammenfassung zweier interner Aussprachen darstellend," n.d., mimeographed six-page open letter; and Gerhard Kunze, "Rom-Wittenberg-Genf," *Monatschrift für Pastoraltheologie*, XL (1951), 80 ff.

constitution, *Munificentissimus Deus.* The long, gradually growing pressure exerted by theologians interested in Mariology to have the dogma defined had begun to reach its climax after the second World War; 1950, a Holy Year, seemed most apt for the proclamation.

Although in many Protestant Churches devotion to Mary in general is non-existent, the same cannot be said of the Lutheran Church. In its first centuries the Lutheran Church was not known for its anti-Marian attitude: Luther had a strong appreciation of devotion to Mary, and he saved the Lutheran Church from iconoclasm. Even today Lutherans celebrate their liturgy in ancient Marian churches. But in the past two hundred years there has been such a growing rejection of the veneration of Mary that in speaking of the growing importance of the veneration of Mary in Catholic life a German Protestant theologian could write, "All that is quite foreign to us, so that many of us can no longer see any basis for reaching an understanding with the Roman Catholics, and regard further discussions as futile, pointless and helpless."[75] Nevertheless there are many contemporary German Lutheran theologians who advocate a Marian devotion: von Loewenich wrote, "We wonder at and love the surrender and spiritual tenderness which had been expressed in the Marian cult and Marian art of earlier centuries."[76] Hans Asmussen said, "Without the virginity of Mary there is no salvation."[77] Such was the situation at the time of the proclamation of the Assumption dogma.

Already in 1948, Friedrich Heiler, whose leaning toward things Catholic was well known, rejected the doctrine of the Assumption and predicted that its definition would bring the Una Sancta Movement to a halt and deliver it a fatal

---

[75]Quoted in Ernst Kinder, "Protestant-Roman Catholic Encounter an Ecumenical Obligation," *The Ecumenical Review,* VII (1955), 338.

[76]Von Loewenich, *Moderne Katholizismus,* 275.

[77]Hans Asmussen, *Maria die Mutter Gottes* (Stuttgart, 1951), 5.

blow. He quoted from an Anglican writer, Victor Bennet, who declared that the Assumption dogma would be ruinous for the reunion movement and complained that the Roman authorities were so insensitive to the yearning for reconciliation that they were prepared to introduce a further doctrinal difference which would require still more centuries to overcome.[78] Also several months before the definition of the Assumption, Edmund Schlink and four other Protestant theology professors of the University of Heidelberg published their opinion of the "new" dogma; it was done "in the interests of the Una Sancta and was supposed to assist in preventing the dogmatization."[79] The dogma was thoroughly discussed and declared to be contrary to the Scripture and Apostolic tradition. The writers went on to say the dogma "would without doubt increase the already existing differences between the Roman and Protestant Churches and deepen the chasm between the faiths of the two Churches";[80] it would at the same time grant great encouragement to those circles in Protestantism which had distrusted any approach to Rome.

"There has arisen, in a manner of speaking, a united front of all non-Roman Churches against the new Marian dogma, and what is most noteworthy is that it includes those who believe in the bodily Assumption as well as those who don't."[81] The Eastern Church, for example, which holds the Assumption as an honored tradition, rejected the dogmatization, saying that it could be done only by an ecumenical council; the Anglican Church provided other examples of theologians who personally believed in the Assumption but objected to its definition. Besides the German bishops the

---

[78]Heiler, "Die Krise," 129-130.
[79]Von Loewenich, *Moderne Katholizismus*, 250.
[80]Edmund Schlink, *Evangelisches Gutachten zur Dogmatisierung der leiblichen Himmelfarht Mariens* (Munich, 1950), 19-20.
[81]Heiler, "Das neue Mariendogma," 42.

bishops of the Evangelical Church of the Augsburg Confession in Austria, the General Synod of the Reformed Churches of the Netherlands, and the Synod of the Waldensian Church of Italy all published statements against the new dogma. The Lutheran bishop of Vienna, Bishop May, in a pastoral letter said, "We Protestants hear it with shame and sadness. For in this time when all Christians should draw closer to each other, the pope tears the cleft between the Roman Catholic Church and the other Christian Churches even wider than it was before."[82] Anders Nygren, the President of the Lutheran World Federation and Bishop of Lund, Sweden, expressed a similar opinion; "While we on our side attempt to tear down walls and build bridges . . . the Roman Church has newly isolated itself by tearing down the bridges and setting up new walls. I am thinking here of the papal encyclical *Humani generis* and proclamation of the dogma of the Assumption of Mary."[83]

PROTESTANTS RECOIL FROM ASSUMPTION DOGMA

When the definition finally came, the reaction of the German Protestant Churches was far greater than the reaction to either the *Monitum* or *Instructio;* most of it of course was unfavorable. One of the most extreme positions taken was that in a main article of the Lutheran newspaper *Kirche und Mann* which was signed "—–er." The writer said that the new dogma threw out the gospel and that "for the sake of the salvation of our souls we can only say 'no' to the whole Marian teaching. And the continuing of the Una Sancta discussions is only possible with men who unanimously repeat this 'no' with us."[84] A continued Una Sancta discussion along these lines, of course, would have

---

[82]"Kommen wir ins Gespräch?" *Der Seelsorger,* XXI (1950), 169.
[83]Loosen, "Gestörtes Gespräch?" 13.
[84]"Una Sancta-Brücke gesprengt," *Kirche und Mann,* III (October, 1950), 7.

been no Una Sancta discussion, for the Catholics who met these requirements would no longer have been Catholics. It is also true that not all Protestants would have found the rejection of the entire Marian teaching acceptable.

Some German Protestants, while not taking such an extreme attitude, nevertheless maintained that the new dogma had wrecked all Una Sancta efforts. Walther Künneth spoke of the Marian dogma as a hail shower in a spring countryside and felt that "The talk of an 'Una Sancta' turned out to be an illusion";[85] a *rapprochement* between the two Churches had been made impossible. Even the bishops of the United Evangelical Lutheran Church of Germany (VELKD) took a very pessimistic view in their special declaration on the new Marian dogma. They said that this decision of the Roman Catholic Church was so fateful, and for them as members of the body of Christ so painful, that as bishops of the Evangelical-Lutheran Church they could not keep silent. In the recent fight against the forces of anti-God the Churches had grown closer together. The basis for this reconciliation was the assumption that "the testimony of the Apostles must be the foundation of the Church's teaching. Because of the now accomplished decision of the Roman Church this foundation has been forsaken. We view with deep concern the consequences which can result from this abandonment of the foundation of the Church."[86]

But a large number of Protestants, though rejecting the new dogma, expressed the desirability and recognized at least the possibility of continuing Una Sancta work. The Landesbischof of Württemberg, Martin Haug, gave a good example of this position when he declared that he had to protest against the new dogma, but he did not wish thereby to give up the working and living together with the Catholic

[85]Walther Künneth, "Das Gespräch um das Mariendogma," *Zeitwende*, XXIII (1951), 119.
[86]*Sonntagsblatt* (Hamburg), November 12, 1950, 19.

Church which had developed in the past few years.[87] Friedrich Heiler, regardless of how much he wrote against the Assumption or how much he maintained it would blight Catholic-Protestant relations, said that in one way the new dogma was an advance for the Una Sancta Movement; it cleared away all illusions, especially that of the possibility of reaching an agreement on specific Roman dogmas.[88] Heiler was again most probably speaking from experience since he almost certainly had been present at the 1934 Protestant-Catholic meeting near Berlin where such a possibility of agreement was entertained by certain members of the *Hochkirchliche Vereingung.* Heiler concluded one article by relating how while at Rome for the proclamation of the Assumption dogma he met an honorable elderly Italian priest who gave him "a profound word of consolation: '*Dobbiamo sperare contro la speranza.*' . . . Nothing in the history of the Church happens without the will of God—perhaps even this dogmatization which appears to hinder the union will hasten it."[89]

One of the most striking examples of how some Protestants placed more emphasis on the continuance of Una Sancta work than on the unacceptability of the Assumption dogma was an article in the basically Protestant *Deutsche Rundschau* which was practically a rebuttal of the anti-Assumption declaration of the Lutheran bishops. It quoted Landesbischof Meiser of Bavaria who, echoing the VELKD bishops' statement, declared that the Marian dogma had made Una Sancta work futile. The author—the unsigned article may well have been written by the editor, Rudolf Pechel—commented that such might be the opinion of one or other

---

[87]*Herder-Korrespondenz,* V (1951), 396.

[88]Heiler, "Das neue Mariendogma im Licht der Geschichte," *Neue Zürcher Zeitung,* January 14, 1951. Blatt 6.

[89]Heiler, "Das neue Mariendogma im Lichte der Geschichte und im Urteil der Oekumene," 43.

Protestant theologian, but there were many Protestant laymen who would not agree. He knew personally many laymen in Una Sancta circles who rejected such statements most sharply, for they wanted to keep what cooperation they had won during the war. The author concluded that it would be fatally dangerous and an irreparable misfortune if confessional peace should be endangered from the Protestant side against the express positive will of so many Protestant laymen.[90]

But probably the most important and sensitive point of contact between Catholics and Protestants was the semiannual meeting of the group of Protestant and Catholic theologians who came together under the leadership of Landesbischof Stählin and Archbishop Jäger. Although Stählin had in 1950 taken a position quite similar to that of the Lutheran bishops,[91] the theologians' meeting took place, contrary to expectations, early in 1951—with the approval of ecclesiastical authorities on both sides.

MANY CATHOLICS PAINED BY ASSUMPTION DOGMA

In the Catholic Church there was no talk of a rejection of the Assumption, but there were those who demurred on the opportuneness of its definition. Such a writer was Anton Fischer, a Catholic priest in southern Germany who had long been active in Una Sancta affairs. In 1948 he wrote an article for Heiler's *Oekumenische Einheit* in which he insisted that a Christo-centric approach in both Churches was a *sine qua non* for effective Una Sancta work—they should, of course, be Christocentric in any case. He bewailed the fact that even after the war peripheral things continued to be placed more in the center, particularly the development of Mariology and the tremendous popularity of

[90]"Vergebliche Una Sancta-Gespräche," *Deutsche Rundschau*, LXXVI (1950), 1062-1064.

[91]*Hessische Nachrichten*, November 1, 1950.

Fatima. He thought too that the definition of the Assumption at that time should be avoided since it would be detrimental to the Una Sancta.[92]

On the other extreme there was the man who actually wrote the dogmatization bull, the Italian Jesuit professor at the Gregorian in Rome, Giuseppe Filograssi. In an article in 1949 he described the dogmatization as "opportune and useful" and thought that an endangering of the reunion of the Churches movement was not to be seriously considered: the Protestants must in any case be reckoned a loss since "their dogmatic teaching is reduced to a shadow."[93]

However, most Catholic writers were more sympathetically concerned with the reactions of Protestants. Robert Grosche remarked that Catholics found it painful to see their Protestant brothers so deeply shaken by the dogmatization and assured the Protestants that Catholics also suffered under the tearing apart of the body of Christ.[94] It was Karl Rahner who recognized the extremely difficult position of the "new" dogma. He wrote that there were not a few Catholics who did not hear the announcement of this definition "with unmixed jubilations of the heart. They are believing (Lord, help my unbelief), but with the hard still faith of the suffering like those who are sensitive before so much light."[95]

But these very theologians, and others, hastened to add that the new dogma did not mean an end to Una Sancta work, for the immediate goal of the Una Sancta Movement is the carrying on of fraternal discussions by the two Churches to find out where they agree and where they disagree; the new Marian dogma is merely another point of disagreement, but not even really a new one, for the Assumption was an

---

[92]Anton Fischer, "Christozentrische Haltung als Weg zur Una Sancta," *Oekumenische Einheit,* I (1948), 39-47.

[93]Von Loewenich, *Moderne Katholizismus,* 244.

[94]Kunze, "Rom-Wittenberg-Genf," 86.

[95]Karl Rahner, "Das 'neue' Dogma," *Wort und Wahrheit,* V (1950), 819-820.

old Catholic tradition. Moreover, there apparently were illusions held by some Protestants and Catholics, though they were not deliberately fostered. The new dogma had cleared the air of these illusions; now the real work could begin. Throughout Christianity people were slowly realizing that the striven and yearned for unity could not be attained through by-passing truth and dogma; the different confessions dare not refrain from declaring openly what they in faith held to be true. "We Catholics can then only hope that the definition does not, contrary to its essence and contrary to our intention, become the occasion for non-Catholic Christians to falter in maintaining an ever-searching will and prayer for the unity of all Christians.[96]

In the months after the definition of the Assumption the Una Sancta Movement appeared to have reached its nadir: in some circles the Protestants withdrew completely; practically no public activities were conducted. But by the latter half or 1951 a number of the Una Sancta circles again took up where they had left off, and there were even quite a number of circles which reported great activity during 1951, such as Munich, Stuttgart, Berlin and Krefeld; of course the Marian dogma was often the center of attention. By October 29, 1951, a year almost to the day after the definition, Father Augustin Bea, S.J., could give a lecture in Rome in which he stated that it was no longer possible to maintain that the discussions between the confessions were being effectively disturbed by the definition.[97]

* *

The cooperation of Christians is in danger. The crisis reached its highpoint at the end of the Holy Year. From the Catholic side there came first of all the much misunderstood *Monitum* of June 1948. There followed the sobering of all "Una-Sancta-circles" through the unambiguous *Instructio* of the Holy Office

---

[96]Rahner, "Das 'neue' Dogma," 820.
[97]*Herder-Korrespondenz,* VI (1952), 156-157.

> from December 20, 1949, on the ecumenical responsibility of the bishops . . . . The papal encyclical *Humani generis* of August, 1950, with its turning against the "false irenicism" appeared to substantiate the concern that Rome is building up a "Catholic ghetto"; and the new Marian dogma found an evaluation in Protestant circles that threatened to make all further discussions with the "papal church which has fallen away from Apostolic tradition" impossible . . . . [98]

But the Una Sancta Movement did not founder in this series of crises. It lost much of its popular appeal, at least for a number of years, but appeared to have deepened its roots in the intellectual, theological fields.

---

[98] Adam Fechter, "Rom und die Evangelischen," *Wort und Wahrheit,* VI (1951), 766.

Chapter Eleven

The Recovery

ALTHOUGH the Una Sancta Movement did not collapse in the years of disillusionment between 1948 and 1950, a state of crisis was spoken of even until 1954. One consequence was that the Una Sancta Movement in the 1950's developed, in contrast to the late 1940's, more on the intellectual and theological levels, as in the increasing number of technical theological discussions in the *Una Sancta* after 1953 indicates. At the 1958 *Katholikentag* in Berlin Dr. Gertrude Reideck admitted that in the beginning the Una Sancta Movement had sometimes shown a spirit of impatience and overzealousness which dreamed of a superficial Christian unity. But, she said,

> It was the childhood illnesses of a movement whose impetuous yearning for unity boiled over, a movement which in these first contacts with the separated brethren immediately became fascinated by the discovery of how profound, despite everything, were the things which already bound us, of how powerfully the bond of Christian faith and baptism drew the separated Christians together. As Christians began to listen to one another and no longer wrangled with one another, they learned to know themselves; as they began to learn to know themselves they began to apppreciate themselves and as the esteem for each other grew they began to love one another; in the ecstasy of the first love Christians succumbed to the illusion that love alone would carry them through to unity. Since then sobriety and prudence on both sides have again taken the tiller firmly in hand.[1]

---

[1]Gertrude Reidick, *Zur Una Sancta Bewegung* (Meitingen, 1959), 16-17.

Though no longer a mass movement the Movement did not become an isolated esoteric group. The dozens of circles that continued meeting, the lectures and discussions attended by hundreds and thousands, and the growth of the number of subscribers to the *Una Sancta* to over ten thousand all show evidence of popular interest and support.

Effects of Crises on Una Sancta Circles

The after-effects of the crises varied in the different Una Sancta circles: some suffered a severe decline; some managed to maintain their equilibrium; others flourished even more during the 1950's than during the 1940's. The circle at Bornstedt which used to meet almost monthly was meeting only once a year by 1952, and the Elsterwerda circle reported a steady decline through the 1950's, having met at first monthly, then quarterly, and finally semi-annually; since the crises the Protestant members appeared "tired." But the Bornstedt circle and the Leipzig circle, among others, reported in 1952 that their activities continued despite the difficulties; the Una Sancta circle at Minden stated that it had twenty-five active members, approximately the same number it initially had. The circles which registered the greatest improvement of participation and activities were those from some of the large cities. Stuttgart, whose Una Sancta circle traced its founding back to Max Metzger in 1940, reported: "Here and there one could read that through the proclamation of the new Marian dogma the bridge between the confessions was broken off; we have noticed nothing of this sort."[2] Its meetings and activities continued to grow in attendance. Nuremberg, which had ceased all activity for a short while after the *Monitum*, gradually began meeting and holding lectures and conferences again and by 1952 was

[2]"Stuttgart," *Una Sancta Rundbriefe*, VII, I (1952), 7.

able to report heavily attended and very promising discussions. The Frankfort Una Sancta circle also reported early in 1958 that "the Una Sancta Movement here has taken a noticeable upswing in the past Winter." A series of lectures brought from 600 to 900 listeners each time. Already in 1957 the Frankfurt circle, drawing from fifty to ninety people to its monthly meetings, had sponsored a series of lectures which were attended by 750 to 1000 persons at a time. The Munich circle, one of the oldest and most active of Una Sancta circles, continued to flourish throughout the 1950's; its secretary described it in 1958 as a "steadily growing community of theologians and laity of all Christian confessions."[3] The monthly meetings, "*Jour fixe*," began with thirty attending and swelled to eighty; Una Sancta topics in lectures were drawing over 1200 listeners.

Probably the most flourishing center of Una Sancta work has been Berlin. Since 1950 there have been an average of thirty public Una Sancta activities and events a year conducted in a total of sixty different Protestant and Catholic parishes; these are in addition to the monthly meetings and monthly theological discussions and yearly joint Catholic-Protestant Advent celebrations.

Outside of Berlin other Una Sancta groups continued to operate in the Soviet zone of Germany, particularly in Leipzig. Some of the circles met monthly, although since the *Monitum* and new dogma signs of discouragement have appeared among some Protestants. Nevertheless as late as 1958 a new Una Sancta circle, made up mostly of Protestants, was formed in Görlitz on the edge of the Neisse border. Besides meeting more or less regularly in these relatively small circles, members also undertook activities of a broader scope, such as retreats for Catholic priests conducted by

---

[3]"Una Sancta Kreis München," *Una Sancta,* XIII (1958), 58.

Protestant theologians and *vice versa* on common themes like the Eucharist, or large public meetings of members of the various confessions like that at Potsdam in 1959 or Berlin in 1958, where over 800 and 1000 respectively attended.

Una Sancta activity around many German universities continued to flourish during the 1950's. In some places like Munich, students and faculty members merely participated in the already existing Una Sancta circle;[4] in others like Heidelberg and Tübingen Una Sancta or Una Sancta-like circles were formed by the student and faculty members themselves. Often confessional sutdent organizations would invite one another to certain lectures and activities. At the University of Leipzig, where the theoloigcal faculty is Protestant, Catholic theologians were regularly invited as guest lecturers.

Many of the Una Sancta circles continued throughout the 1950's the practice started earlier of sponsoring public lectures, sometimes individually at various times during the year, or in a series within a week or several weeks, but also especially during the Church Unity Octave, January 18 to 25. The Una Sancta circle at Munich printed a schedule for the Unity Octave of 1960 in which at least one special liturgical or religious service or lecture or sermon was arranged for each day; most of these services and lectures in the churches of different confessions drew mixed audiences of several hundred persons apiece.[5] Arrangements were also made during this week to broadcast three lectures on Una Sancta subjects over the Bavarian Radio Station. The various Una Sancta public lectures throughout the year were also well attended, often with 500 or 1000 persons present. When Professor Heinrich Fries gave a series of six lectures on the

---

[4]University students constituted about ten per cent of the Munich circle in 1958 to 1960.

[5]The high point of the week was the service in Munich's cathedral.

Una Sancta in different communities of southwest Germany during the spring of 1959, the average attendance was between three and four hundred; some lectures drew over eight hundred listeners. A year later Fries went on a similar tour with like success.

This situation was recognized in a pamphlet put out by the Catholic diocese of Rothenburg in 1954 to inform the clergy of the Una Sancta Movement. It stated:

> The Catholic clergy must not overlook the fact that the Catholic people are very largely sympathetic to this and similar efforts toward unity. And it is not merely that the conferences and lectures where usually a Catholic and Protestant clergyman speak on the *Una Sancta* are well attended; the people applaud heartily when a speaker emphasizes that we Catholics wish to live in peace with Protestants and we thank them for all they have done (granting of the use of churches, etc.).[6]

The practice of sponsoring conferences of several days' length also continued throughout the 1950's; these were sometimes annual as at Nuremburg, but in other places such as at Frankfurt, Hamburg, Kiel, and Schleswig, theye were irregular. Sometimes there was a sort of joint conference of Una Sancta circles or groups such as when the Munich circle was invited to an Una Sancta conference in Kiel by Propst Hans Asmussen, or when the "East-West Conference" at Berlin in 1956 drew over a thousand persons. The Protestant and Catholic academies at Hohenheim and Bad Boll continued to hold yearly joint Una Sancta conferences during Pentecost week, the academies alternating as host. In 1954 the first national Una Sancta conference drew 150 participants of both confessions to Berlin; that their determination was not essentially weakened is indicated by the

---

[6]"Die Una-sancta-Bewegung," in *Materialdienst des Bischöflichen Ordinariats Rottenburg,* (April, 1954), 1.

fact that they "directed an urgent plea to the Protestants and Roman Catholics in Germany to work in act and prayer for the overcoming of the division in Christendom."[7] Two years later, from June 28 to July 1 of 1956, two hundred representatives from "almost every Una Sancta circle in Germany" were present at the second national Una Sancta conference at Burg Rothenfels, earlier the scene of many "*Quickborn*" activities. One of the participants, Walter Rupprecht, came as the representative of Bishop Dietzfelbinger, Lutheran bishop of Bavaria; Bishop Dietzfelbinger had been delegated special responsibility for Una Sancta work by the Lutheran bishops of Germany, much as Archbishop Jäger on the Catholic side. In reporting on the conference in the *Nachrichten der Evangelisch-Lutherischen Kirche in Bayern,* Rupprecht suggested that in Germany the special task of Lutheranism, which holds a middle position in the ecumenical movement between the Orthodox-Anglican and Reformed wings, is to serve as a link between the ecumenical movement and Roman Catholicism. "We should not draw back from the task."[8] The next year, 1957, a notice appeared in the *Una Sancta* stating that there would be no national Una Sancta conference that year; reference was made at the same time to the joint conference of the Protestant and Catholic Academies of Bad Boll and Hohenheim planned for that Pentecost week and to an Una Sancta retreat to be held in the new *Haus der Begegnung.* Since then no further national Una Sancta conferences have been held.

NEW INSTITUTIONS SPRING UP

The "House of Meeting," *Haus der Begegung,* was opened in 1956 in a new wing of the Benedictine Abbey of Niederaltaich on the Danube not far from the "Iron Curtain" of

---

[7]"Una Sancta Konferenz, "*Universitas,* X (1955), 101.
[8]Quoted in Thomas Sartory, "2. Gesamtdeutsche Una Sancta Tagung Burg Rothenfels 28. June–1. Juli 1956," *Una Sancta,* XII (1957), 48.

Czechoslovakia. Niederaltaich's abbot is Emmanuel Heufelder, a friend of Max Metzger and a pioneer in Una Sancta work; the abbey was also the home of Father Thomas Sartory, the editor of the *Una Sancta* from 1953 to 1963. The *Haus der Begegnung* contains two libraries, the smaller one with material on the Eastern Churches and a larger one holding Protestant-Catholic Una Sancta books and periodicals; there are also guest rooms, and dining rooms. The *Haus der Begegnung* not only supplies the place and materials to study Una Sancta matters, but also furnishes a place where Orthodox, Anglican, Protestant and Catholic Christians can meet with each other in a religious atmosphere. "Una Sancta" retreats and conferences were inaugurated in 1956 and have grown in importance each year. But besides these planned activities the *Haus der Begegnung* has been a constant source of inter-confessional contact; in December of 1957 the director could write: "How many have already found the way to us! In our guestbook we find the names of Christians of all confessions from all continents and all leading nations."[9] The attitude of Protestant theologians toward the *Haus der Begegnung,* both before and after its founding, is indicative of its importance. Already in 1954 Ernst Kinder, a Lutheran theologian of wide repute, especially in ecumenical circles, wrote: "How wonderful it would be if the Una Sancta work had at its disposal a house, a *Haus der Begegnung.* We should strive for this."[10] Just a year after the opening of the *Haus der Begegnung,* a plan for a Lutheran institute for the study of the different confessions (*Konfessionskundliches Institut*) was submitted to the meeting of the Lutheran World Federation at Minneapolis, stressing among other things the

[9]Benedikt Ewaldt, " 'Haus der Begegnung' in Niederalteich," *Una Sancta,* XII (1957), 233.

[10]Ernst Kinder, "Was erwartet die evangelische Kirche von der Una Sancta-Arbeit?" *Una Sancta,* IX (1954), 8.

need for a place of contact with Catholics; it added, "We

call attention to the fact that the Roman Catholic Church has erected a *Haus der Begegnung* in Germany (Niederaltaich) to which Lutheran theologians from all Europe are continually invited."[11]

The nineteenth of January, 1957, opened a new phase in the history of German theology. Fifty representatives from almost all the Catholic theological faculties of Germany attended as Archbishop Jäger dedicated the new Johann-Adam-Möhler Institute in Paderborn. The aims of the new institute were outlined: 1. Scientific investigation and presentation of the doctrine, cult, order and life of the Protestant confessions; 2. Explanation of the Roman Catholic faith in its fullness in answer to the Protestant questions; 3. Communication of the results particularly to pastors. The psysical plant of library, study and conference rooms is used by the group of Catholic theologians, usually with different fields of specialization, who study new developments in their specialties in Protestant theology and make periodic reports at meetings of the institute members. The institute essentially has taken over the "*Konfessionskunde*" work of Konrad Algermissen, who is also a member of the institute; this work was felt to be growing beyond the capacity of one man. The institute produces a small bulletin periodically and has also assumed the editorship of the *Catholica,* previously edited by Robert Grosche both before the war and after. In addition the institute began the publication of a series of books; the first of this series was Hans Küng's *Rechtfertigung. Die Lehre Karl Barths und eine katholische Besinnung* (1958).[12]

---

[11]*Evangelisch-lutherische Kirchenzeitung* (Berlin), XI (1957), 363-364; "Konfessionskundliches Institut des Lutherischen Weltbundes," *Una Sancta,* XII (1957), 238.

[12]Franz Herre, "Brückenschlag der Theologen," in *Priester-Jahrheft 1957* (Paderborn, 1957), 31-32; Interview with Professor Heinrich Fries, a charter member of the Möhler Institute, January 1958.

At the August, 1957, meeting of the World Lutheran Federation in Minneapolis a plan for a *"konfessionskundlichen"* institute was presented by the German National Committee. The plan is of special interest not only for its own sake or because it parallels the Catholic Johann Adam Möhler Institute, but also because it reflected the thinking of an influential section of German Lutheran theologians on the Una Sancta problem. In a published Memorandum describing the plan for the new institute, Oberkirchenrat Schnell stated that the present situation in the Lutheran and Catholic Churches had caused a large number of European, particularly German, Church leaders and theology professors to declare the founding of a *"konfessionskundlichen"* institute to be necessary and urgent. The discussion with the Catholic Church was proclaimed to be the ecumenical task of the Lutheran Church. "We also cannot ignore the fact that many Catholic theologians see in the Lutheran Church their essential discussion partner and wish to clarify their own theology in the give-and-take with Lutheran theology. In the coming years the discussions with Roman Catholicism cannot be and ought not be avoided."[13]

Of the specific reasons given at Minneapolis for studying Catholicism the main one corresponded with the first goal of the Una Sancta Movement, the elimination of widespread misconceptions. The radical difference between the Catholic Church of today and that of four hundred years ago was cited. The work of Lortz and other Una Sancta-minded Catholic historians and theologians was acknowledged in the statement: "How many Catholic theologians today realize that the Reformation is a serious theological problem; we must also recognize in Catholicism a problem which cannot be lightly done away with.[14] A second goal of the Una

[13]"Konfessionskundliches Institut," 235.
[14]*Ibid.*, 237.

Sancta Movement also found an echo in the *Konfessionskunde* plan, the coming to know one's own position better, followed by a constructive self-criticism. The Lutheran plan summed up this notion: "The intensive working with Catholicism could give Lutheran theology a new direction, loose it from certain rigidities and overworked formulations of questions."[15]

In the plans for the new institute limits, goals and means were carefully defined. Although it was considered desirable sometime in the future to expand the institute into an ecumenical institute dealing with all Christian groups, the authors of the Minneapolis plan suggested that for a considerable length of time the institute, for the sake of effectiveness, concern itself with Catholicism alone. Four major aspects of the institute were envisioned, to a large extent complementing Una Sancta work already begun by Catholics. The prime overall function of the institute was to be fundamental research in "Catholic theology (with the greatest emphasis on modern Catholicism), Catholic Church history (with particular concern for the present day situation including the relations to the state, to culture, and to the intellectual life), Catholic practical piety."[16] This work would be carried on with the closest contact and even sometimes cooperation with the university theological faculties, and in coordination with the World Lutheran Federation so as to eliminate duplication. Work similar to that of the Möhler Institute, the publication of a series of monographs, was planned, plus smaller writings and the creation of a *konfessionskundlichen* supplement to the *Lutherische Rundschau*. It was also intended that the most gifted theologians would be given a year free to study at the institute and

[15]*Ibid.*
[16]*Ibid.*, 238.

participate in a research project and then to bring this knowledge and experience back to their own local church areas, for "we need men who have learned to know Catholicism from within and who know why they are Evangelical-Lutheran Christians."[17] It was also hoped that the new institute would serve as a point of personal contact between Lutherans and Catholics; it was in this connection that attention was called to the *Haus der Begegnung.* Finally, the institute was to function as an information service.

A committee of four was appointed at Minneapolis, Dr. Vajta and Professor Skydsgaard[18] from Denmark and Bishop Dietzfelbinger and Professor Peter Brunner from Germany, to work on setting up the institute, which was originally located in Copenhagen, with Professor Skydsgaard as the first director, and has since been transferred to Strassburg, the German-French speaking city on the French-German border.

An Ecumenical institute had already been established at the University of Heidelberg by Protestant theology Professor Edmund Schlink, another at the University of Marburg by Professor Ernest Benz, and a third at the University of Tübingen by Professor Rosenkranz; an ecumenical center was founded at Frankfurt by the central autrority of the EKD under the direction of Pastor Wilhelm Menz, while at the University of Munich an ecumenical house was erected. These institutions, unlike the planned *konfessionskundliches* institute, are concerned with all the Christian Churches, not merely Catholicism.

---

[17]*Ibid.,* 236.

[18]"Kristen Ejner Skydsgaard, the Danish Lutheran theologian, is the man who has probably devoted the most study to the problems of the relationship between Protestants and Roman Catholics at a deeper level." Ernst Kinder, "Protestant-Roman Catholic Encounter an Ecumenical Obligation," *The Ecumenical Review,* VII 1955), 343.

PROTESTANT LITERATURE

During the 1950's an amazing amount of literature of all types on Una Sancta matters continued to come off the German presses, much of which is important in the development of the Movement. Among Protestant writers, Kinder, von Loewenich and the "Sammlung" were especially important.

In an article called "What does the Protestant Church Expect from the Una Sancta Work?" published in 1954, Ernst Kinder argued that the Una Sancta Movement was very important for the Protestant Church because discussion with the Catholic Church is "essential and indeed necessary for the life" of the Protestant Church. His two most significant demands were that Catholics and Protestants learn through Una Sancta work to know each other and themselves better, a primary goal constantly proclaimed by Una Sancta leaders, and that the Una Sancta work be more strongly participated in by the Churches as such. The following year at the conference of the Lutheran bishops and Church leaders of the VELKD both Professor Kinder and Professor Peter Brunner again insisted on the necessity of the Protestant Church entering into discussion with the Catholic Church. Kinder continued this train of thought in an article in the *Ecumenical Review.* "Our relation to the Roman Catholic Church is still influenced far too strongly by a widespread *mythical* conception of that Church, which fascinates while it repels us, and which is really born of a sense of inferiority among Protestants, and is often the source of irrelevant illusion and of equally irrelevant resentment. We must free ourselves from this mythical conception in order to perceive reality."[19]

Walther von Loewenich published in 1956 a book entitled *Die moderne Katholizismus* (it has since been translated

[19]Kinder, "Protestant-Roman Catholic Encounter," 343.

into English: *Modern Catholicism*, New York, 1959) which dealt comprehensively with the Catholic Church in the twentieth century, covering the developments of theology, of various movements, and of popular piety. Among the movements discussed by von Loewenich was the Una Sancta. Like Kinder and Heiler, among others, von Loewenich brought up the objection not infrequently raised by Protestants: the Una Sancta Movement is just under-cover Catholic convert-making. Von Loewenich denied this:

> the discussions as such do have a positive value. We really can learn from each other; we know each other much too little. Unchristian resentments and irrational feelings can be eliminated through personal contact; the same is true of apparently ineradicable misunderstanding. . . . We do the Una Sancta Movement an injustice when we look upon it as merely Roman Catholic propaganda. The genuine yearning for unity, which was so alive in its founders, has still not died in her.[20]

Reaction to von Loewenich's book was favorable on both sides: the Catholic *Herder-Korrespondenz* reviewer wrote that the book indicated a strong desire for a greater union with Rome; writing for the *Ecumenical Review,* a Protestant reviewer stated that "'von Loewenich's book contains extensive and reliable information, and is in every respect a standard work. But it is more than that: *it is a programme for discussion on the question of truth both within the Churches and between them.*"[21]

A number of works appearing in the 1950's by Protestant exegetes showed a renewed concern for the problem of Peter and the papacy. The Protestant pastor Kurt Hutten remarked that the "Tu es Petrus" passage of Matthew

[20]Walther von Loewenich, *Der moderne Katholizismus* (Witten, 1956), 360.

[21]J. P. Böndermaker, "Der moderne Katholizismus," *The Ecumenical Review,* X (1958), 207.

16:8-19, long regarded by Protesants as apocryphal, is now

accepted as authentic. He went on to state, "The Catholic theology sees therein and in the related greater appreciation of Peter and his commission a promising sign of *rapprochement.*"[22] One of the most comprehensive historical investigations of this problem was undertaken by Oscar Cullmann in his book *Petrus, Jünger–Apostel–Märtyrer* of 1952. Although he concluded that Peter did not hand on his commission from Christ in the foundation of the Church. Catholic as special among the apostles and as having a unique commission from Christ in the foundation of the church. Catholic theologians considered the manner in which Cullman handled the controversial theme of the papacy "an extraordinary step forward which also meant a step on the path to unity."[23]

THE GATHERING OF THE "SAMMLUNG"

In the middle 1950's there appeared a new group of German Protestants "which may prove to have repercussions far more profound than the Oxford Movement of England, which this development strikingly resembles."[24] The group, which called itself the *Sammlung* or "Gathering," was a union of Protestant, mostly Lutheran, men and women, lay and cleric, who heard God's call to overcome the division of Christendom; their purpose was to work and pray that the Churches of the Reformation find their "necessary" place in the one, catholic and apostolic Church, not only for their own fulfillment but also for the future of the entire Church of God.[25] For some decades there have been Protestants who felt less and less at home in their Churches; immedi-

---

[22]Kurt Hutten, "Die katholischen und die evangelischen (IV)," *Materialdienst* (Stuttgart), XVII (1954), 207.

[23]Quoted in *ibid.*, 212.

[24]Adolph Schalk, "Reformation in Germany," *The Commonweal,* LXXV (November 28, 1958), 229.

[25]Hans Asmussen, Ernst Fincke, Max Lackmann, Wolfgang Lehmann, Richard Baumann, *Katholische Reformation* (Stuttgart, 1958), 241.

ately after the last war a number of men began to voice this feeling in periodicals. They thus became aware of each other and began to correspond and finally to meet with one another. Eventually the *Sammlung* was formed to "gather" or win back those "catholic" or universal truths which had been viewed one-sidedly, forgotten, or allowed to atrophy in the Protestant Church.[26] The members of the *Sammlung* felt that they must come in contact with the Roman Catholic Church which has kept many of the Catholic truths, such as the sacramental aspect of Christianity, much better than the Lutheran Church. One of the leaders, Pastor Max Lackmann, expressed it: "We can only truly find ourselves, even historically, by re-discovering our communion with the Catholic Church."[27] This approach of course brought from fellow Protestants accusations of catholicizing tendencies. Max Lackmann's answer, was, "One is either a catholic Christian or one is no Christian." Hans Asmussen retorted, "I have no catholicizing tendencies, but rather a catholic passion."[28]

In 1954 four Lutheran clergymen, Hans Asmussen, Max Lackmann, Ernst Fincke and Wolfgang Lehmann, decided to communicate these ideas to other Protestants via a circular letter; thus was the *Sammlung* born. These letters, seven over a period of three years, went out to thousands of Protestants in Germany, Austria, and Switzerland. Major points of theology were discussed, and throughout it was stressed that the Protestant "alone" did not necessarily contradict the Catholic "and." For example, concerning the crucial problem of the relation of faith and good works to salvation the *Sammlung* stated:

---

[26]Heinrich Fries, "Der Kreis der 'Sammlung' und die 'Katholische Reformation,'" *Una Sancta,* XIII, (1958), 53.

[27]Schalk, "Reformation," 230; cf. Asmussen et al., *Katholische Reformation,* 27.

[28]Fries, "Der Kreis," 53.

It is likewise a catholic truth that God does not save us without ourselves. The apparent contradiction which lies in these statements finds its solution in that when God leads us to salvation He is not to be circumscribed by the categories of classical, rational, causal thinking. Therefore it is necessary to show in Holy Scriptures that God rewards in time and in eternity every good work of the believing and the unbelieving. This truth does not contradict the other that we obtain salvation as a gift.[29]

By the middle of 1958 some 1200 Protestants had given their support to the *Sammlung*, and an additional 300 Catholics had "assisted the group continually with their prayers, their love and their unremitting appeal for understanding in their own ranks."[30] But the early reaction of most Protestants was unsympathetic; in their seventh circular letter (May, 1957) the *Sammlung* complained that the only group within Protestantism to enter into conversations with them was the *Michaelsbruderschaft*. They however felt that the matters they discussed in their letters, the various aspects of the Catholic question, were beginning to be discussed more and more by Protestant bishops, theologians and Church authorities. And by the end of 1958 Lackmann could say "there are also Lutheran leaders who recommended *bona fide* theological disputations with the *Sammlung*, its writings and its aim, but in a friendly and brotherly manner."[31]

For the most part Catholic reaction was very encouraging.[32] Following their expressed aim of coming into closer contact with the Catholic Church, the *Sammlung* took great pains to keep Catholic leaders informed of their work,

---

[29]Asmussen *et al.*, *Katholische Reformation*, 66.
[30]Schalk, "Reformation," 229.
[31]*Ibid.*, 229.
[32]Cf. *ibid.*, 230; and *Il Quotidiano* (Rome), July 11, 1957; and *Rheinischen Merkur*, August 2, 1957; and *Allgemeine Sonntagszeitung* (Würzburg), July 7, 1957.

and not only in Germany. A number of the leaders of the *Sammlung* privately and individually visited Rome several times to speak with leading Catholic churchmen "to inform them about us and to be informed about Rome. The Holy Father too knows about our work."[33] Professor Fries in reviewing one of the writings of the *Sammlung* said that Catholics can only "heartily and gratefully rejoice" over what is expressed in the book. He pointed out that the *Sammlung* and their friends have problems within their own community and that it would be tragic and unjust if they were repulsed by adverse Catholic criticism.[34] Nevertheless, some Catholic theologians have regarded the *Sammlung* as dangerous because they felt it suggested modification of Catholic dogma.

Besides the seven circular letters the *Sammlung* also sent out twenty thousand copies of twelve theses containing the burden of their message; the reaction to the latter was encouraging. In 1958 they also published a book containing their earlier circulars and a number of essays, *Katholische Reformation* (*The Unfinished Reformation*, Fides, 1962).[35]

---

[33]Schalk, "Reformation," 230.

[34]Fries, "Der Kreis," 59.

[35]The following is a sampling of publications of some of the *Sammlung* leaders: Hans Asmussen and Otto Karrer, *Trennung und Einigung im Glauben* (Stuttgart, 1956); Hans Asmussen, *Um die Einheit der evangelischen Kirche in Deutschland*, (Stuttgart, 1947); Hans Asmussen, *Warum noch Lutherische Kirche?* (Stuttgart, 1949); Hans Asmussen and Wilhelm Stählin (eds.), *Die Katholizität der Kirche* (Stuttgart, 1957); Max Lackmann, *Ein Hilferuf aus der Kirche für die Kirche* (Stuttgart, 1958); Max Lackmann, *Reformatorische Rechtfertigungslehre* (Stuttgart, 1953); Max Lackmann, *Das Geheimnis der Schöpfung*, (Stuttgart, 1952); Max Lackmann, *Katholische Einheit und Augsburger Konfession* (Cologne, 1959); Max Lackmann, *Credo Ecclesiam Catholicam* (Cologne, 1960). A later member of the *Sammlung's* leaders group, Richard Baumann, was also an active writer on the Protestant-Catholic question, e.g., *Fels der Welt–Kirche des Evangeliums und Papstum* (Tübingen, 1956); *Herr bist Du es?* (Stuttgart, n.d.); *Primat und Luthertum* (Tübingen, 1953). Unfortunately for the *Sammlung* both Baumann and Lackmann were suspended from pastoral activity in the Lutheran Church.

The *Sammlung* was entirely a movement within the Protestant Church and consequently not specifically connected with the Una Sancta Movement as such. But its avowed aim of recovering and deepening certain catholic truths and practices it considers best preserved by the Roman Catholic Church, as well as its concern for unity in the Church placed it within the more general Una Sancta Movement. But the *Sammlung* did not intend to convert to Roman Catholicism or prepare the way for it. If unity comes, they insisted, it will not come as an unconditional surrender

> but rather it may come about in such a way that the Evangelical Church will return for itself within the Catholic. Too many Catholic theologians think that it is all a very easy matter. They say all Protestants must simply become Catholics. But in this way nothing will be learned. We are not conversion-conscious; we still regard our confession seriously.[36]

This idea is similar to those suggested by Heiler in the 1930's and Adam in the 1940's.[37]

THE LEAGUE FOR EVANGELICAL-CATHOLIC REUNION

Not all of the *Sammlung* were willing to work toward unity by a slow inward catholic renewal of the Protestant Church. Three members under the leadership of Pastor Max Lackmann decided to form a League for Evangelical-Catholic Reunion. The ideas of the League are essentially the same as those of the *Sammlung* except that it aims at the setting up of an ecclesiastical organization which would be the means of corporate reunion with Rome; the goal of the League is to form a separate Evangelical Church united with the

---

[36]Schalk, "Reformation," 230.

[37]After the second session of Vatican II the *Sammlung* leaders decided to disolve their organization because they felt their primary aim of bringing the Protestant and Catholic Churches into serious high-level dialogue was sufficiently inaugurated.

Roman Catholic Church. It would thus be analogous to the Eastern Uniate Churches, having its own church order, canon law, liturgy, married clergy and catechism, but united to the Roman Catholic Church.

> Although this presupposes the fundamental agreement of such an Evangelical fellowship with the Roman Catholic faith, cultus and constitution, it must also be remembered that the preservation of everything legitimately Evangelical is guaranteed. Specifically this includes Evangelical and biblical doctrine (in so far as this does not contradict the Roman Catholic faith in principle); the unique forms of Evangelical theology which operate more in biblical or contemporary philosophical categories than in terms of medieval scholasticism; Evangelical forms of piety and devotion (liturgy, hymns, prayers) which have come into existence during the past 400 years; Evangelical forms of parish administration in which laymen share the responsibility and work with pastors and bishops.[38]

Already in the early 1960's the League completed a new formula for an "Evangelical Mass" (published in number 5 of its periodical *Bausteine*) which was thoroughly discussed with Roman Catholic specialists. It was felt that the formula contained what is best in the Evangelical tradition while complying essentially with Roman Catholic doctrine and tradition, but incorporated many of the reforms long advocated by Catholic liturgists.

The League does not wish either to settle or to ignore the confessional differences among Protestant groups. It believes these differences will be overcome only through catholic rethinking and incorporation into Catholic unity; each denomination must work in its own area gathering members toward the goal of corporate reunion. At the same time, however, the League agrees with the critique of Rome's union practice by Uniate Patriarch Maximos IV, "Uniformity cannot be

---

[38]Max Lackmann, "Toward Corporate Reunion," *Perspectives* VII, No. 4 (July-August, 1962), 3.

reconciled with catholic universality." Each denomination should maintain and cultivate its unique evangelical-catholic content and charism, and seek through catholic renewal to overcome its own errors, distortions and one-sidedness. "The admission and toleration of differing confessions in the joint work of the League has, therefore, nothing to do with contemporary union practice among Protestants. The goal, limitations and norm for all our doctrinal statements remains the universal Roman Catholic Church with its living Teaching and Pastoral Office in the Petrine See."[39]

The Protestant Churches naturally have not embraced the new Evangelical-Catholic League; for the present they seem to be content to watch in silence. Put since the fall of 1960 the League has been gathering members throunghout Europe and America; so far it has found recruits in Germany, Austria, Switzerland, Denmark, Sweden, The Netherlands, France and the USA.

The Catholic reaction to the League is mixed, much as with the *Sammlung*. However, the German Catholic bishops, through Archbishop Jäger of Paderborn, have appointed Abbot Laurentius Klein, O.S.B., consultor to the League, and stated that Catholics in Germany may attend conferences of the League without special permission. Put most significant is the fact that the work of the League is known to, and has the private encouragement of, members of Cardinal Bea's Secretariat for the Fostering of Christian Unity.

The great difference between the League and earlier similar plans is that things have moved from the discussion stage to the actual setting up of preparatory organizational machinery. Whether the League will have any more success than the somewhat similar Anglican proposals in the recent past will depend both on the Protestant and Catholic response.

---

[39]*Ibid.*, 4.

Of course some elements within German Protestantism have opposed all ecumenical work with Catholics, although these grew fewer as the 1950's wore on. One vocal opponent was Martin Niemöller, who, although he had been very popular because of his celebrated resistance against the Nazis, lost many of his followers when he not only took a strong stand against Rome but also became very critical of the Bonn government for its strongly pro-Western policy. A more serious stumbling block to inter-confessional work is the growing importance of Rudolf Bultmann and his "demythologization," which, although it is an attempt to make the Bible more meaningful to modern man, in effect is very near the old liberal theology approach to Scriptures. This difficulty is modified in several ways, however. On the Protestant side there is much opposition to Bultmann's approach, including public disavowals by Bishop Haug and Bishop Dibelius among others. On the other hand there have been Catholic theologians who have attempted to deal sympathetically with his work, such as Heinrich Fries in his book *Bultmann Barth und die katholische Kirche* (English translation by Leonard Swidler, Pittsburgh: Duquesne University Press, 1966). Also the development of form criticism in Catholic biblical studies has made the Catholic biblical position a little less antithetical to Bultmann's kerygmatic approach.

Catholic Una Sancta Literature

Throughout the 1950's German Catholic theologians and writers were deeply involved in the Una Sancta Movement, probably even more than their Protestant counterparts, many of whom were directing more and more energy toward the ecumenical movement. There were writings dealing with single trends in Protestant theology or with the work of one man or one aspect of his work, as Hans Urs von Balthasar's *Karl Barth, Darstellung und Deutung seiner Theo-*

logie (Karl Barth, Presentation and Significance of His Theology) and Gottlieb Söhngen's work with natural theology and Barth. Other men like Michael Schmaus, Karl and Hugo Rahner, and Franz Arnold, who were either in Una Sancta circles or the Protestant-Catholic theologians' circle, occasionally wrote articles or lectured on Una Sancta subjects or took part in Una Sancta discussions and conferences. Others, such as, Heinrich Fries and Thomas Sartory, became involved in the Una Sancta discussion on a broader front through books, articles, lectures, editing and joint projects with Protestant writers.

Heinrich Fries rose to particular prominence in Una Sancta work during the decade. Already in the 1940's he concentrated on a study of John Henry Newman, the same subject that earlier helped bring Matthias Laros to Una Sancta work, and has since assumed editorial responsibilities in publishing material on Newman, his thought, theology and ecumenicity.[40] Professor Fries has also published a number of articles and books on Barth, Bultmann, and the Una Sancta;[41] he is a member of the Möhler Institute and co-editor of the quarterly *Catholica.* In addition to his writings on ecumenical matters Fries has held public discussions with Protestant theologians and has given lectures on Una Sancta subjects on the radio and from Berlin to Paderborn to southern Germany. Even his inaugural lecture at the University of Munich

---

[40]Cf. Heinrich Fries and Werner Becker (eds.), *Newman Studien* (Nuremberg, 1948, 1954).

[41]Cf. Heinrich Fries, "Das Anliegen Bultmanns im Licht der katholischen Theologie," *Catholica,* X (1954), 1-14; "Karl Barth und die katholische Theologie," *Hochland,* XLV (1953), 260-268; "Zur Theologie der Entmythologiesierung," *Hochland,* XLIV (1952), 354-360; *Kirche als Ereignis* (Düsseldorf, 1958); *Bultmann, Barth und die katholische Theologie* (Stuttgart, 1955); *Antwort an Asmussen* (Stuttgart, 1958); *Der Beitrag der Theologie zur Una Sancta* (Munich, 1959. For a complete bibliography and analysis of Fries' work see: Günter Biemer, "Theology of Encounter," *Journal of Ecumenical Studies,* I, 2 (Spring, 1964), 213-242.

was entitled "The Contribution of Theology to Una Sancta,"[42] and since his arrival in Munich Professor Fries has been very active in the Una Sancta circle there, taking a leading part in the discussions.

Thomas Sartory, was a monk of the Benedictine Abbey at Niederaltaich, which already in the 1930's was becoming a center of ecumenical activities under the leadership of Abbot Emmanuel Heufelder.[43] In the years after the war Father Sartory was sent by Abbot Heufelder to the Universitly of Munich to obtain a doctorate in theology, with particular emphasis on ecumenical matters; at Munich he worked particularly under the ecumenical inspiration of Professors Schmaus and Söhngen. His doctoral dissertation, *Die ökumenische Bewegung und die Einheit der Kirche* (*The Ecumenical Movement and the Unity of the Church*), re-emphasized the direction of his theological interests. In 1953 Sartory was appointed by the German Bishops' Conference as editor of the periodical *Una Sancta*, previously edited as the *Una Sancta Rundbriefe* by Matthias Laros, and after the founding of the Möhler Institute he was responsible for the sector of theology concerning Protestant piety and "religious orders."

One of the most important of Dr. Sartory's many ecumenical activities was the editing of the *Una Sancta*. The *Una Sancta Rundbriefe* when edited by Matthias Laros from 1946 to 1949 rarely went over a dozen pages. After Laros laid down the editing burden at the end of 1949, the *Rundbriefe* appeared only occasionally under the joint editorship of Max Metzger's Kyrios Publishing Company at Meitingen and the Munich Una Sancta circle; it remained an eight or sixteen page pamphlet with no cover. This quasi-

---

[42]Heinrich Fries, *Der Beitrag der Theologie zur Una Sancta* (Munich, 1959).

[43]Benedikt Ewaldt, "In Christo Unum," *Die Beiden Türme* Sonderheft, (1958), 39 ff.

editorless period of the *Rundbriefe* corresponded with the nadir of the Una Sancta Movement in general.

In 1953 Father Sartory took over the editorship of the *Rundbriefe* in conjunction with the Kyrios Publishing Company. Under his direction the *Rundbriefe* became a regular quarterly, and its size increased from 22 pages to 125 or 150 per issue by 1960; in 1954 the name was changed to *Una Sancta.* In 1954 Johannes Straubinger could say that the *Una Sancta* had few readers, particularly among the clergy;[44] by 1960 the subscriptions had risen to over 11,000, of which over a third were Protestant and the rest mainly Catholic, with many clergy on both sides included.

The content of the *Una Sancta* also changed greatly. Laros had originally written the entire issue himself. Later the copy was written by many people; for the most part the contributions were short. Under Sartory's editorship the articles have lengthened and branched out to discuss questions of doctrine, piety and practical life of inter-confessional interest; the magazine also includes reports on inter-confessional activities and cooperation, letters from readers taking positions on various problems, and reviews of Catholic books by Protestants and *vice versa.* The articles are written by theologians and laymen, mostly Protestants and Catholics but occasionally also Orthodox. In 1957 Father Sartory noted, in answer to the query why Catholic articles are more numerous than Protestant, that articles by Protestants were not forthcoming in sufficient quantity. Walter Rupprecht in his favorable review of the *Una Sancta* in a January, 1958, issue of the *Evangelisch-Lutherische Kirchenzeitung* complained similarly, "The *Rundbriefe* of the Una Sancta presents a duty for Protestant theology. The readers of this periodical expect the Protestant position to be given along

[44]Juan C. Ruta and Johannes Straubinger, *Die katholische Kirche in Deutschland und ihre Probleme* (Stuttgart, 1954), 120.

with the Catholic on these decisive questions between the confessions . . . . We should not fail in this duty."[45] Sartory suggested that perhaps the reason for this imbalance is that Protestant theologians already deeply involved in the ecumenical movement are reluctant to take on an additional burden. However, in three out of the next five issues, in 1958 and 1959, Protestant contributions outnumbered the Catholic; there were also four articles written by Orthodox Christians in these two years.

The Una Sancta books coming out in the last few years of the sixth decade tended more and more to take a dialogue form; one writer may specifically direct his ideas toward someone in the other camp, as Otto Karrer in his *On the Unity of Christians. The Petrine Question. A Conversation with E. Brunner, O. Cullmann, H.v. Campenhausen*[46] and Fries in *Answer to Asmussen,*[47] or a collection of essays by members of one confession may be directed toward the other, as in *The Catholicity of the Church* edited by Hans Asmussen and Wilhelm Stählin.[48] Even farther in this direction were books written jointly by Catholics and Protestants. One joint venture, *Conversation between the Churches,*[49] by E. Przywara, S.J., and H. Sauer, discussed the differences between the Catholic and Protestant concepts of Church. Asmussen collaborated on several, with Grosche in *Do We Need a Pope?*[50]and Karrer on *Division*

---

[45]Walter Rupprecht, "Das Gespräch zwischen den Konfessionen," *Evangelisch-lutherische Kirchenzeitung* (Berlin), January 15, 1958, 29.

[46]Otto Karrer, *Um die Einheit der Christen. Die Petrusfrage Ein Gespräch mit E. Brunner, O. Cullmann, H. v. Campenhausen.* (Frankfurt, 1953).

[47]Fries, *Antwort an Asmussen.*

[48]Asmussen and Stahlin, *Die Katholizität der Kirche.*

[49]E. Przywara and H. Sauer, *Gespräch zwischen den Kirchen* (Nuremberg, 1957).

[50]Hans Asmussen and Robert Grosche, *Brauchen wir einen Papst?* (Cologne, 1957).

and Unity in Faith.[51] In still another book, *Discussion Between the Confessions,*[52] Asmussen cooperated with Sartory; over a dozen key topics were discussed by each author. Two other books involved a number of Protestant and Catholic theologians. The one, *Christian Religion,*[53] is an encyclopedia in a paper-back edition; over forty Catholics and Protestants contributed, often with parallel essays. The other work, *Meeting of Christians,*[54] is also a collection of parallel essays by Protestant and Catholic theologians. The growing number of these "dialogue" books toward the end of the decade also strongly suggests that the Una Sancta Movement had recovered from its setbacks earlier in the decade and was drawing continually greater participation of theologians and laymen on both sides.

ATTITUDE OF CATHOLIC HIERARCHY TOWARD UNA SANCTA

What was the attitude of the Catholic hierarchy toward the Una Sancta Movement during the 1950's? It was tacitly accepted that the "ecumenical" powers granted to bishops by the *Instructio* were extended indefinitely. The official appointment by the German bishops' conference of Father Sartory as the editor of the *Una Sancta* implied a desire to encourage the Una Sancta Movement; the bishops later made this approval and encouragement even more explicit both as a group in the bishops' conference and in personal letters of encouragement to Father Sartory. Archbishop Jäger retained his commission from the German

[51]Asmussen and Karrer, *Trennung und Einigung im Glauben.*
[52]Hans Asmussen and Thomas Sartory, *Gespräch zwischen den Konfessionen* (Frankfurt, 1959).
[53]Oskar Simmel and Rudolph Stählin (eds.), *Christliche Religion* (Frankfurt, 1957).
[54]Maximilian Rösle and Oskar Cullmann (eds.), *Begegnung der Christen* (Stuttgart, 1959).

bishops' conference to look after ecumenical affairs; he also maintained his leadership of the Catholic half of the Catholic-Protestant theologians semi-annual conferences. He reemphasized his vital concern for the work when he sponsored the founding in his diocesan seat, Paderborn, of the Möhler Institute. Recognition of his leadership in ecumenical work came from Rome when he was appointed a member of the Secretariat for the Fostering of Christian Unity in preparation for the Second Vatican Council.

Outside of Archbishop Jäger a number of bishops have shown by their public actions a very strong sympathy for Una Sancta work. Dr. Albert Stohr, bishop of Mainz until his death in 1962, wrote a pastoral letter in 1952 to his clergy describing and discussing the ecumenical movement and recommended that his clergy concern themselves with it: "Let us above all follow with great interest the ecumenical movement, particularly in those developments which touch on our Fatherland. . . . The ecumenical question certainly is one of the pressing tasks given by God to our age."[55] He gave further evidence of his vital concern by sponsoring three Catholic-Protestant conferences in 1956 and 1957.

In September, 1957, Würzburg received a new Catholic bishop, Dr. Josef Stangl. At his consecration two Protestant pastors, official representatives of the Evangelical Church, participated in the kiss of peace ceremony. In this ancient ceremony the celebrant, Archbishop Schneider, gave the symbolic kiss to the newly consecrated Bishop Stangl with the words *pax tecum;* Bishop Stangl answered with *et cum spiritu tuo* and then turned to the next cleric and repeated the ceremony, which in chain-like fashion was continued, including the two Protestant pastors. So reported the *Evangelisch-Lutherische Kirchenzeitung.* After this somewhat aus-

[55]Quoted in Thomas Sartory, "Die katholische Kirche und das Problem der Una Sancta," *Klerusblatt* (Munich), XXXV (1955), 132-133.

picious beginning, Bishop Stangl continued his support of the Una Sancta Movement, as is amply shown by his sermon for the Church Unity Octave, published in the *Una Sancta*. He spoke of the Eucharist as the sacrament of unity, which, he said, "obliges us to unremitting prayer for our separated brothers and sisters"; the Holy Eucharist makes such a demand of unity in the Church that every deepening of division must be felt as violation of the sacrament. "May the Lord guide the coming Council with his rich grace and grant fulfillment to that which serves unity and contact."[56]

Bishop Stangl's predecessor at Würzburg, Julius Döphfner, has had for many years the reputation of being very sympathetic toward Una Sancta work. His attitude was very aptly phrased in his Church Unity Octave sermon of 1957.[57] He stated that "for us Catholics in the ecumenical discussion of the present time humility, the spirit of penance and the readiness to learn are indispensable."[58] He expressed himself even more forcefully and dramatically when he said,

> It is possible that in theological thought and in the consciousness of faith in a certain epoch part of revelation recedes into the background; it is not denied but is given less attention. Therefore, all obligations toward the ecclesiastical teaching office notwithstanding, the participation also of Catholics in ecumenical discussions is stimulating and fruitful. We do not stand sated and content among our searching brothers. We acknowledge openly and gratefully that we are indebted to the insight of Protestant theology which we would not wish to miss. Certainly the *Instructio* . . . says of converts, "One may not so present things that the impression is aroused that through their conversion they bring something essential to the Church

[56]Josef Stangl, "Die heilige Eucharistie—'Sakrament der Einheit,'" *Una Sancta*, XV (1960), 7-8.

[57]Cf. also Julius Döpfner, "Die alleinseligmachende Kirche," *Una Sancta*, X (1955), 3 ff.; and "Apostolat im Geiste Christi," *Una Sancta*, XI (1956), 50 ff.

[58]Julius Döpfner, "Kirche Christi unterwegs," *Una Sancta*, XII (1957), 6.

which she lacked until then." The sentence, at which offense is often taken, must be rightly understood. They add nothing to the real, essential permanent truth; but they can enrich the Church in the realized, developed understanding of the truth, as the example of great converts shows.

Therefore we must painfully regret when representatives of the Church's teaching office, or any Catholics, fall into a rigid narrowness, into an unjustified attitude of infallibility.[59]

These were strong words for a Catholic bishop before Vatican II. Nevertheless Bishop Döpfner was since then made a Cardinal. Also, essentially the same position was taken by Pope John XXIII when he declared that the reunion of Christians depends on the inner renewal of the Catholic Church, and Vatican II has carried this trend of thought even further.

At the end of this same sermon, delivered just a few days after he was named Bishop of Berlin, Bishop Döpfner reminded his congregation that in his years at Würzburg the reunion in faith had always been his heart's desire and that now, going to a diaspora diocese, he would need an ecumenical attitude even more. Berlin was already probably the most active of Una Sancta centers, but shortly after Cardinal Döpfner's arrival a new step was taken. The Protestant chancery and the Catholic chancery in Berlin formed a committee of three theologians each, which was to carry on Una Sancta work under an official ecclesiastical commission. "Very soon three laymen each will also be chosen by the committee . . . . By this a decisive step forward has been taken, for both Church chanceries have officially announced their will to remain in conversation with each other."[60] The *Una Sancta,* of course, eagerly commended this step as a great service to the Una Sancta Movement and

[59]*Ibid.*
[60]"Una Sancta-Kreis Berlin," *Una Sancta,* XIII (1958), 171.
[61]Sartory, "Vorwort," *Una Sancta,* X (1955), 3.

recommended it as a model for the Protestant and Catholic hierarchy in other areas to follow in discharging their responsibilities to work for a united Christianity.

One of the most significant reactions of the Catholic hierarchy to the Una Sancta Movement came from Rome. In 1955 Father Sartory reported to the Vatican authorities on the developments of the Movement. He wrote, "I can assure you the ecumenical work as we strive to conduct it is looked upon with good will in Rome."[61] In 1957 Father Sartory visited Cardinal Ottaviani, the Prosecretary of the Holy Office, to report on the work of the Movement; Ottaviani "blessed and approved the work of Father Sartory and exhorted him to continue and extend it with all his power."[62] It is from the Holy Office that the *Monitum* and *Instructio* of 1948 and 1949 had been issued.

PROTESTANT ATTITUDE TOWARD THE UNA SANCTA MOVEMENT

The attitude of the Protestant Church leaders after the crisis period gradually grew ever more sympathetic toward the Una Sancta Movement. The VELKD in 1955 arranged to look further into the matter of relations with Rome, and under the leadership of the ecumenical-minded Bishop Hans Lilje made tolerance and more particularly relations with the Catholic Church the theme of the 1956 Synod at Hanover. At this synod Bishop Dietzfelbinger of Bavaria delivered a speech with such a wide understanding and sympathy for Una Sancta work that it "won for him the trust of many Catholics."[63] Shortly afterwards it was announced that the VELKD had made Bishop Dietzfelbinger responsible for

---

[62]Die Mitarbeiter des Hauses der Begegnung, *Haus der Begegnung* (Meitingen, 1958), 2. This is a pamphlet accompanying the May 1958 *Una Sancta.*

[63]"Bischof Dietzfelbinger Beauftragter für Catholica," *Herder-Korrespondenz,* XI (1957), 230.

questions of relations with the Catholic Church much as Archbishop Jäger had been similarly appointed by the Catholic Bishops; many Catholics greeted this "with joy." It was likewise planned that each member Church of the VELKD would appoint someone responsible for Una Sancta work within the Church. Dietzfelbinger was one of the first to put this into action by appointing Walter Rupprecht as responsible for Bavaria and H. Schmidt specifically for the Munich area. One further appointment was made by the VELKD, that of a committee of theologians to work out guides for Protestants engaged in Una Sancta work.

Prayer and Sacrifice for the Una Sancta

Throughout the 1950's the notion that Protestants and Catholics should not only discuss theology together but should pray together continued to grow stronger, as is indicated by the founding of the *Haus der Begegnung* and by the common prayer at the numerous Una Sancta conferences; at the Catholic-Protestant theologians' meetings Compline was said jointly every evening, alternating German and Latin.

Walter von Loewenich remarked, "We are convinced that all the Una Sancta efforts without prayer for unity remain unfruitful."[64] In line with this idea many individuals and groups began to take up the practice of praying for the unity of Christianity; this is in addition to those groups, such as the Ecumenical Marian Sisters (Lutheran), who were doing so before 1950. Already in 1940 the "Votive Mass for the Removal of Division in the Church" was translated into German and set to simple Gregorian melody; the Mass and melody, republished in 1953, was used by Una Sancta groups. Thursday in particular was often chosen for Una Sancta prayer, for it was on a Thursday that Christ instituted the

---

[64]Von Loewenich, *Der moderne Katholizismus,* 361.

Eucharist, "the Sacrament of Unity," and recited the prayer found in John 17:11-23, which has become the anthem of all ecumenical work. It is from the most pertinent part of this prayer, "that all may be one as thou Father in me and I in thee, and that they may be one in us," that the motto "that all may be one" on the Una Sancta candles came; these German art candles first made in the 1930's at Niederaltaich are also often burned on Thursdays in conjunction with prayers for unity.

The number of groups praying for the Una Sancta grew through the decade: a Cistercian convent in Thyrnau promised to delegate a sister each day to pray for the Una Sancta. A convent of Poor Clares in Düsseldorf and a convent of Carmelites in Cologne also pledged daily prayer; the Dominican nuns of Altenhohenau and Social Women's Schools in Aachen and Heidelberg were added to the growing number as were also a group of school children in southern Germany. Reports came in also from outside Germany, from the Benedictines at St. Paul's in Rome, the institute *Pro civitate Christiana* in Assisi, the Benedictine High School in San Anselmo, and from many French groups, including the Trappists of Normandy and the Great Carthusians. Even a mission station in South Africa and an Indian village of Christians on the edge of the jungle in Mexico wrote of the Una Sancta prayers being offered; in "a satellite country a 'candle' burned every Thursday."[65] The clerics of the Collegium Germanicum in Rome reacted to hearing of the Una Sancta Movement by writing to Father Sartory: "In the week after your lecture all those who were particularly moved by your ideas gathered together in a discussion to consider the next step. It appeared most important that we start from within, so we will keep Thursdays as special days of prayer for the Una Sancta . . . . Once a month we celebrate Holy

[65]Thomas Sartory, "Das Licht wächst," *Una Sancta* IX (1964), 7.

Mass as a votive Mass for the men and women in Una Sancta work. Each month one of us will read at table a report on the progress of the Una Sancta Movement with news on the situation in individual lands, special events, difficulties, and so forth.[66] These prayer groups are in the spirit of the Una Sancta Movement—they do not seek conversions but ultimate unity according to God's will.

Related to the idea of prayer and sacrifice for the Una Sancta was the suggestion made by the Protestant theologian Oscar Cullmann in Basel in January of 1957. He suggested that one way to further the search for unity would be for the churches to take up collections for one another once a year, preferably during the Church Unity Octave, somewhat as St. Paul did among the Gentile Christians for the needy Jewish Christians. The response was immediate. Some Protestant parishes in Zürich collected funds for a needy Catholic village; a Swiss Catholic parish did the same for a Reformed congregation; the Waldensian theology students in Rome had a collection for Catholics, as did also the Catholic seminarians of Chur, Switzerland for Protestants. Cullmann repeated his suggestion in a speech at the Swiss Institute in Rome before a responsive audience of several hundred, including an unusually large number of Catholic priests and Church dignitaries. The idea spread to other Christian groups; the Catholic community of Heriliberg, Switzerland, took up a special collection for the Russian Orthodox Emmigrant Church in Zürich.

ADDITIONAL AREAS OF COOPERATION

The Protestant and Catholic press continued in the decade after the *Instructio* to grow in understanding of the other Church. Kurt Hutton, editor of the *Materialdienst* section of the Protestant periodical *Für Arbeit und Besinnung*, wrote

[66]Sartory, "Vorwort," 2.

a very sympathetic description of Catholic-Protestant relations in the middle 1950's in which he praised particularly the Catholic press for its ecumenical spirit. "The openness of many organs of the Catholic diocesan and daily press toward the other confessions is an effective instrument for the good. There are leading Catholic periodicals which have on their staff a Protestant representative. They and the Catholic newspapers do not ignore the Protestant Church; they do not limit themselves to events in the Catholic Church."[67]

Cooperation between the Catholic and Protestant press reached a new phase at the general synod of the VELKD in 1956. Here several Protestant and Catholic publicists conceived the idea of having a Catholic and Protestant publicists' conference to discuss common problems and to exchange information. In March of the following years, at the Evangelical Academy of Loccum, eighty Protestant and Catholic editors met for four days to listen to lectures by theologians from both sides and to discuss common problems among themselves. This first meeting was so stimulating and fruitful that they decided not only to continue the meetings regularly in the future and expand them by specialized conferences but also to set up a continuation committee whose members in pressing situations could exchange needed information on inter-confessional questions. A second such publicists' meeting took place less than a year later when in December of 1957 over one hundred publicists of both confessions met in a Catholic institute in Dortmund; a third conference of over 60 people followed in September, 1958, at the Evangelical Academy at Tutzing. The last such conference of the decade was held at Maria Laach Abbey in June of 1959; over 150 were present. The huge increase in

[67]Kurt Hutten, "Die Katholischen und die Evangelischen (II)," *Materialdienst* (Stuttgart), XVII (1954), 180.

numbers may have been partly due to Pope John XXIII's proclamation of a new Council with questions of union high on the agenda; the coming Council was the theme of this conference.

The unusually good relations between the *Katholikentag* and the *Kirchentag* were continued throughout the 1950's. Often representatives from the other confession would speak at the opening or closing assembly. In 1950, for example, the President of the Evangelical *Kirchentag*, Reinold von Thadden-Trieglaff, spoke at the *Katholikentag* at Passau. He said, "We wish to do everything possible to retain the 'togetherness' which God granted us in the recent years of need and want."[68] Cooperation on the physical level also continued as when at the 1952 *Katholikentag* in Berlin Cardinal Wendel from Munich stayed with Protestant Bishop Dibelius of Berlin, and many Catholics were housed by Protestants; the favor was returned in 1959 when Cardinal Wendel urged all Catholics of Munich to extend their hospitality to Protestant participants in the *Kirchentag*.[69]

Although the Una Sancta work in Germany naturally mainly confined itself to Protestants and Catholics, as in the 1940's so also in the 1950's there was some participation by Orthodox theologians in Una Sancta meetings. The contributions to the *Una Sancta* by Orthodox increased sharply after the January, 1959, announcement of the new Council. Niederaltaich abbey pointed more of its efforts toward the Orthodox by expanding its Eastern rite section, ordaining monks in the Eastern rite, constructing a Byzantine chapel, celebrating the Eastern litury, doing research and publishing and conducting Eastern Churches study weeks for theology students.

---

[68]*Ibid.,* 179.

[69]Requests for lodging for visitors of the *Kirchentag* were made in all Catholic churches in Munich.

A somewhat new dimension was added to the work particularly by a group of intellectuals in southeastern Germany who started the *Freiburger Rundbrief* (*Freiburg Circular for the Fostering of Friendship Between the Old and New People of God—in the Spirit of Both Testaments*) in 1948; the periodical apppeared approximately every six months. There were also other Christian-Jewish societies formed to do what they could to counterbalance the crimes committed against the Jewish people. What helped give the *Freiburger Rundbrief* group its particular Una Sancta direction was that two of the editors were involved in the Una Sancta Movement: Karlheinz Schmidthüs also edited the *Herder-Korrespondenz*, and Karl Thieme had been the editor of the pioneering *Religiöse Besinnung* in the early 1930's. In April, 1957, Karl Thieme spoke at a conference between Catholics, Protestants and Jews in the Evangelical Academy in Berlin. The report on the conference in the *Una Sancta*, entitled "Una Sancta with the Jews?" stated, "Whoever is involved in Una Sancta work may be happy that the two Christian Churches invited representatives of Judaism to meet with us in discussion."[70] This lead was later followed by a conference announced for September, 1960, at the *Haus der Begegnung*, a "Christian-Jewish Conversation. (In conjunction with the *Freiburger Rundbrief* Circle and our Protestant friends)."

The Una Sancta Movement in Germany is essentially a discussion between Catholics and Lutheran and, to a much lesser extent, Reformed Protestants; as such it was not connected with the ecumenical movement with its headquarters in the World Council of Churches at Geneva, Switzerland. Father Sartory, whose doctoral dissertation dealt with the ecumenical movement, complained in 1953 that the Una Sancta Movement had isolated itself too much from the world ecu-

[70]Johann Allendorff, "Una Sancta mit den Juden?" *Una Sancta*, XII (1957), 132.

menical activities and asked that the members of the Una Sancta Movement take a greater interest in the ecumenical movement. The Protestant Ernst Kinder noted a little over a year later that very recently the activities of the ecumenical movement were being followed very acutely and energetically among the Una Sancta circles,"–actually more enthusiastically and earnestly than in many purely Protestant circles!"[71] But he also strongly urged Protestants not to succumb to the temptation to forget about Rome as far as the ecumenical movement was concerned, and at the same time pleaded with the Una Sancta Movement to enter even more into contact with the ecumenical movement.[72] By the end of the decade the situation was such that much of the best Protestant energy was being channelled into ecumenical movement activities, sometimes leaving the Catholics in the Una Sancta Movement without sufficient discussion partners. On the other hand the Catholics formed the international circle of Catholic theologians to explain a Catholic position on problems submitted to it by the World Council of Churches; Sartory was a member of this circle..

CONCLUSION

The Una Sancta Movement appeared in Germany and not elsewhere for a number of reasons. Germany was the only large country in Europe with anything like an equal number of Catholics and Protestants. In France there was a good deal of ecumenical work on the intellectual level, but it was done mostly by Catholics, and understandably so, since Protestants, except in certain areas, are as plentiful in France as are Catholics in Scandinavia. In Holland there was a religious population situation similar to Germany's, and there was a considerable amount of ecumenical activity, but this

[71]Kinder, "Was erwartet die evangelische Kirche?", 6.

[72]*Ibid.;* and Ernst Kinder, "Protestant-Roman Catholic Encounter an Ecumenical Obligation," *The Ecumenical Review,* VII (1955), 339.

activity seemed usually to follow Germany's example. Outside of the traditional creativeness of German theology, Protestant and Catholic, one factor that gave Germany the advantage over Holland in Catholic-Protestant affairs is that Dutch Protestantism is mostly Calvinist and the strongest Protestant element in Germany is Lutheran, a form of Protestantism that is closed to Catholicism in a number of ways, particularly in regard to sacramental theology, liturgical practice and church structure. Consequently, the liturgical movements of the twentieth century did more to bring the Lutheran and Catholic Churches together than the Calvinist and Catholic, and it was within the Lutheran ecclesiastical framework that the position, and even name, of the bishop was reemphasized. Another differentiating factor between Germany and the rest of Europe in the sphere of Catholic-Protestant relations was the greater length and intensity of the Nazi persecution of the Christian Churches. Moreover following the war it was most particularly Germany that experienced the tremendous transfer of population and its inter-confessional consequences.

Since the war the memory of the Nazi persecution served as a continuing, though gradually fading, ecumenical force in Germany and to some extent its place was taken by the Communist oppression of religion. This was especially true in East Germany of course, but because of the immediateness of the iron curtain and the passage back and forth of persons and mail West Germany was also affected. Nevertheless the presence of Communism did not seem to make too great a difference; if it had not been there during the last two decades the Una Sancta Movement would no doubt have developed essentially the same way it actually did. The same, however, could not have been said about Naziism. The beginnings of the Una Sancta Movement were already there before the Nazi persecution, but the Movement would never have developed so rapidly or broadly had there been no *Kirchenkampf*.

The fact that the Roman Catholic Church today is so definitely committed to ecumenical activity is due in large measure to the pioneer work in this field by the Una Sancta Movement of Germany, and just as much of the present Catholic ecumenical leadership comes from the ranks of the German Una Sancta Movement, so also does the greatest amount of experience among Protestants in Catholic-Protestant exchanges come from German Protestants. Germany, the starting place of the Reformation in the sixteenth century and its consequent divisions, has become in the twentieth century the land of the Una Sancta Movement with its drive for Christian unity.

Appendix

The *Monitum* of June, 1948, as found in *Acta apostolica sedis* 40 (1948), 257:

Supreme Sacra Congregatio Sancti Officii, Monitum. Cum compertum sit variis in locis, contra Sacrorum Canonum praescripta et sine praevia S. Sedis venia, mixtos conventus acatholicorum cum catholicis habitos fuisse, in quibus de rebus fidei tractatum est, omnibus in memoriam revocatur ad normam canonis 1325 #3 prohibitum esse, quominus his conventibus intersint, sine praedicta venia, cum laici, tum clerici sive saeculares sive religiose. Multo autem minus catholicis licitum est huiusmodi conventus convocare et instituere. Quapropter Ordinarii urgeant, ut haec praescripta ab omnibus adamussim serventur.

Quae autem potiore jure observanda sunt, cum agitur de conventibus quos "oecumenicos" vocant, quibus catholici, sive laici sive clerici, sine S. Sedis praevio consensu, nullo modo interesse possunt.

Cum vero, tum in praedictis conventibus tum extra ipsos, etiam actus mixti cultus haud raro positi fuerint, denuo omnes monentur quamlibet in sacris communicationem ad norman canonum 1258 et 731 #2 omnino prohibitum esse.

Datum Romae, ex Aedibus S. Officii, die 5. juni; 1948.

Petrus Vigorita Notarius.

Canons 1325 #3; 1258 #1, 2; 731 #2, as found in *Codex juris canonicai* (Typis Polyglottis Vaticanis, 1948):

Can. 1325 #3. Caveant catholici ne disputationes vel collationes, publicas praesertim, cum acatholicis habeant, sine venia Sanctae Sedis aut, si casus urgeat, loci Ordinarii.

Can. 1258 #1. Haud licitum est fidelibus quovis modo active assistere seu partem habere in sacris acatholicorum.

#2. Tolerari potest praesentia passiva seu mere materiales, civilis officii vel honoris causa, ob gravem rationem ab Episcopo in casu dubii probandum, in acatholicorum funeribus, nuptiis similibusque sollemniis, dummodo perversionis et scandali periculum absit.

Can. 731 #2. Vetitum est Sacramenta Ecclesiae ministrare haereticis aut schismaticis, etiam bona fide errantibus eaque petentibus, nisi prius, erroribus reiectis, Ecclesiae reconciliati fuerint.

Statement of the Sacred Congregation of the Propaganda of the Faith on March 8, 1625, as found in Justiniani Seredi (ed.), *Codicis juris canonici fontes* (Typis Polyglottis Vaticanis, 1935), VII, 1:

S.C. de Prop. Fide, 8 mart. 1625.

S. Congregatio jussit publicas disputationes non fiere cum haereticis, quia plerumque vel ob loquacitatem vel audaciam aut circumstantis populi acclamationes veritas falsitate praevalente opprimitur; et si aliquando huiusmodi disputationes excusari non possent, primum de illis certior fiat S. Congregatio, quae juxta temporis et personarum qualitatem quid agendum sit peculiariter praescribet.

Statement of the Sacred Congregation of the Propaganda of the Faith on February 7, 1645, as found in *Codicis juris canonici fontes,* VII, 11:

S.C. de Prop. Fide (c.P.), 7 febr. 1645.

S.C. respondit: 1. Colloquia et disputationes publicas catholicorum cum haereticis aliquando esse licitas, cum scilicet spes habetur maioris boni, et concurrunt aliae conditiones, quae a theologis recensentur, ut patet ex iis disputationibus quas habuit S. Augustinus contra Donatistas ac alios haereticos.

2. Sanctem Sedem Apostolicam et Romanos Pontifices, quod huiusmodi colloquia, plerumque sine bono, aut etiam cum malo exitu peracta fuerint, illa frequenter prohibuisse, as suis ministris scripsisse ut illa evaderent; si vero non possent impediri, curarent ne fierent sine auctoritate Apostolica, insisterentque ut per viros doctos, qui possent et valerent defendere veritates catholicas id perageretur; et saepissime id ipsum S. C. de Prop. Fide rescripsit ad suos missionaris eosque monuit ut a publicis disputationibus cum haereticis abstinerent.

Appendix

Statement of the Sacred Congregation of the Propaganda of the Faith on December 18, 1662, as found in *Codicis juris canonici fontes,* VII, 42:

S.C. de Prop. Fide, 18 dec. 1662.

De conferentiis et publicis congressibus seu disputationibus missionariorum cum haereticis monetur Generalis (Capucin.) ut omnino prohibeat, cum S. Sedes plurimis experimentis exacta semper eas prohibuerit; quo vero ad interventum concionibus haereticorum, hoc etiam prohibueatur, sicut a S.C. S. Officii semper fuit prohibitum, nec omnibus indifferenter absolute expediat; quod si aliquis adsit insignioris doctrinae et prudentiae, supplicet in particulare pro licentia.

Index